DONOR-ADVISED FUNDS
LAW AND POLICY

BY BRUCE R. HOPKINS

DORRANCE
PUBLISHING CO
EST. 1920
PITTSBURGH, PENNSYLVANIA 15238

Dorrance Publishing Co
585 Alpha Drive
Suite 103
Pittsburgh, PA 15238
Visit our website at *www.dorrancebookstore.com*

ISBN: 978-1-6470-2508-3
eISBN: 978-1-6470-2684-4

TABLE OF CONTENTS

PREFACE

Feeding my addiction to writing about nonprofit law, I decided to focus on donor-advised funds. (In today's climate, it is impossible to avoid that subject.) When that decision expanded to the idea of a book, my first reaction was that there was insufficient material for a book. After all, the existing law of donor-advised funds is skimpy. That reaction was reversed when I became more deeply ensconced in the project, reviewing this vehicle's history, criticisms, and legal issues (and even statistics).

My goal with this book is to capture in one volume all that can be said about donor-advised funds—not just the law surrounding them but all the policy issues swirling about them. This is an elusive objective, if only because of the ongoing rush of commentary (usually adverse) about these funds. I think I have identified all the criticisms and legal issues but new perspectives (and wordplay) about them keeping rolling out as the articles and reports pile up.

My plan at the outset was to write this book but not publish it until an analysis of the proposed regulations being developed at the Department of the Treasury and the IRS could be included. When the book was otherwise completed, at the end of 2019, and these proposed regulations seemed far away (with the writing of guidance implementing the Tax Cuts and Jobs Act and the Taxpayer First Act a higher priority), I decided to publish the book in advance of issuance of the proposal.

Publication of these proposed regulations, and the many writings of others about donor-advised funds to come in the interim, will make for a sumptuous second edition of this book.

Bruce R. Hopkins

CHAPTER ONE:
The Donor-Advised Fund Legal Landscape

Donor-advised funds and the environment in which they function are the subjects of these pages, principally from a law standpoint. History and statistics are also part of the narrative. This book is a detailed look at these vehicles, the support and opposition they are generating (the latter predominating), and the new spurt in attempts by the federal government to regulate them.

This chapter, following some opening thoughts and illustrative quotes, summarizes the law as to *funds*, briefly defines the term *donor-advised funds*, places

1

donor-advised funds in the public charity/private foundation context, discusses the federal tax law of community foundations, summarizes the rules as to *material restrictions*, explains the matter of "reservation of rights," defines *donor-directed funds*, addresses the concept of the *conduit*, explores the rationale for tax-exempt charitable status for grantmaking entities, summarizes the commensurate test, and inventories the reasons for the popularity of donor-advised funds.

OPENING THOUGHTS

The donor-advised fund is one of nonprofit law's hottest topics—perhaps the most heated of them all. The text of a report on donor-advised funds observed that "[d]onor-advised funds are one of the fastest-growing charitable giving vehicles in the United States, due to the flexibility and ease with which they streamline donors' giving."[1] The author of a law review article wrote that recent years have seen "exponential growth in the creation and funding of donor advised funds."[2] Law professors Roger Colinvaux and Ray Madoff wrote that donor-advised funds "are a fundraising phenomenon that make it easy to set aside dollars for good causes and get significant tax benefits right away."[3] An article written by community foundation leaders states that the "rapid growth of donor-advised funds is one of the major stories in charitable giving."[4] A cost-benefit analysis of donor-advised funds opened with the statement that they "are now a major source of charitable dollars in the United States, responsible for 1 in 10 dollars donated to charity in 2015."[5] The report on donor-advised funds for 2019 issued by the National Philanthropic Trust states that the "rapidly increasing number of individual donor-advised fund accounts makes them the fastest-growing vehicle in philanthropy, and the rising value of charitable dollars granted from donor-advised funds also makes them the most active type of charitable giving vehicle."

---

[1] "The Data on Donor-Advised Funds: New Insights You Need to Know" 11 (Giving USA (2018)). It is submitted that donor-advised funds are *the* fastest-growing of these charitable giving vehicles.

[2] Hussey, "Avoiding Misuse of Donor Advised Funds," 58 *Clev. St. L. Rev.* 59, 62 (2010).

[3] Colinvaux and Madoff, "A Donor-Advised Fund Proposal That Would Work for Everyone," *Chron. of Phil.* (Sep. 23, 2019).

[4] Kridler, Philipp, Slutsky, Seleznow, and Williams, "Donor-Advised Funds: How to Make Sure They Strengthen Our Communities," *Nonprofit Quar.* (Aug. 20, 2018).

[5] Andreoni, "The Benefits and Costs of Donor-Advised Funds," National Bureau of Economic Research (978-0-226-57752-4 (2018)).

Although donor-advised funds have been in existence for decades and disputatious for years, the level of controversy is intensifying as the amount of giving to donor-advised funds continues to rapidly rise, private foundations make greater use of these funds, and the federal government's regulatory apparatus begins to seriously focus on them. This increase in controversy is sparking growth in the ranks of donor-advised funds' advocates and critics, which stokes still more controversy.

Every statistic demonstrates the dramatic increase in utilization of donor-advised funds: the sheer number of them, the size of the larger sponsoring organizations, the amount of giving to donor-advised funds, and the amounts of grants from these funds.[6] There are record-breaking analyses of donor-advised funds, many articles about them, and more presentations about them at nonprofit law conferences.

The government's tax law establishment has, for decades, been suspicious of donor-advised funds, believing them to be vehicles to sidestep the private foundation rules. This is seen as nefarious, if not outright illegal, behavior. In fact, donor-advised funds are an alternative to private foundations—in most legitimate and effective ways.

Foes of donor-advised funds have never been able to get beyond the notion that these funds are fundamentally flawed and thus tarnished because they are rested on a *legal fiction*. The "fiction" is that sponsoring organizations own and control the contributed money. The "reality," from the critics' viewpoint, is that the true control remains with the donors, inasmuch as the "advice" proffered by them is not really "advice" at all, since it is nearly always followed by the sponsors. All of this is seen, in these quarters, as nothing more than wealthy individuals playing economic games at the expense of charities serving the poor and disadvantaged.

Opponents of donor-advised funds are also unhappy because there can be a delay between the making of a charitable contribution and use of the money for charitable ends. This is indisputably true. The same can be said, however, with respect to gifts to other charitable vehicles, such as private foundations, supporting organizations, and charitable remainder trusts. (Of course, these entities also have their critics.)

THE FRENZY

By 2018, when levels of contributions to donor-advised funds began reaching spectacular heights, critics of donor-advised funds had worked themselves into an anti-

---

[6] See Chapter 3.

DAF frenzy, the likes of which the nonprofit world had never seen before. Advocates of donor-advised funds, by contrast, were rather quiet. Critics of these funds were blasting them in all forms of media, using inflammatory terminology in an effort to force further federal regulation of donor-advised funds.

Here is a sampling:[7]

- *Atlantic*, in May, 2018, ran an article titled "The 'Black Hole' That Sucks Up Silicon Valley's Money."
- *Forbes*, in May, 2018, published an article titled "Foundations of Hedge Fund Managers Gave Big to Controversial Donor-Advised Funds."
- The Institute for Policy Studies, in July, 2018, published a report titled "Warehousing Wealth: Donor-Advised Charity Funds Sequestering Billions in the Face of Growing Inequality."
- The *Nonprofit Quarterly*, in its Summer 2018 issue, published three articles critical of donor-advised funds.[8] One is titled "Three Simple Steps to Protect Charities and American Taxpayers from the Rise of Donor-Advised Funds."
- *The New York Times*, in August, 2018, ran an article with the headline "How Tech Billionaires Hack Their Taxes With a Philanthropic Loophole."
- Paul Streckfus, in his *EO Tax Journal*, in August, 2018, wrote that "[a]ll of us need to keep beating the drums and demanding legislative action because the alternative is moral bankruptcy for the entire nonprofit sector."
- In August, a law professor blogged that "you first must begin with the self-evidently true factual proposition that the independence of the DAF from the donor is a sham."
- The *Chronicle of Philanthropy* published an article on August 22, 2018, with the title "How I helped Create the Donor-Advised Fund Monster – Inadvertently."
- *Wealth* magazine came forth, on October 3, 2018, with "The Super-Rich Are Stockpiling Wealth in Black-Box Charities."
- The *Chronicle of Philanthropy* published an article in September 2019, titled "Put a Stake in 'Zombie Charity.' Philanthropy Is for the Living."

[7] These and other publications referenced here are in Chapter 5.
[8] The editors of this publication stated: "We also invited others to write about why broad-based congressional attention was not now needed [concerning donor-advised funds] and to speak up about what additional, but more limited, regulations were needed, but we mostly got demurrals."

WHAT ARE WE TALKING ABOUT?

The subject matter of this book is, of course, the *donor-advised fund*. The statutory definition of this vehicle is discussed in more detail later. At this point, let's just say that a donor-advised fund is a fund within a public charity, with the charity termed a sponsoring organization. Gifts are made to the sponsoring organization but, instead of being placed in the charity's general treasury, the gift amount is placed in a fund, which usually bears the name or names of the donors. The gift amount—money or other property—is owned and controlled by the sponsoring organization. The donor, and/or someone designed by the donor, is accorded the ability to recommend (or advise) charities to receive grants from the donor-advised fund.

The IRS provided this pre-statutory definition of the term "donor-advised fund": It "was understood to refer to separate funds or accounts established and maintained by public charities to receive contributions from a single donor or group of donors. The charities had ultimate authority over how the assets in each account were invested and distributed, but the donors, or individuals selected by the donors, were permitted to provide nonbinding recommendations regarding account distributions and/or investments." Many of the characteristics of a donor-advised fund are echoed in the tax regulations concerning community foundations and the rules concerning material restrictions on transferability.

Here is an illustration of use of a donor-advised fund. Annabelle Clark just inherited $50,000. Not needing the money for her day-to-day existence, Annabelle decides to give the money to charity. She is happy to have the resulting charitable deduction(s) but is reluctant to simply scatter the $50,000 over a handful of charities. After consulting her favorite nonprofit lawyer, Sam, she decides to create a donor-advised fund. Annabelle lives in the city of Clio. With Sam's help, Annabelle finds her way to the Clio Community Foundation, a public charity that, among a range of programs, maintains donor-advised funds.

Annabelle executes a donor-advised fund agreement with the Clio Community Foundation, creating the Annabelle Clark Charitable Fund. This agreement gives Annabelle the privilege of advising the Foundation, from time to time, as to the making of grants from the Fund and advising the Foundation as to investment of the Fund's assets. It also names Sam as the donor advisor. The Foundation owns the

5

assets and income of the Fund, and controls it. Annabelle gives the Foundation a check for $50,000, which is deposited in the Annabelle Clark Charitable Fund.

Six months after establishing the Annabelle Clark Charitable Fund, Annabelle contacts the community foundation in a town by the name of Clio and requests that a grant in the amount of $1,000 be made to one of Annabelle's favorite charities, the Clio Environmental Protection Society. The Foundation duly considers this advice, then decides to make the grant. In due course, the Clio Community Foundation sends a check, showing the payor as the Annabelle Clark Charitable Fund, to the Clio Environmental Protection Society. The Society records the grant as coming from the Fund. During this six-month period, the Fund earned $750. Following this grant, the balance in the Fund's account is 49,750.

PUBLIC CHARITIES AND PRIVATE FOUNDATIONS

Organizations that sponsor (maintain) donor-advised funds are public charities. Most of them are publicly supported charities.

Pursuant to the federal tax law, a tax-exempt charitable organization is either a public charity or a private foundation.[9] Exempt charities are presumed, by the federal tax law, to be private foundations.[10] This presumption is rebutted by a showing by the charitable entity, to the IRS, that it qualifies as one of the types of public charities.[11]

A private foundation essentially is a tax-exempt charitable organization that generally is initially funded from one source (e.g., an individual, family, or for-profit company), is funded on an ongoing basis by investment income, and makes grants for charitable purposes. Technically, from a law standpoint, a private foundation is an exempt charitable entity that does not qualify as a public charity.[12]

Public charities are of three basic types: the institutions, publicly supported charities, and supporting organizations. The institutions are charitable entities such as churches, associations and conventions of churches, schools, hospitals, medical research

---

[9] Internal Revenue Code of 1986, as amended, section (IRC §) 509(a).
[10] IRC § 508(b).
[11] Usually, public charity status is demonstrated (if it can be) as part of the process by which an organization seeks recognition of exemption as a charitable entity (Rev. Proc. 2020-5, 2020-1 I.R.B. 243 § 6).
[12] IRC § 509(a).

organizations, and agricultural research organizations.[13] Supporting organizations are essentially exempt charitable subsidiaries of exempt charitable organizations.[14]

Publicly supported organizations generally fall into two categories: the donative-type publicly supported charity[15] and the service provider publicly supported charity.[16] The federal tax statutory law defines the types of revenue that qualifies as public support and the amount of public support that is required to enable a charitable organization to consider itself publicly supported.

For example, the donative-type publicly supported charity[17] is generally required to receive a substantial part of its financial support in the form of public support.[18] The tax regulations define this requirement to mean at least one-third of financial support in the form of public support,[19] as measured over the organization's most recent five years. Financial support from any person (individual, tax-exempt entity, or for-profit entity) generally is public support to the extent it does not exceed an amount equal to two percent of the organization's total support.[20] Financial support from another donative-type publicly supported charity, however, generally constitutes public support in its entirety.[21]

These distinctions are based on language in the operative statute that differentiates between *direct* and *indirect* public support. A gift or grant to a publicly supported charity (or an entity that is striving to qualify as such or an entity that is described in the definition of the publicly supported charity) generally is a form of direct public support (and thus subject to the two percent limitation). A grant from a donative-type publicly supported charity to another donative-type publicly supported charity is the principal (if not the only) form of indirect public support. The underlying concept, in connection with the indirect public support rule, is that donors who made gifts directly to the grantor publicly supported charity are indirectly donors to the grantee publicly supported charity; this is why the grant funds retain their character as public support in full.

---

[13] IRC § 509(a)(1), by reference to IRC § 170(b)(1)(A)(i)-(v), (x).
[14] IRC § 509(a)(3).
[15] IRC § 509(a)(1), by reference to IRC § 170(b)(1)(A)(vi).
[16] IRC § 509(a)(2).
[17] Most organizations that sponsor donor-advised funds (see Chapter 4, p. 91) are donative-type publicly supported charities.
[18] IRC § 170(b)(1)(A)(vi).
[19] Treasury Regulations (Reg.) § 1.170A-9(f)(2).
[20] Reg. § 1.170A-9(f)(6)(i).
[21] *Id.*: Reg. § 1.170A-9(f)(6)(v). This rule lies at the heart of one of the major controversies concerning the law of donor-advised funds. See Chapter 6, pp 156-169.

Organizations funding publicly supported charities, particularly private foundations, need to be careful that their grants are not of an amount that causes the grantee to lose its public charity status.[22] Grant-making to this extent, such as an amount in excess of the two percent threshold, is informally termed "tipping." That is, the grant causes the grantee to be tipped from what might otherwise be public charity status into private foundation status.

CONCEPT OF THE FUND

Generally, when a donor makes a contribution to a charitable organization,[23] the donor parts with all right, title, and interest in the gift property (including money) and the gift property is thereafter owned by the recipient charitable organization. Exceptions to this general rule abound. This is because of two fundamental (and overlapping) concepts in the federal tax law of charitable giving: funds and restrictions.

Often, the word *fund* is used to describe something other than a separate legal entity. That is, a fund frequently is akin to an account, held and maintained by a charitable organization. The federal tax law does not provide any limitation as to the type or number of funds that a charitable organization may have. Thus, as examples, a church may hold one or more endowment funds, a college or university may hold one or more scholarship funds, and a scientific institution may hold one or more research funds. (By contrast, a "fund" itself may be a separate legal entity, such as a private foundation[24] or a pooled income fund,[25] or a separately formed endowment fund.)

A donor may make a charitable gift outright or make a gift that is restricted as to its use. Thus, to continue one of the foregoing examples, a donor may make an outright gift to a church or a restricted gift to a church, the latter requiring that the

---

[22] Private foundations generally confine their grants to public charities; this is the "safe" way of ensuring that the grants are "qualifying distributions," eligible for credit toward the mandatory payout (IRC § 4942), and are not "taxable expenditures" (IRC § 4945). A private foundation can avoid the latter body of law by exercising "expenditure responsibility" over the grant (IRC § 4545(h)). But a private foundation that makes a grant to a public charity, believing that neither of these bodies of law are implicated, can find itself facing two sets of excise taxes if the grant is sufficiently large to tip the grantee into private foundation status, so that the grantor private foundation has inadvertently made one or more grants to another private foundation (without exercising expenditure responsibility).

[23] A "charitable organization," for these purposes, is an entity that is federally tax-exempt pursuant to IRC § 501(a) by reason of description in IRC § 501(c)(3).

[24] IRC § 509(a).

[25] IRC § 642(c)(5).

gift be placed in an endowment fund. The charitable donee is legally bound by the restriction, once the gift is accepted, although the charitable donee owns the gift property. A restricted gift, therefore, may be made to a charitable donee pursuant to a document stipulating the restriction or by means of a gift to a fund maintained by the charitable donee.

Usually, the restriction is imposed by the donor at the time of the gift transaction, with the donor having no further involvement as to use of the gift property. But that is not always the case; this is where the concepts of funds and restrictions blend. In this context, the distinction is generally made among two types of funds: the donor-advised fund and the donor-directed fund. The distinguishing features of these types of funds is the extent of ongoing donor control over the gift property and the role of the fund as a conduit.

COMMUNITY FOUNDATIONS

The history of donor-advised funds, and perhaps much of their future, is tied to entities known as *community foundations*. These foundations, sometimes referred to as community trusts, are designed primarily to attract large contributions of a capital or endowment nature for the benefit of a specified community or area. Often, these contributions initially are derived from a small number of donors. These gifts are often received and maintained in the form of separate trusts or funds, which are subject to varying degrees of control by the community foundation's governing body. Community foundations generally have a governing body composed of representatives of the community or area.[26]

A community foundation, to qualify as a publicly supported organization, must meet the financial support requirements for a donative publicly supported charity,[27] which may include satisfaction of a facts-and-circumstances test.[28] As to the latter, the requirement of attraction of public support will generally be satisfied if a community foundation seeks gifts, bequests, and devises from a wide range of potential donors in the community or other area served, through banks or trust

---

[26] Reg. § 1.170A-9(f)(10).

[27] IRC § 170(b)(1)(A)(vi). See Hopkins, *The Tax Law of Private Foundations* (5th ed. 2018) (*Private Foundations*) §15.4.

[28] The facts-and-circumstances test is the subject of Reg. § 1.170A-9(f)(3)(ii). See *Private Foundations* § 15.4(c).

companies, through lawyers or other professionals, or in other appropriate ways that call attention to the community foundation as a potential recipient of gifts and the like made for the benefit of the area served. A community foundation is not required to engage in periodic, community-wide fundraising campaigns directed towards attracting a large number of small contributions in a manner similar to fundraising efforts conducted by organizations that are community chests or united funds.[29]

A qualified community foundation is a single entity, as opposed to an aggregation of separate funds. The foundation may be created as a nonprofit corporation, trust, or unincorporated association. All funds in the community foundation must be treated as component parts of the organization.[30]

To be regarded as a component part of a community foundation, a trust or fund must be created by gift, bequest, or similar transfer to a community foundation that is treated as a separate entity and may not be subjected by the transferor to a material restriction[31] with respect to the transferred assets.[32]

To be treated as the requisite separate entity, a community foundation must be appropriately named, conveying the concept of a capital or endowment fund supporting charitable activities in the community it serves.[33] The foundation must be structured so that its funds are subject to a common governing instrument.[34] The organization must have a "common governing body," which directs or, in the case of a fund designated for specific beneficiaries, monitors the distribution of all of the funds exclusively for charitable purposes.[35]

The governing body of a community foundation must have the power, by provision in the governing instrument or other document, to (1) modify any restriction or condition on the distribution of funds for any specified charitable purposes or to specified organizations if, in the sole judgment of the body, the restriction or condition becomes, in effect, unnecessary, incapable of fulfillment, or inconsistent with the charitable needs of the community served; (2) replace any participating trustee, custodian, or other agent for breach of fiduciary duty under state law; or (3)

---

[29] Reg. § 1.170A-9(f)(10). Thus, the facts-and-circumstances test for community foundations is different than that for donative publicly supported charitable organizations generally.

[30] Reg. § 1.170A-9(f)(11)(i).

[31] See text accompanied by *infra* notes 43-54.

[32] Reg. § 1.170A-9(f)(11)(ii). These requirements are summarized in Priv. Ltr. Rul. 9807030 (Nov. 19, 1997). Reg. § 1.170A-9(f)(12) concerns situations where there is a failure to meet these requirements.

[33] Reg. § 1.170A-9(f)(11)(iii).

[34] Reg. § 1.170A-9(f)(11)(iv).

[35] Reg. § 1.170A-9(f)(11)(v)(A).

replace any participating trustee, custodian, or agent for failure to produce a reasonable return of net income over a reasonable period of time.[36]

If a power described in a provision of these documents is inconsistent with state law, even if the power were expressly granted to the governing body by the governing instrument and were accepted without limitation under an instrument of transfer, the community foundation is treated as meeting the requirements of the provision if it meets the requirements to the "fullest extent possible" consistent with state law.[37]

The governing body of a community foundation must commit itself to exercise the foregoing powers in the best interests of the organization. The body will be considered to not be so committed where it has grounds to exercise a power and fails to exercise it by taking appropriate action. This type of "appropriate action" includes consulting with the appropriate state authority prior to taking action to replace a participating trustee.[38]

In addition to the foregoing requirements, the governing body of a community foundation must commit itself to obtain information and otherwise take other appropriate steps with the view to seeing that each participating trustee, custodian, or agent, with respect to each restricted trust or fund that is, and with respect to the aggregate of the unrestricted trusts or funds that are, a component part of the community foundation, administer the fund or trust in accordance with the terms of its governing instrument and "accepted standards of fiduciary conduct" to produce a reasonable return of net income or perhaps appreciation, with "due regard" to safety of principal, in furtherance of the exempt purposes of the community foundation (except for assets held for the active conduct of the foundation's exempt activities). The tax regulations state that, in the case of a low return of net income, and perhaps, appreciation, the IRS will "examine carefully" whether the governing body has, in fact, committed itself to take the appropriate steps.[39] For these purposes, any income that has been designated by the donor of the gift or bequest to which the income is attributable as being available only for the use or benefit of a broad charitable purpose, such as the encouragement of higher education or the promotion of better health care in the community, will be treated as unrestricted. Any income that has

---

[36] Reg. § 1.170A-9(f)(11)(v)(B).

[37] Reg. § 1.170A-9(f)(11)(v)(D).

[38] Reg. § 1.170A-9(f)(11)(v)(E).

[39] This sweeping warning of IRS audit capacity does not match the state of today's IRS, which is underfunded and understaffed, and overwhelmed with other responsibilities, such as implementation of recent tax legislation.

been designated for the use or benefit of a named charitable organization or for the use or benefit of a particular class of charitable organizations, the members of which are readily ascertainable and are less than five in number, will, however, be treated as restricted.[40]

A community foundation must prepare periodic financial reports that treat all funds held by the community foundation, directly or in component parts, as its funds.[41]

Contributors, grantors, and other transferors to community foundations may rely on the publicly supported charity status of these foundations under circumstances that are the same as those applicable to reliance in the case of other categories of public charities.[42]

Material Restrictions

As noted, to be regarded as a component part of a community foundation, a trust or fund must be created by gift, bequest, or similar transfer to a community foundation that is treated as a separate entity and may not be subjected by the transferor to a material restriction with respect to the transferred assets.[43]

In order to effectuate this type of transfer, a transferor entity may not impose any material restrictions or conditions that prevent the transferee public charity from freely and effectively employing the transferred assets, or the income derived from the assets, in furtherance of its tax-exempt purposes. Whether a particular condition or restriction imposed on a transfer of assets is *material* must be determined from all of the facts and circumstances of the transfer.[44]

Some of the more significant facts and circumstances to be considered in making this determination are whether the public charity is the owner in fee of the assets it receives from the transferor, whether the assets are held and administered

---

[40] Reg. § 1.170A-9(f)(11)(F).
[41] Reg. § 1.170A-9(f)(11)(vi). An illustration of an organization satisfying these requirements is the subject of Priv. Ltr. Rul. 201307008 (Nov. 19, 2012). The IRS ruled that an exempt community foundation and a corporation that is a supporting organization with respect to the foundation will be treated as a single entity for law purposes (Priv. Ltr. Ruls. 201936002 (June 3, 2019), 201936003 (June 3, 2019).
[42] Reg. § 1.509(a)-7.
[43] See text accompanied by *supra* note 32.
[44] Reg. § 1.507-2(a)(8)(i).

by the public charity in a manner consistent with one or more of its tax-exempt purposes, whether the governing body of the public charity has the ultimate authority and control over the assets, and the income derived from them, for its tax-exempt purposes, and whether and to what extent the governing body of the public charity is organized and operated so as to be independent from the transferor.[45]

Whether a governing body is *independent from the transferor* is to also be determined by the facts and circumstances.[46] Some of the more significant facts and circumstances to be considered are whether and to what extent members of the governing body are individuals who are selected by a transferor that is a private foundation or disqualified persons with respect to it[47] each member of the governing body may serve.[48]

Acceptable Terms

The presence of some or all of the following four factors is not considered to prevent the transferee from freely and effectively employing the transferred assets, or the income derived from them, in furtherance of its tax-exempt purposes: (1) the fund is given a name or other designation that is the same as or similar to that of the transferor entity or otherwise memorializes the creator of the transferor, or the transferor itself, or his or her family; (2) the income and assets of the fund are to be used for a designated purpose or for one or more particular organizations that are not private foundations and the use is consistent with the charitable basis for the exempt status of the public charity; (3) the transferred assets are administered in an identifiable or separate fund, provided that the public charity is the legal and equitable owner of the fund and exercises ultimate and direct authority and control over the fund; and (4) the transferor transfers property the continued retention of which by the transferee is required by the transferor and is important to the achievement of charitable purposes in the community.[49]

Unacceptable Terms

The presence of any of the following seven factors is considered to prevent the transferee from freely and effectively employing the transferred assets, or the income generated by them, in furtherance of its tax-exempt purposes:

---

[45] *Id.*
[46] Reg. § 1.507–2(a)(8)(ii).
[47] IRC § 4946. See *Private Foundations*, Chapter 4.
[48] Reg. § 1.507–2(a)(8)(ii).
[49] Reg. § 1.507–2(a)(8)(iii).

The transferor reserves the right, directly or indirectly, to name the persons to which the transferee public charity must distribute, or to direct the timing of these distributions as, for example, by a power of appointment.

The terms of the transfer agreement, or any express or implied understanding between the transferor and the transferee, require the public charity to take or withhold action with respect to the transferred assets that is not designed to further one or more of the exempt purposes of the public charity, and the action or withholding of action would, if performed by the transferor, if it is a private foundation, with respect to the assets, have subjected the transferor to one or more of the private foundation excise taxes.

The public charity assumes leases, contractual obligations, or liabilities of the transferor entity, or takes the assets of the transferor subject to the liabilities, for purposes inimical to the purposes or best interests of the public charity.

The transferee public charity is required by a restriction or agreement (other than a restriction or agreement imposed or required by law or regulatory authority), express or implied, to retain, or not dispose of, any securities or other investment assets transferred to it by the transferor, either permanently or for an extended period of time.

An agreement is entered into between the transferor and the transferee public charity in connection with the transfer of securities or other property that grants to persons connected with the transferor a first right of refusal to purchase at fair market value the transferred securities or other property, when and if disposed of by the public charity.

An agreement is entered into between the transferor and the transferee public charity that establishes irrevocable relationships with respect to the maintenance or management of assets transferred to the public charity, such as continuing relationships with banks, brokerage firms, investment counselors, or other advisors with regard to the investments or other property transferred to the public charity.

Any other condition is imposed on action by the public charity that prevents it from exercising ultimate control over the assets received from the transferor for purposes consistent with its exempt purposes.[50]

With respect to the first of these seven factors, the IRS is to examine carefully whether the seeking of advice by the transferee from, or the giving of advice by, a transferor after the assets have been transferred to the transferee constitutes an indi-

---

[50] Reg. § 1.507–2(a)(8)(iv).

rect reservation of a right to direct the distributions. In this type of a case, the reservation of this type of right will be considered to exist where the only criterion considered by the public charity in making a distribution of income or principal from a transferor's fund is advice offered by the transferee. Whether there is a reservation of this type of right is to be determined on the basis of all of the facts and circumstances.[51]

This factor went to the heart of an issue that burns today—whether the right to advise constitutes in fact an ongoing form of control over the contributed property by the donor.[52] In an example, under the terms of a transfer of funds to a community trust, the donor retained the right to determine what charities are to receive distributions from the fund; the community trust lacked any right to vary the donor's direction as to distribution of the monies. This was deemed to be an adverse restriction on the transferred funds.[53] This matter has been resolved—at least as a matter of law—by statute.[54]

RESERVATION OF RIGHTS

As illustrated by the acceptable and unacceptable conditions outlined in the foregoing section, the transfer of assets in this context must be complete. The recipient public charity must have absolute dominion and control over the use of the assets it receives. Similar to terms allowed in connection with donor-advised funds, however, transferors can ask that they be allowed to advise about use of the funds. The tax regulations outline the conditions under which a transferor may reserve rights in regard to the transfer of assets.

The presence of some or all of the following factors indicates that the reservation of this type of right does not exist: (1) there has been an independent investigation by the staff of the public charity, evaluating whether the transferor's advice is consistent with specific charitable needs most deserving of support by the recipient charity; (2) the public charity has promulgated guidelines enumerating specific char-

[51] Reg. § 1.507–2(a)(8)(iv)(A)(1).
[52] See Chapter 5, pp. 132-133.
[53] Reg. § 1.507–2(a)(8)(v), Example (4). By contrast, a donor-advised arrangement in a community trust that adhered to the requirements of Reg. § 507-2(a)(8) is the subject of Priv. Ltr. Rul. 200028038 (April 14, 2000).
[54] See Chapter 4, pp. 87-89.

itable needs consistent with its charitable purposes, and the transferor's advice is consistent with these guidelines; (3) the public charity has instituted an educational program publicizing these guidelines; (4) the public charity distributes funds in excess of amounts distributed from the transferor's fund to the same or similar types of organizations or charitable needs as those recommended by the transferor; and (5) the solicitations for funds by the public charity state that it will not be bound by advice offered by the grantor.[55]

The presence of some or all of the following factors indicates that the reservation of a right exists: (1) the solicitation of funds by the public charity states or implies, or a pattern of conduct on its part creates an expectation, that the transferor's advice will be followed; (2) the advice of the transferor (whether or not restricted to a distribution of income or principal from the transferor's trust or fund) is limited to distributions of amounts from the transferor's fund (and certain factors are not present);[56] only the advice of the transferor as to distributions of the transferor's fund is solicited by the public charity and no procedure is provided for consideration of advice from persons other than the grantor with respect to the fund; and for the years involved and all prior years, the public charity follows the advice of all transferees with respect to their funds substantially all of the time.[57]

The presence of any of the foregoing factors is, as noted, considered as preventing the transferee from "freely and effectively" utilizing the transferred assets or income from them in furtherance of exempt purposes. To have application of these rules be deemed something less than a full transfer for termination purposes, however, a restriction, right, or condition must also be material.[58]

DONOR-DIRECTED FUNDS

There is little law as to the concept of the donor-directed fund; there is no general federal statutory law.[59] It is generally understood that, in the case of a donor-directed fund, the donor or a designee of the donor retains the right to direct in-

---

[55] Reg. § 1.507–2(a)(8)(iv)(A)(2).

[56] Namely, the first two of the factors in text accompanied by *supra* note 50.

[57] Reg. § 1.507–2(a)(8)(iv)(A)(3).

[58] See text accompanied by *supra* note 44.

[59] The Internal Revenue Code provides for a "pooled common fund" which is a type of private foundation (IRC §§ 170(b)(1)(A)(vii), 170(b)(1)(E)(iii)).

vestment of the fund's assets and/or to direct grants from the fund for charitable purposes. This right is a true legal right, as opposed to an opportunity to merely render advice as to investments and/or grant-making, as is the case with respect to donor-advised funds.

The principal court case on the point illustrates the distinction between a donor-advised fund and a donor-directed fund. The organization solicited contributions and made grants for charitable purposes. The IRS argued that the organization was operating a group of donor-directed funds; that argument was rejected by the court, which found that the organization was the only separate legal entity and that the organization retained full control and ownership of the donated funds and was not obligated to use the funds in the manner requested.[60]

Contributions to donor-directed funds are deductible as charitable gifts but the extent of deductibility is determined by the tax status of the ultimate recipient, inasmuch as the donor-directed fund is considered a conduit of the gift properties. There is no limit on the number of donor-directed funds that may be maintained by a charitable organization. A donor-directed fund is considered a conduit of the funds from the original donor to the ultimate grantee.

CONCEPT OF THE CONDUIT

The rule by which indirect public support constitutes public support in its entirety[61] does not apply where the amount transferred is earmarked by the donor as being for or for the benefit of the ultimate recipient.[62] This is informally referred to as a "conduit" arrangement. (The concept of the *conduit* in this context is the fundamental distinction between the donor-advised fund and the donor-directed fund.) Whether an arrangement amounts to a conduit structure is determined by the relevant facts and circumstances.

The federal tax law as to conduit arrangements in the tax-exempt organizations context is the most developed in connection with the charitable giving rules involving the deductibility of contributions where the gift proceeds are expended in countries other than the United States. Essentially, the matter comes down to

---

[60] National Foundation, Inc. v. United States, 87-2 U.S.T.C. ¶ 9602 (Ct. Cl. 1987). Likewise Fund for Anonymous Gifts v. Internal Revenue Service, 99-1 U.S.T.C. ¶ 50,440 (D.C. Cir. 1999).

[61] See text accompanied by *supra* note 21.

[62] Reg. § 1.170A-9(f)(6)(v). Cf. Reg. § 1.509(a)-3(j)(1)-(3).

whether the contribution is *earmarked* for the use and benefit of a particular person (earmarking and conduit arrangements being essentially the same thing).

Following a basic American tax law principle, deductibility of a contribution does not necessarily depend on whether the transfer is to a qualifying organization. If the gift is earmarked for a further destination, it is necessary to look beyond the immediate recipient (even if it is a qualifying organization) to determine whether the payment is a charitable contribution that will result in an income tax deduction to the donor.

As an illustration of earmarking, in one of the rare cases outside of those concerning use of gift proceeds by foreign charities, a court considered the question as to whether amounts paid to a foster home (a charity) for the care of a named individual were furnished for the use and benefit of the home and hence qualified as deductible charitable contributions. The earmarking in this instance transformed the gift, ostensibly to the foster home, into a gift to a particular individual. In the view of the court, the contributions were not to be used in any manner as deemed appropriate by the home but were for the use of a single individual in whom the donor felt a keen fatherly and personal interest. The charitable contribution deduction, in this circumstance, was denied.[63]

Charitable contributions by individuals to foreign charities generally are not deductible for federal income tax purposes.[64] (Exceptions may be found in tax treaties.) Charitable contributions to U.S. charities, that in turn make grants to foreign charities, are deductible as long as the intermediate entity is not functioning as a mere conduit of (or intermediary as to) the funds to the foreign charity.

The IRS provided guidance as to when these arrangements constitute conduits.[65] Generally, these arrangements are not conduits where the intermediate entity makes an independent determination as to when to distribute the funds and perhaps in what amounts. By contrast, the IRS wrote, "it seems clear that the requirements of . . . [the federal income tax law] would be nullified if contributions inevitably committed to a foreign organization were held to be deductible solely because, in the course of transmission to a foreign organization, they came to rest momentarily in a qualifying domestic [i.e., U.S.] organization."[66] The IRS added: "In such case

---

[63] Thomason v. Commissioner, 2 T.C. 441 (1943).
[64] IRC § 170(c)(2)(A). See Hopkins, *The Tax Law of Charitable Giving* (5th ed. 2014) (*Charitable Giving*) § 18.2.
[65] Rev. Rul. 63-252, 1963-2 C.B. 101; Rev. Rul. 66-79, 1966-1 C.B. 48.
[66] Rev. Rul. 63-252, 1963-2 C.B. 101.

the domestic organization is only nominally the donee; the real donee is the ultimate foreign recipient."[67]

"A given result at the end of a straight path is not made a different result because reached by following a devious path."[68]

IRS ruling policy permits a U.S. charitable organization to fund a foreign charitable organization (or perhaps one or more individuals) where (1) the domestic organization's purpose can be furthered by granting funds to one or more foreign entities, (2) the domestic organization has reviewed and approved the foreign entity's purposes, and (3) the grants are paid from general funds rather than from special funds solicited on behalf of the foreign organization.[69]

Difficulty arises, from the IRS's point of view, when a domestic charity is operating in such a way that it is no more than an agent or trustee for a particular foreign organization, has purposes so narrow that its funds can go only to a particular foreign organization, or solicits funds on behalf of a particular organization.

The IRS analyzed five situations:

A foreign organization causes a domestic organization to be formed to conduct a fundraising campaign in the United States, pay administrative expenses from the collected funds, and remit any balance to the foreign organization.

Certain persons in the U.S., desirous of furthering the work of a foreign organization, form a domestic charitable organization to receive contributions and send them periodically to the foreign organization.

A foreign organization and a domestic organization that had previously received a ruling from the IRS that contributions to it are deductible as charitable gifts enter into an agreement under which the domestic organization is to conduct a fundraising campaign on behalf of the foreign organization, representing to prospective contributors that the raised funds will be transferred to the foreign organization.

A domestic organization, that conducts a variety of charitable activities in a foreign country, sometimes grants funds to a foreign charitable organization to further the domestic organization's purposes. These grants are made for purposes that the domestic organization has reviewed and approved, and the grants are made from the organization's general funds rather than from a special fund raised on behalf of the foreign organization.

---

[67] Id.

[68] Griffiths v. Helvering, 308 U.S. 355, 358 (1939); Minnesota Tea Co. v. Helvering, 302 U.S. 609, 613 (1938).

[69] Rev. Rul. 63-252, 1963-2 C.B. 101.

A domestic organization that does work in a foreign country forms a subsidiary in that country to facilitate its operations. The subsidiary is formed for administrative convenience; the domestic organization controls all facets of its operation. The domestic organization will solicit funds for the specific purpose of carrying out its charitable activities in the foreign country, as it did before forming the foreign subsidiary but will now transmit the funds directly to the foreign subsidiary.[70]

A common theme in the first three of these cases is that the organizations are charitable organizations nominally created in the United States. They are organized or operated solely to solicit funds on behalf of preexisting foreign entities. The domestic entities are effectively agents or conduit organizations for the foreign beneficiaries. As such, contributions to them are not deductible under U.S. law as charitable gifts.

Examples 4 and 5 describe organizations that solicit funds without any express understanding that the donations will be forwarded to foreign entities. They are independent organizations with their own charitable programs. These organizations exercise discretion and control over the funds solicited from U.S.-based sources. Consequently, gifts to them are deductible under U.S. law.

The IRS's view is that the true donees in the first, second, and third of these situations are the foreign organizations; hence, contributions ostensibly to the domestic organization are not deductible under U.S. law. By contrast, the IRS concluded that contributions to the domestic organizations in the fourth and fifth situations are deductible as charitable gifts because the domestic organizations in these situations actually receive and essentially control the use of the funds.

The seminal IRS ruling on these points ends with recognition by the IRS that "special earmarking of the use or destination of funds paid to a qualifying charitable organization may deprive the donor of a deduction." The case law, the IRS wrote, "indicate[s] that an inquiry as to the deductibility of a contribution need not stop once it is determined that an amount has been paid to a qualifying organization; if the amount is earmarked [,] then it is appropriate to look beyond the fact that the immediate recipient is a qualifying organization to determine whether the payment constitutes a deductible contribution." The IRS continued: "Similarly, if an organization is required for other reasons, such as a specific provision in its charter, to turn contributions, or any particular contributions it receives, over to another organization, then in determining whether such contributions are deductible, it is appropriate

---

[70] Id.

to determine whether the ultimate recipient of the contribution is a qualifying organization." The IRS concluded that the "requirements of . . . [the federal tax law] would be nullified if contributions inevitable committed to go to a foreign organization were held to be deductible solely because, in the course of transmittal to the foreign organization, they came to rest momentarily in a qualifying domestic organization" and, in these cases, the domestic organization is "only nominally the donee; the real donee is the ultimate foreign recipient."[71]

The IRS, in its private letter rulings, is adding another criterion in this context, which is that the grantor of funds is expected to undertake some form of expenditure responsibility.[72] For example, the IRS observed that the board of directors of a grantor organization was to "review" and "monitor" the use of granted charitable funds.[73] In another instance, the IRS wrote of a requirement of "periodic accounting" for the monies granted; in this ruling, the IRS found the requisite control, in part because of the existence of a monitoring procedure.[74] Monitoring is referenced in other private letter rulings.[75] In one ruling, the IRS suggested that granting organizations must maintain some form of "control" over the granted funds.[76]

More recently, the IRS announced that it was in the process of revoking the tax-exempt charitable status of a U.S. entity, on the ground that it is a mere conduit of funds it raises in the U.S. and distributes to a foreign charity.[77] The agency's examination yielded no information about the organization's control or discretion over the grantee's use of the funds (what the IRS termed "expenditure responsibility") or how the foreign organization utilizes the funds. As the IRS stated the matter, the federal tax law[78] "would be nullified if contributions inevitably committed to go to a foreign organization were held to be deductible solely because, in the course of transmission to the foreign organization, they came to rest momentarily in a qualifying domestic organization."

---

[71] *Id.*

[72] The IRS should not go too far in this regard, however, in that Congress imposed expenditure responsibility requirements only on private foundations (IRC § 4945(h)). See *Private Foundations* § 9.7.

[73] Priv. Ltr. Rul. 8839029 (June 29, 1988).

[74] Priv. Ltr. Rul. 8714050 (Jan. 6, 1987).

[75] E.g., Priv. Ltr. Rul. 8408051 (Nov. 23, 1983).

[76] Priv. Ltr. Rul. 8408054 (Nov. 23, 1983).

[77] Priv. Ltr. Rul. 201751015 (June 21, 2017).

[78] IRC § 170(c)(2)(A).

FUNDRAISING CHARITIES

Tax-exempt, charitable activity is considered, by the IRS and courts, to occur where contributions are made to a qualified organization and that entity makes grants to other charitable entities. Grantmaking is the exempt function. That is, the law focuses on the grantmaking function rather than the process used to procure, or the source of, the granted funds.

It has been IRS policy since 1924 that a nonprofit organization that carries on operations that involve generation and receipt of contributions (and usually also investment income) and distribution of its income to charities is eligible to receive recognition of tax exemption as a public charity.[79] This principle of law was restated by the IRS in 1967, when it considered the case of an organization formed for the purpose of providing financial assistance to several types of charitable organizations. The IRS ruled that this organization, that "carrie[d] on no operations other than to receive contributions and incidental investment income and to make distributions of income to such exempt organizations at periodic intervals," was eligible for tax exemption as a charitable entity.[80]

In a 1960s case reviewed by the IRS, a resulting technical advice memorandum states that "[c]haritable organizations have traditionally engaged in fund raising activities as a means of raising funds to carry out their charitable purposes." This memorandum concludes: "The mere fact that an organization derives its income primarily from such fund-raising activity is not considered to defeat either the primary purposes or the substantial activity tests" in the tax regulations concerning charitable exempt status.[81]

Another considered by the IRS in the 1970s involved a "social fund raiser," the objective of which was to "raise money for charity through members, family and friends sponsoring socials, lunches and dinners, and donations for the affairs to be given for various charitable organizations." This entity owned a clubhouse where these events took place. In a technical advice memorandum, the IRS wrote: "Many charitable organizations do not engage in active charitable undertakings themselves, but rather assist the work of religious, charitable, educational or similar organizations by contributing money to them," adding that "[p]roviding financial assistance to such organizations is a charitable activity justifying exemption."[82]

[79] I.T. 1495, III-1 C.B. 273 (1924).
[80] Rev. Rul. 67-149, 1967-1 C.B. 133.
[81] 1982 EO CPE Text at 6-7.
[82] *Id.* at 9.

In another case from the 1970s, an organization operated a beer "kegger" for the benefit of local charities, producing considerable revenue. The IRS ruled that the organization qualified for exemption as a charitable entity.[83] Presumably, this organization granted an appropriate amount of this revenue for charitable purposes.

An early version of the IRS's *Exempt Organizations Handbook* contains this observation: "Many charitable foundations do not engage in active charitable undertakings themselves, but rather assist the work of religious, charitable, educational, or similar organizations by contributing money to them. The foundation's funds may be dedicated to purposes as broad as but no broader than, the purposes set out in IRC [§] 501(c)(3). These foundations are charitable in the broad sense of the word."[84]

A court observed: "It seems well settled that an organization need not engage in a functional charitable activity to be organized and operated for charitable purposes within the meaning of section 501(c)(3). . . . Such charitable purposes may be accomplished solely by providing funds to other exempt [charitable] organizations."[85] Another court similarly stated: "In determining whether an activity is organized for educational purposes and so exempt from social security taxes, the purposes for which it spends its income and not the means whereby it obtains income are conclusive."[86]

The foregoing body of law is directly applicable to sponsoring organizations maintaining donor-advised funds. Writing about national sponsoring organizations, the Department of the Treasury stated that the "main characteristic of [them] is that the sponsorship of the DAFs and other similar accounts or funds generally appears to constitute the principal activity performed by the sponsoring organization," adding that these organizations "largely focus on receiving contributions, converting non-cash donations into a more liquid form, facilitating grant-making, and managing the investment of DAF assets, rather than the direct provision of charitable services."[87] This report also observed that sponsoring organizations are entities "whose primary role is to serve as intermediaries between donors and a broad range of charities."[88]

---

[83] *Id.* at 9-10.

[84] *Id.* at 33.

[85] Golf Life World Entertainment Golf Championship, Inc. v. United States, 65-1 U.S.T.C. ¶ 9174 (S.D. Cal. 1964)).

[86] Southeastern Fair Association v. United States, 52 F. Supp. 219 (Ct. Cl. 1943).

[87] Department of the Treasury, Report to Congress on Supporting Organizations and Donor Advised Funds 49 (2011) (Treasury Report). See Chapter 3, pp. 73-75.

[88] Treasury Report at 21.

This distinction made between organizations that engage solely in fundraising and grantmaking ("intermediaries") and organizations that engage in the "direct provision of charitable services" was not a criticism by Treasury, it was an observation. This observation is a direct reflection of the IRS's ruling, in 1967, that organizations that "receive contributions" and "make distributions" to other charitable entities are themselves tax-exempt charitable entities.[89] It also directly reflects the observation of the federal district court that stated that an organization "need not engage in a functional charitable activity to be organized and operated for charitable purposes."[90] As the tax regulations have stated for decades, the term *charitable* is "used in section 501(c)(3) in its generally accepted legal sense and is, therefore, not to be construed as limited by the separate enumeration in section 501(c)(3) of other tax-exempt purposes which may fall within the broad outlines of 'charity' as developed by judicial decisions."[91]

Yet critics of donor-advised funds and their sponsors continue to advance the argument that donor-advised funds are not "really" charities. These critics criticize DAFs for not being "working" charities or "actual" charities.[92] Professor Roger Colinvaux writes that sponsoring organizations "in effect are no more than fundraising organizations."[93] He is absolutely correct. Then, he writes that, when considering sponsoring organizations as fundraising organization, the "case for [their] 501(c)(3) status is qualitatively weak."[94] That is not correct, as the foregoing summary of the law, dating back to 1924, illustrates. Clearly, fundraising charities are tax-exempt charities. Conceding that the "fundraising rationale for exempt status is longstanding," Professor Colinvaux inexplicably concludes—in the face of much authority to the contrary—that the "501(c)(3) fundraising organization stands at the edge of legitimacy."[95] How can that be? His answer: "Charity is accomplished in the doing"[96] and "[t]o grant 'charitable' status to a shell seems awkward and counterintuitive."[97]

---

[89] Rev. Rul. 67-149, 1967-1 C.B. 133.

[90] Golf Life World Entertainment Golf Championship, Inc. v. United States, 65-1 U.S.T.C. ¶ 9174 (S.D. Cal. 1964)).

[91] Reg. § 1.501(c)(3)-1(d)(2).

[92] One commentator in this regard pronounces donor-advised funds to be "zombie" charities (Arnold, "Put a Stake in 'Zombie Charity.' Philanthropy Is for the Living," 31 *Chron of Phil.* (Issue 11) 31 (Sep. 2019)).

[93] Colinvaux, "Donor Advised Funds: Charitable Spending Vehicles for 21st Century Philanthropy," 92 *Wash. L. Rev.* 39, 62 (2017)..

[94] *Id.* at 64.

[95] *Id.*

[96] *Id.*

[97] *Id.* at 65.

But, again, as this body of law makes amply clear, fundraising and grantmaking are among the ways of accomplishing the "doing" and fundraising charities (including sponsoring organizations) are not mere "shells."

But there is more. The federal tax statutory law providing tax exemption for charitable organizations[98] certainly does not make this distinction between fundraising intermediaries and charities that engage in "functional" programs. By contrast, however, the tax regulations that accompany and expand on this body of exemption law openly recognize and encourage this distinction. For example, schools are tax-exempt because they are educational institutions,[99] various types of research facilities are exempt because they are scientific institutions,[100] and churches are exempt because they are religious institutions. Yet, many types of nonprofit organizations are exempt as charitable organizations because they engage in activities that collaterally support and benefit these and similar institutions. These entities are termed the *advancement* organizations. Thus, an entity can be an exempt charity because it advances education, advances science, and/or advances religion.[101] True, some of these advancement organizations have "functional" programming but others have "intermediary" functions, such as fundraising and holding of endowments. Often, supporting organizations fall into these classifications. Donor-advised funds are sometimes sponsored by educational institutions; some sponsoring organizations confine their efforts (their "doings") to discrete fields, such as religion.

Consequently, there is no basis in the law for bifurcating the charitable sector on the basis of these functional distinctions—the members of this sector have equal status when it comes to tax exemption. Efforts to downgrade and denigrate charities that focus only on fundraising and grantmaking are not supported by the law. These are merely artifices deployed by DAF critics.[102]

---

[98] IRC §§ 501(a), 501(c)(3).

[99] Reg. § 1.501(c)(3)-1(d)(3).

[100] Reg. § 1.501(c)(3)-1(d)(5).

[101] Reg. § 1.501(c)(3)-1(d)(2).

[102] This distinction is manifested in the *Chronicle of Philanthropy's* current criteria for ranking "America's Favorite Charities." In the ranking published late in 2019, sponsoring organizations are left out, because the "focus" is on "groups with defined charitable missions," as opposed to donor-advised funds that are merely "financial tools to hold and distribute charitable funds" (Stiffman and Haynes, "Can the Boom Times Last?," 32 *Chron. of Phil.* (Issue 1) 8, 10 (Nov. 2019). Among other outcomes, this approach distorts the rankings. For example, United Way Worldwide is cast as number one, having raised over $3 trillion in 2018, although the Fidelity Charitable Gift Fund raised $9 trillion during that year and is not included. The *Chronicle* does not include contributions made to donor-advised funds held by community foundations in compiling its list either, causing only one community foundation to be on the list of the nation's top fundraising charities. In general, see Chapter 3, p. 68.

Having reviewed the law concerning fundraising charities, there is another aspect of it that directly pertains to sponsoring organizations and donor-advised funds—the commensurate test.

COMMENSURATE TEST

A test that is related to the venerable operational test[103] was developed by the IRS and unveiled in 1964: the commensurate test.[104] Pursuant to this test, the IRS is empowered to assess whether an organization, to be tax-exempt as a charitable entity, is maintaining program activities that are commensurate in scope with its financial resources. In the facts underlying this initial ruling, the organization derived most of its income in the form of rent, yet was successful in preserving its exempt status because it satisfied the commensurate test in that it was engaging in an adequate amount of charitable functions notwithstanding the extent of its rental activities. These charitable functions consisted of making grants to other charitable organizations.

In 1990, the IRS revoked the tax-exempt status of a charitable organization on a variety of rationales, including the ground that its fundraising costs were too high and thus violated the commensurate test. In a technical advice memorandum,[105] the IRS concluded that the test was transgressed because of its finding that the charity involved in the case expended, during the years under examination, only about 1 percent of its revenue for charitable purposes; the rest was allegedly spent for fundraising and administration. The matter of the organization's exempt status was ultimately resolved in court, albeit without application of the commensurate test; the case turned out to be one involving private inurement.[106]

The commensurate test and the primary purpose test[107] have an awkward coexistence. For example, a charitable organization was allowed to retain its tax-exempt

---

[103] One of the fundamental requirements for tax exemption as a charitable entity is that the organization be operated exclusively for one or more exempt purposes (Reg. § 1.501(c)(3)-1(c)(1). See Hopkins, *The Law of Tax-Exempt Organizations* (12th ed. 2019) (*Tax-Exempt Organizations*) § 4.5.

[104] Rev. Rul. 64-182, 1964-1 C.B. 186 (Part 1).

[105] This technical advice memorandum is reproduced at 4 *Exempt Org. Tax Rev.* (No. 5) 726 (July 1991).

[106] United Cancer Council, Inc. v. Commissioner, 109 T.C. 326 (1997), *rev'd and rem'd*, 165 F.3d 1173 (7th Cir. 1999). The private inurement doctrine is the subject of *Tax-Exempt Organizations*, Chapter 20.

[107] See *Tax-Exempt Organizations* § 4.4.

status while receiving 98 percent of its support in the form of unrelated business income, inasmuch as 41 percent of the organization's activities were charitable programs.[108] Likewise, an organization retained its exemption despite the fact that two-thirds of its operations were unrelated businesses.[109] Yet a public charity had its tax exemption revoked by application of the commensurate test, because, in the two years under examination, although its bingo game gross income was 73 percent and 92 percent of total gross income, only a small amount of this money was distributed for charitable purposes.[110] Likewise, an organization had its exemption as a charitable entity revoked because it was conducting Motto games "while making no significant charitable donations."[111]

The commensurate test can be invoked in connection with organizations that seek to be tax-exempt charitable entities where their functions consist of fundraising and grantmaking for exempt purposes. On occasion, the IRS will rule that this type of organization cannot qualify for exemption.[112] Nonetheless, in one instance, the IRS wrote that an organization that conducts bingo games may be exempt as a charitable entity "if it uses the proceeds from bingo to conduct a charitable program, commensurate in scope with its financial resources, of making grants to other charitable organizations."[113]

Case law is essentially the same. For example, an organization conducted bingo games as its principal activity; its stated purpose was to conduct these games and provide financial assistance for the care of needy children and children's charities. The organization made grants to charitable entities that were insubstantial when compared to its gross receipts from the games. A court held that this organization did not qualify for exemption as a charitable entity because it did not engage in any charitable activities and principally operated the bingo game business.[114]

---

[108] Tech. Adv. Mem. 9711003 (Nov. 8, 1995). The IRS concluded, by application of the commensurate test, that the tax-exempt status of four charities should not be revoked because of the small amount of money they granted for charitable purposes (Field Service Adv. Mem. 199910007 (Nov. 24, 1998).

[109] Tech. Adv. Mem. 200021056 (Feb. 8, 2000).

[110] Priv. Ltr. Rul. 200825046 (Mar. 11, 2008).

[111] Priv. Ltr. Rul. 201415003 (Dec. 19, 2013).

[112] The IRS once classified these entities as "unproductive" fundraising organizations (1982 EO CPE Text, at 54).

[113] Priv. Ltr. Rul. 201103057 (Oct. 25, 2010).

[114] Help the Children, Inc. v. Commissioner, 28 T.C. 1128 (1957).

A TRIPARTITE CLASSIFICATION

Although this is not a matter of law, the landscape of donor-advised funds is sometimes viewed from the perspective of three categories of sponsoring organizations:
community foundations, single-issue charities, and the national sponsoring organizations. One report notes that this approach to classification of sponsoring organizations "provide[s] a useful way to explain the evolution of donor-advised funds in
the United States".[115] That is, the "history of donor-advised funds tracks closely
with that of community foundations."[116]

The National Trust for Philanthropy's 2019 report on donor-advised funds is
based on data concerning 989 sponsoring organizations. Community foundations
comprise 603 of these sponsoring organizations. The other two categories of sponsoring organizations are 332 single-issue charities and 54 national charities.

"As time passed" [i.e., about 60 years], this report continues (in a striking understatement), the community foundations' model of donor-advised funds "caught
the attention of commercial investment managers and financial firms that recognized
the potential of the model."[117] In addition, the report notes, "single-issue charities
such as those devoted to religious causes or education saw that it was possible to
house donor-advised funds in addition to other funds."[118]

As to the latter, "nonprofits not traditionally in the business of donor-advised
funds are establishing them."[119] For example, donor-advised funds are becoming
popular at colleges and universities, where money management has long been strong
because of these institutions' endowment funds. One report, published at the close
of 2018, states that a dozen of these institutions, including Dartmouth, Harvard,
Notre Dame, Stanford, and Yale Universities, "have garnered a total of $1.2 billion
in endowment-managed donor-advised funds."[120] In these instances, of course, most
of the grants involved must be made to the college or university.

---

[115] "The Data on Donor-Advised Funds: New Insights You Need to Know" (Giving USA (2018)) (Giving USA 2018 DAF Report), at 13.

[116] *Id.* See Chapter 2.

[117] Giving USA 2018 DAF Report, at 13. See Chapter 2.

[118] Giving USA 2018 DAF Report, at 13.

[119] Blum, "In-House Donor-Advised Funds," 30 *Chron. of Phil.* (Issue 8) 28 (June 2018)). This article
features this opening caption: "Seeing the stunning success of advised-fund sponsors like Fidelity, more
nonprofits are getting in on what they hope will be a good thing for them, too."

[120] Lorin, "Got $5 Million? Yale Will Invest It," *Bloomberg Businessweek* (issue 4596 (Dec. 17, 2018)).

POPULARITY OF DAFS

A recent article opens with this: "Over the last few years, the charitable giving world has undergone a major transformation. Instead of contributing directly to a charity or, in the case of high-net-worth individuals, creating a private foundation from which to donate, Americans of all stripes are increasingly using donor-advised funds for their giving needs."[121] Simply put, donor-advised funds are "one of the fastest-growing charitable-giving vehicles in the U.S."[122]

This rising popularity of donor-advised funds is attributable to many factors. Some of these factors are the simplicity of establishing these funds (as opposed to, for example setting up a private foundation[123]), the centralizing of charitable giving in a single account and the resulting record of gifts, the opportunity to have the maximum in deductibility of contributions,[124] the ability to grow the amounts in the funds without taxation (through investment earnings and/or additional gifts), and the ability to integrate DAF contributions with the donors' other financial plans.[125] As to the latter factor, "[p]otential donors are becoming increasingly aware of DAFs through the advice of their financial planners, tax advisors, and stock-brokers."[126]

Donor-advised funds took on a significant role in the aftermath of enactment of revised tax laws in late 2017, which caused the standard deduction amount to be nearly doubled and thus drastically shrank the number of taxpayers who itemize tax deductions. This law development has led to the concept of "bunching" of charitable contributions in a single year to gain the maximum tax advantages for the giving

---

[121] Borzykowski, "The Rapid Rise of Donor-Advised Funds," 201 *Forbes* (Issue 8 (Oct. 31, 2018)).

[122] Mullich, "Donor-Advised Funds: The Fastest-Growing Vehicle for Charitable Giving," 200 *Forbes* (Issue 5 (Nov. 14, 2017)).

[123] One analysis of this point states that a donor-advised fund "can be set up immediately with no start-up costs, whereas starting a private or family foundation can take weeks or months and incurs certain compulsory initial legal fees" (Giving USA 2018 DAF Report at 15). It is true that legal fees are usually entailed when establishing a private foundation but it is unusual to characterize them as "compulsory."

[124] The federal tax laws favor public charities over private foundations when it comes to the deductibility of charitable contributions. For example, gifts of money to public charities are generally annually capped at 50 percent of individual donors' adjusted gross income (and in some instances up to 60 percent of AGI), gits of money to private foundations are annually capped at 30 percent of AGI (with carryovers in both instances). Also, gifts of appreciated property may give rise to a greater tax deduction in the case of donee public charities.

[125] See Chapter 2, p. 40.

[126] Smith and Morris, "Donor-Advised Funds: A Well-Kept Secret," 71 *CPA Jour.* (Issue 9 (Sep. 2001)). Obviously an out-of-date title!

year, with donors claiming the standard deduction in other years. A large gift to a donor-advised fund in the giving year can smooth out the rate of distributions to charities over the multi-year period.[127] Fidelity Charitable elegantly described this phenomenon as donors "adjusting the cadence of their [donor-advised fund] contributions in order to maximize their tax benefit."[128] The sponsoring organization wrote that donor-advised funds "are helping donors maintain a consistent level of support to the charities they care about, while allowing them to time their contributions for the maximum tax deduction," adding that it "expect[s] that the unique structure of donor-advised funds will encourage donors to maintain their consistent pace of granting."[129]

An illustration of this bunching technique posits a married couple, filing jointly, who typically contributed $5,000 annually to charity. This couple pays $8,000 per year in mortgage interest and $10,000 per year in state and local taxes. With the bunching approach, the couple contributes $15,000 every three years into their donor-advised fund. Over a six-year period, the couple itemizes their deductions in year one and year four (obviously the same years in which they make their charitable gifts), and claims the standard deduction in years two, three, five, and six.[130]

Donor-advised funds can facilitate the charitable contribution of complex assets (such as privately traded securities, real estate, interests in partnerships and limited liability companies, and cryptocurrencies), by assisting with the conversion and liquidation of them, and maximize the deduction for these types of gifts.[131] This is an interesting and positive development, although DAF critics often do not see it that way.[132] Fidelity Charitable appears to be leading the way in this regard, observing that, while most charitable contributions in the U.S. are made in cash or cash equivalents (e.g., checks and debit and credit cards), donors to its advised funds "reach beyond charitable giving and embrace charitable planning."[133] This sponsoring or-

---

[127] E.g., Rothey, "A Surprising Benefit of the New Tax Law," Bloomberg BNA, *Daily Tax Report* (No. 65) G-11 (April 4, 2018).

[128] Fidelity Charitable, *2019 Giving Report*, at 11.

[129] *Id.*

[130] Greater Kansas City Community Foundation website.

[131] For example, gifts of this nature to private foundations are generally confined, from the standpoint of calculation of the deduction, to an amount equal to the donors' basis in the property (IRC § 170(e)(1)(B)(ii)).

[132] E.g., Institute for Policy Studies, "Warehousing Wealth: Donor-Advised Charity Funds Sequestering Billions in the Face of Growing Inequality" (July 25, 2018), where it is written that the "primary attractions for the use of DAFs among the super-wealthy are the advantages related to the relief of capital gains tax burdens, and the easy donation of non-cash appreciated assets – an area of charitable giving rife with potential abuses" (at 3).

ganization reports that 63 percent of contributions made to it in 2018 were in the form of "strategic non-cash assets," including publicly traded securities and non-publicly traded assets.[134]

Donor-advised funds can also be a means for including family members in charitable giving. This is often a major factor in the private foundation context.[135] It is now equally applicable in the donor-advised fund setting, where DAFs that "involve both parents and children in grant-making can be a rich training ground to pass on family values and establish a tradition of family philanthropy."[136]

Some individuals use donor-advised funds to plan their philanthropic giving over a lengthy period of time. A principal model here is to make charitable contributions to these funds during the years when donors are earning money, then distribute the funds during their retirement years when they have more time to focus on philanthropic pursuits. One set of commentators referred to this utilization of donor-advised funds as "spread[ing] philanthropic activity across the life cycle."[137] Another variation on this theme is for hedge fund managers to make contributions to a donor-advised fund during a high-earnings phase, then focus on making distributions from the DAF after the hedge fund has wound down.[138]

An underutilized aspect of donor-advised funds' existence is their prospective role in enhanced charitable fundraising. For example, consultant Ron Ries has written that charities, facing declines in giving due to the shrinking base of deduction itemizers, should seek support from donors who have established DAFs because they have "greater flexibility in their requests, since they know assets have been specifically set up to meet these charitable needs" and charities should also contact sponsoring organizations because "these fund managers have considerable influence and authority to grant distributions as they see appropriate as part of their fiduciary responsibilities."[139]

Nonprofits advisor Ken Nopar appears to be among the first to raise this point. He rejected the claims that the primary purpose of donor-advised funds is to help "wealthy people . . . receive tax benefits" and that these funds are diverting charitable

---

[133] Fidelity Charitable, *2019 Giving Report*, at 14.
[134] *Id.*
[135] See Chapter 6, p. 186.
[136] Foord, "Philanthropy 101: Donor-Advised Funds," *Jour. of Financial Planning* (Nov. 2003).
[137] Harris and Hemel, "Don't Delay Deductions for Gifts to Donor-Advised Funds," *Chron. of Phil.* (Oct. 7, 2019).
[138] Ebeling, "The $80 Billion Charity Stash: Donor-Advised Funds Reach Record Highs" (Forbes.com (Nov. 15, 2016).
[139] Ries, "First Look at the Tax Cuts and Jobs Act: The Impact on Donor Advised Funds," 88 *CPA Jour.* (Issue 4 (April 2018)).

contributions. He wrote that "[n]early all families and individuals who establish donor-advised funds have a strong desire to support their favorite charities and causes."[140] The main point of his article is that the existence of funds at sponsoring organizations, including the national ones, "has made it easier for financial, tax, and legal advisors to talk to their clients about philanthropy—and that is leading to more giving now and in the future." Nopar outlines some "simple steps" that charitable organizations can take to "encourage more DAF holders to support their organizations." His view is that "[n]onprofit organizations should view DAFs as friends, not enemies," adding that "[e]verybody in the nonprofit world should support any technique that creates more opportunities for charitable giving." Without donor-advised funds, he notes, the "charitable conversation between advisers and clients would occur less often, and fewer assets would be allocated for charitable purposes." Nopar concludes that, "if new and more onerous restrictions are applied, that situation will grow even worse."[141]

The Council on Foundations issued a statement in mid-2108, stating that "[d]onor advised funds have long served as a philanthropic tool to transfer charitable dollars to organizations that need it most.[142] "Unfortunately," the Council continued, "recent news articles have mischaracterized donor advised funds, which are far from a loophole designed for the wealthy."[143] The statement continued: "The fact is that donor advised funds and their relatively low startup costs have enabled the philanthropic spirit of millions of middle-class families and have empowered donors to remain engaged in charitable efforts beyond a one-time contribution."

An analysis of these points concluded that, "[f]or many donors, the benefits of donor-advised funds make these giving vehicles a key component of their philanthropic activity."[144] These developments are correspondingly leading to the "growth of diversity of philanthropy," in the sense that, by means of donor-advised funds, "we are opening philanthropy to a new segment of the American population" and, in doing so, are "literally democratizing philanthropy."[145]

---

[140] Nopar, "Savvy Nonprofits Can Reap Big Benefits," XXVII *Chron. of Phil.* (No. 2) 29 (Nov. 6, 2014).

[141] An illustration of a public charity's successful fundraising efforts using the resources of donor-advised funds is in Lindsay, "Raising Money From Donor-Advised Funds: It's There for the Asking; You Just Have to Ask," 31 *Chron. of Phil.* (Issue 7) 47 (May 2019).

[142] Statement reprinted in *EO Tax Jour.* 2018-176 (Sep. 7, 2018).

[143] See Chapter 5, pp. 131-132.

[144] Giving USA 2018 DAF Report, at 15.

[145] Gunderson, "Current Trends in Philanthropy," 84 *Jour. of Jewish Communal Service* (No. 1/2) 91, 92 (Winter/Spring 2009).

CHAPTER TWO:
Evolution of and Thinking
about Donor-Advised Funds

The history of donor-advised funds spans over 100 years. This history features six major phases: (1) the beginning of these funds with the emergence of the community foundation in the early 1900s, (2) the impact of the Tax Reform Act of 1969, (3) the consequences of a major court decision, (4) the rise of the so-called national (or "commercial"[146]) donor-advised funds, (5) enactment of the Pension Protection Act of 2006, and (6) the issuance of federal tax regulations concerning donor-advised funds. There have been other significant developments, interspersed throughout these phases.

HISTORICAL AND SOCIOLOGICAL PERSPECTIVES

Americans have always had a certain antipathy toward the wealthy. Throughout the nation's history, there has been distrust among the citizenry of amassed wealth in all forms, whether held by individuals, for-profit companies, or charitable institutions. And yet, just about any American would gladly join the ranks of the rich if they could (as participation in state lotteries attests). This contradiction in attitude has played out over the decades; it is manifest today, as the controversy over donor-advised funds rages on.

Donor-advised funds, often being huge accumulations of wealth, are magnets for criticism for a variety of reasons. One of these reasons is that these funds are seen, in some quarters, as playthings of the rich and facilitators of various abuses by the wealthy. Thus, these funds are the most recent inheritors of Americans' love-hate relationship with those who are financially successful beyond the dreams of the vast majority of citizens.

One of the early legal devices that facilitated massive accretions of wealth was the long-term trust, sometimes referred to as the *dynastic trust*.[147] The fundamental purpose of these trusts was to hold and manage capital assets, such as securities, land, and businesses. The law did not always favor these arrangements—witness the complex rule against perpetuities—but they persisted and endured. Indeed, the rule embodying the prudent investor standard sprang from this body of law.[148]

The concept of the dynastic trust gave birth to the long-term charitable trust. The great historian of American law, Lawrence M. Friedman, wrote that "[c]harities, so goes

---

[146] The term *commercial donor-advised fund* is used, in a derogatory fashion of course, in reference to donor-advised funds maintained by sponsoring organizations that are affiliated with investment management companies. As a matter of law, however, these organizations and the donor-advised funds in them are not commercial at all. In connection with litigation (see text accompanied by *infra* notes 115-118), a national sponsoring organization repeatedly denied in its answer that there is any "legal significance" to the characterization of a donor-advised fund as a "commercial" donor-advised fund.
[147] E.g., Friedman, A History of American Law, Third Edition 184 (Simon & Schuster, New York: 2005).
[148] See *infra* note 152.

the maxim, are favorites of the law," although the "favor was not always very obvious."[149] He continued: "In the early nineteenth century, charity was associated with privilege, with the dead hand, with established churches (especially the Roman Catholic Church), with massive wealth held in perpetuity"—none of these being "particularly popular".[150]

As Friedman noted, "[h]ostility toward charitable trusts weakened, but only slowly."[151] An important case, decided in 1830 by a Massachusetts court, upheld what was then a major transfer of wealth ($50,000) to a hospital and a college, the latter for endowment of a chair in history.[152] Friedman dryly concluded that a "college endowment, consisting of stocks and bonds, and supporting a professor of history, was not as frightening as a barony or church."[153] (Yet, there is more to this case from the standpoint of evolution of nonprofit law; it laid down the modern-day standard for the conduct of trustees of charitable trusts.)

Later, the U.S. Supreme Court upheld the validity of the concept of the charitable trust in the United States, even in states where there was no authorizing statute, holding that chancery courts have the inherent power to administer trusts.[154] This case concerned a devise establishing a college, where nothing in the transfer was said to be in opposition "to any known policy" of the state involved.[155]

The courts in New York struck down the validity of a multi-million-dollar charitable trust as recently as 1891; the state's legislature changed the law in 1893. Some states had passed statutes—termed *mortmain* laws—prohibiting death-bed gifts to charity. Friedman observed that, behind these laws, was the "fantasy of the evil priest, extorting ransom for the Church from a dying man, as the price of absolution."[156] (Public antipathy toward trusts persists today. Thus, the body of law designed to minimize monopolies and eliminate most restraints of trade is still termed anti-*trust* law.)

In 1867, a state court invoked the *cy pres* doctrine—a rule long in use in England—to help perpetuate a long-term dynastic charity.[157] It concluded that, since a chancery court has equity jurisdiction over charitable trusts, and that support of those trusts is of concern to the "whole public" and are allowed by law to be per-

---

[149] Friedman, *supra* note 147, at 185.
[150] *Id.*
[151] *Id.* at 186.
[152] Harvard College v. Amory, 26 Mass. (9 Pick.) 446, 461 (1830).
[153] Friedman, *supra* note 147, at 186.
[154] Vidal v. Girard's Executors, 43 U.S. 127 (1844).
[155] *Id.* at 201.
[156] Freidman, *supra* note 147, at 185.
[157] Jackson v. Phillips, 96 Mass. 539 (1867).

petual, the court has inherent authority to apply the doctrine.[158]

Friedman noted that the "changing nature of American wealth" had the effect of weakening restrictions on charitable gifts and charitable trusts.[159] That was a wry reference to the phenomenon of the emergence of the "barons of finance, oil, and steel" beginning to "give away conscience money."[160] He observed, in that context, that the great foundations were still far in the future."[161] Those foundations were not that far away, however; they were speedily coming and would transform and greatly enhance American philanthropy.[162] The names and philanthropies of individuals such as Carnegie, Mellon, Julliard, and Rockefeller would soon enter the history books.

Another reason that the discussions about donor-advised funds is so subjective and harsh is that they are being undertaken in the context of the tenor of our time. We are not, to state the matter mildly, in an era treasuring civil and rational discourse. Charges of "fake news" swirl about. These days, it seems, everyone is a critic and everything needs to be criticized. In this environment, the attitude frequently is that criticism must be ferocious to be effective, with plenty of hyperbole and chunks of inaccuracy thrown in to stoke the heat. Thus, the bombast, the hurtling of words, in the donor-advised fund context, such as "sham," "loophole," "fraud," and "black-box."

Still another reason, one that intersects the antipathy-toward-the-wealthy and tenor-of-our-times reasons, is the class divide, which apparently is widening.[163] Part of this is partisan politics, but the one-percenters are attracting great vitriol. Soak the rich (as in heavily tax them) is back in vogue. The wealthy are ridiculed with photographs of mansions and yachts. Much of the media pushes the view that the recent tax law changes benefit only those already financially well off. The college admissions bribe scandal afforded many the opportunity to posture about the excesses, if not the evils, of the rich. So, stories about billionaires stashing huge amounts

---

[158] *Id.* at 580.

[159] Friedman, *supra* note 147, at 318.

[160] *Id.*

[161] *Id.*

[162] Private foundations are frequently referenced throughout this book. In general, *Private Foundations*. For a thorough analysis of the history of private foundations, see Hammack and Anheier, *A Versatile American Institution: The Changing Ideals and Realities of Philanthropic Foundations* (Brookings Institution Press, Wash., DC: 2013).

[163] E.g., General Accountability Office, "Income and Wealth Disparities Continue Through Old Age" (GAO-19-587 (Aug. 9, 2019)); this report found disparities in income and wealth among older households have become greater over the past three decades. Yet, the Census Bureau reported on Sep. 10, 2019, that the poverty rate declined in 2018 to 11.8 percent, the lowest level since 2001, according to the *New York Times* (Fadulu, "Gap Between Rich and Poor Gets Bigger," Sep. 11, 2019, at A15).

of highly appreciated property in donor-advised funds, with total lack of interest in authentic charity, fit right in with anti-wealth narratives.

Charities have existed in this country from its beginning, of course. The march of history in this regard reflects emergence of the charitable trust, followed by community chests and community foundations, private foundations, endowments, and, now, donor-advised funds. Each of these types of charitable funds were maligned along the way.

Assemble the pieces of today's arguments against donor-advised funds: The super-rich are avoiding (or hacking) taxes by stockpiling (or warehousing) complex assets in non-transparent (or black-box) fake charities at the expense of real (or working) charities and the poor these authentic charities serve in increasingly tough economic times (which are getting tougher because the rich are getting richer). Matters worsen because the national sponsoring organizations are untrustworthy.

IMPORT OF COMMUNITY FOUNDATIONS

It is generally recognized that the birth of the donor-advised fund is closely related to development of the community foundation.[164] The report on these funds issued by the Lilly Family School of Philanthropy states the matter flatly: "The history of donor-advised funds tracks closely with that of community foundations."[165]

Unique charitable giving vehicles began to emerge early in the twentieth century. Most notable are the private foundation, the community foundation, and the charitable remainder trust.[166] For long periods of time, these entities were not recognized in formal law. As will be discussed, that state of affairs eventually changed—in each case.

Historian Lila Corwin Berman, who has written the most detailed history of donor-advised funds,[167] commenced her narrative with a brief summary of the development of federal statutory tax law: the 1894 tariff, the overturning of that legislation by the U.S. Supreme Court, ratification of the Sixteenth Amendment to the

---

[164] For a discussion of the formal legal requirements for community foundations, see Chapter 1, text accompanied by notes 26–42, and *Private Foundations* § 15.4(d).

[165] Giving USA, *The Data on Donor-Advised Funds: New Insights You Need to Know* (Jan. 2018), at 13.

[166] Charitable remainder trusts are largely outside the scope of this book. In general, *Charitable Giving*, Chapter 12.

[167] Berman, "Donor Advised Funds in Historical Perspective," paper published in connection with the Boston College Law School Forum on Philanthropy and the Public Good (2015) (Berman Paper).

U.S. Constitution, and adoption of tax legislation in 1913 and 1917.[168] The 1984
and 1913 legislation introduced the feature of tax exemption for charitable and like
entities; the 1917 legislation brought the charitable contribution deduction. Berman
wrote that Congress, in crafting this legislation, was "careful to protect the structures
of private associationism and denominationalism that had emerged as central to
American democracy in the prior century."[169] Noting that the 1917 legislation was
enacted in support of American efforts in World War I, she explained the charitable
deduction (a "mechanism . . . to deplete treasury dollars") as reflecting an "enduring
commitment to private modes of governance: allowing individuals to make decisions
about and for the public good."[170] She added: "Changing ideals about the proper
balance between public and private governance in a healthy democracy shaped tax
policy and philanthropic structures."[171]

This matter of emerging "philanthropic structures" is a significant part of Berman's launch of her description of the birth of donor-advised funds. She observed
that, "[b]y the first few decades of the twentieth century, several new vehicles for
philanthropic activism emerged, including private foundations, community chests,
and community foundations."[172] Another part of this description is Cleveland—"an
important hub for philanthropic creativity."[173]

Cleveland formed the first community chest entity in the nation, in 1913. The
first community foundation was established in Cleveland in the next year. This model
of the community foundation made use of the endowment fund. The foundation had
a governing board of, as Berman wrote, "prominent community leaders" who made
"philanthropic decisions by committee."[174] Thereafter, she continued, "[t]hroughout
the 1920s and 1930s, powerful and wealthy leaders in various cities created community
foundations and pledged themselves to an endowment model of charitable aggregation, with a professionalized approach to distribution decisions."[175]

The first donor-advised fund began operations in 1931, within the New York
Community Trust (a community foundation). The term *donor-advised fund* was not
then used, however. Berman stated: "Still, in their unnamed infancy, community

---

[168] Berman Paper at 9–10.
[169] *Id.* at 10.
[170] *Id.* at 11.
[171] *Id.*
[172] *Id.* Charitable remainder trusts and other planned giving vehicles are also in that mix.
[173] Berman Paper at 11.
[174] *Id.* at 12.
[175] *Id.* at 13.

foundation funds supported an endowment model of charitable giving and offered the individual the opportunity to name their funds and, often, suggest a purpose for their earnings to the board."[176] Also: "At the same time, by aggregating funds in community foundations, donors also agreed to a collective process of rule by a professionalized board that would extend beyond their lifetime."[177] Further: "Community foundation boards, historically comprised of wealthy community leaders who also kept their money in the community foundation, protected individual donors' charitable interests and gave informal, if not formal, methods of accounting for how their money was spent."[178]

TAX REFORM ACT OF 1969

Enactment of the Tax Reform Act of 1969[179] is the most important occurrence in the development of the federal statutory law of nonprofit organizations. This legislation essentially created the federal law of tax-exempt organizations. Before this body of law came into being, lawyers representing nonprofit organizations did not have much statutory federal tax law as guidance.[180]

A major feature of the Tax Reform Act was introduction of a statutory definition of the term *private foundation*, which caused the universe of tax-exempt charitable organizations to be split between these foundations and *public charities*.[181] Private foundations became subject to heavy tax penalties should they engage in a wide range of self-dealing transactions, fail to meet a mandatory payout requirement, hold excessive interests in business enterprises, make speculative investments, or make expenditures for political, lobbying, and various other ends.[182] An excise tax was imposed on foundations' net investment income.[183] Charitable contributions became less deductible in the case of foundations.[184] In most instances, public charity status became more favorable than private foundation status.

---

[176] *Id.*
[177] *Id.*
[178] *Id.*
[179] Pub. L. 91-172, 91st Cong., 1st Sess. (1969).
[180] About all there was, pre-1969, was the prohibition on substantial lobbying by public charities (1934), the unrelated business law (1950), and the ban on political campaign activity by public charities (1954).
[181] IRC § 509. In general, *Private Foundations* §§ 1.2, 15.1.
[182] IRC §§ 4941-4945. In general, *Private Foundations*, Chapter 5-9.
[183] IRC § 4940. In general, *Private Foundations*, Chapter 10.
[184] In general, *Private Foundations*, Chapter 14.

Professor Berman credits tax lawyer Norman Sugarman for successfully advocating the idea that community foundations qualify as public charities and the concept of donor advisory authority in connection with contributed charitable dollars. After the law was passed, Sugarman secured a private letter ruling for the Cleveland Jewish Federation, holding that the federation was a publicly supported charity.[185] He exploited the fears of some who had private foundations, persuading them to avoid what was then viewed as oppressive regulation under the new law by terminating their foundations and transferring the assets to public charities, such as community foundations, retaining some form of recommendatory authority over the assets on an ongoing basis. Sugarman obtained a private ruling from the IRS in late 1970, with the agency recognizing the concept of establishment of a "philanthropic fund" where donors to the fund could recommend charities to receive grants from the fund.[186] The ruling undoubtedly was the first from the IRS expressly approving what would come to be known as a donor-advised fund. Professor Berman wrote that "[o]nly in the mid-1980s did Jewish Federation and community foundation professionals begin calling them donor-advised funds."[187]

Notwithstanding the private letter ruling Norman Sugarman obtained in 1970, the federal government subsequently aggressively fought the concept of the donor-advised fund. The IRS initially viewed the donor-advised fund as a device to deviously circumvent the private foundation regulatory rules enacted in 1969. In a sense, this perception was quite accurate!

The donor-advised fund is, in many ways, an alternative to the private foundation. In the right set of circumstances, it can be an attractive alternative. With the private foundation, one must incur the costs, including legal fees, of establishing the charity, forming a board of trustees, developing the necessary documents (e.g., by-laws, policies, board meeting minutes), procuring recognition of tax-exempt status from the IRS, and obtaining state and local tax exemptions.

The donor-advised fund obviates the need to organize anything. There is no requirement to form an organization, construct a governing board, or pursue recognition of exemption with the IRS. The approach accords automatic public charity status, facilitates the receipt of contributions that are deductible to the greatest extent, avoids state and local considerations, and eliminates the necessity of filing annual

---

[185] Berman Paper at 19. The classification is under IRC §§ 170(b)(1)(A)(vi) and 509(a)(1). In general, *Private Foundations* § 15.4.

[186] Berman Paper at 20.

[187] *Id.* at 21.

information returns. This leaves the founder free to see to grantmaking and, if wanted, fundraising.

COURT CHALLENGES

The first court case the IRS brought resulted in a devastating loss to the government. It involved an organization by the name of the National Foundation—a precursor to today's donor-advised fund. The Foundation, formed in 1983, administered what it termed "projects," each of which was the subject of internally segregated accounts. The projects were the ideas of others, who were both applicants to the Foundation to house their projects and donors to the Foundation. An individual who wanted to start a charity could do so by submitting a project proposal application ($100 fee) and making a charitable contribution to the Foundation ($500 minimum). (At the time of the court opinion in this case, the National Foundation was administering 695 projects.) The Foundation levied a fundraising and administration charge equal to 2 ½ percent of contributions.

The National Foundation reviewed the projects to be certain they conformed to the federal tax rules for classification as charitable undertakings. It retained full control and discretion over the funds contributed, and was not obligated to use the funds in the manner requested. Nonetheless, a donor could request that the funds donated be used for a particular charitable project. If the Foundation concluded that a project was not charitable in nature, the initial contribution was returned to the donor or, at the donor's request, was contributed to a charity or retained by the Foundation as an undesignated contribution. If a donor became dissatisfied with the manner in which the funds were being spent or the project supervised, he or she could request that the unspent funds be transferred to another charitable organization.

The Foundation sought recognition of tax exemption as a charitable entity, on the ground that it operated to raise and distribute funds to charitable organizations (in the manner of, e.g., the United Way), and operated to fund and administer a wide variety of charitable, educational, religious, scientific, and literary projects. The government, conversely, characterized the Foundation as a commercial enterprise, that merely provides services to a collection of clients and does not perform any exempt activities itself. Further, the government expressed displeasure that the

Foundation is a "device" to, in the language of the opinion, "first, to avoid Internal Revenue Service scrutiny of individual activities, and, second, to escape from classification as a private foundation, with the attendant restrictions and supervision."[188] The government also asserted that the donors retained "full control" of the contributed funds.[189]

The court in this case was eloquent. The court first found that donors to the Foundation "relinquish all ownership and custody of the donated funds or property" and that the organization is "free to accept or reject any suggestion or request made by a donor."[190] Noting that the Foundation's "methods of operating may be somewhat unique and innovative," the court wrote that it "offers another way to harness both the sensitivity to local community needs and the charitable creativity of public-minded citizens throughout the country."[191] The Foundation's goal, the court continued, "is to create an effective national network to respond to many worthy charitable needs at the local level which in many cases might go unmet."[192] "By drawing upon this grass roots network of resources, creativity, and knowledge of local needs," said the court, the Foundation "initiates, funds, and administers many small local charitable projects which would otherwise not be supported."[193] There was more: the Foundation's "activities promote public policy and represent the very essence of charitable benevolence as envisioned by Congress in enacting § 501(c)(3)" and it "truly functions in the 'spirit of charity.'"[194] Lavish words by a court about a charity.

Two aspects of this case warrant further attention. One is the degree of autonomy the Foundation really had over the contributions to and for the projects. The government asserted that the donors to the projects retained control over the funds, so that the Foundation acts only as a "conduit" for its donors and is merely a "device for circumventing the authority and responsibility of the Commissioner of Internal Revenue."[195]

The court, however, rejected the conduit theory. Reviewing the facts, the court concluded that the donors "relinquish all ownership and custody of the donated funds or property" and that the Foundation "exercises full control over the

---

[188] National Foundation, Inc. v. United States, 87-2 U.S.T.C. ¶ 9602 (Ct. Cl. 1987), at 491.
[189] Id.
[190] Id. at 493.
[191] Id.
[192] Id.
[193] Id. at 493–494.
[194] Id. at 494.
[195] Id. at 492.

donated funds and exercises independent discretion as to the charitable disposition of the funds."[196]

Second, the government asserted that the Foundation was nothing more than an aggregate of separate organizations, because of the 2 ½ percent administrative charge on each donation. The court somewhat sidestepped this issue, observing that "[f]ew, if any, charitable organizations can claim that 100 per cent of each donation reaches the charitable objective, for every organization bears some operating expense," with the court concluding that the Foundation is a "unitary organization which does not assess a 'fee' on each donation."[197]

In my newsletter, I commented that this opinion is "controversial"; I was correct about that. I also observed that the government is "certain to appeal the decision"; I was wrong there. Then, I offered the thoughts that the "idea of the National Foundation is indeed an 'innovative' one and it will be interesting to see where this approach leads."[198] Again, I was correct on both counts, albeit way understating the latter. It has been a long run from the date of this decision to the date of the final donor-advised fund tax regulations.

IRS ATTEMPTS DAFs REGULATION

One of the articles in the IRS's Continuing Professional Education text, issued in 2000, analogized to Dickens' *A Tale of Two Cities* and the *Star Wars* saga, expressing the agency's view that there is a "dark side in the Exempt Organizations Universe." The IRS stated that it has been "confronted" with a number of "aggressive tax avoidance schemes." One of these schemes is "certain donor directed funds." (Note the use of that term, rather than "donor-advised funds.")

The IRS wrote that it is continuing to review the "issue of donor control in donor-advised funds." The agency asserted that the donor-advised fund that qualifies as a tax-exempt charitable entity must have "appropriate control over the donated funds." The IRS reiterated that, in measuring levels of control in this context, the *material restriction* rules relating to termination of private foundation status[199] are applied.

The most striking aspect of this stage of IRS administration of the law of

---

[196] *Id.* at 493.
[197] *Id.*
[198] *The Nonprofit Counsel,* Jan. 1998, p. 3.
[199] See Chapter 1, pp. 12-15.

donor-advised funds is that the agency attempted to administratively impose the private foundation rules (which, of course, the IRS lacks the authority to do). The IRS announced the following "representations" that were to be made if tax exemption is to be recognized:

The sponsoring organization expects that its grants for a year will equal or exceed 5 percent of its average net assets on a fiscal year rolling basis.

If this level of grant activity is not attained, the organization will identify the donor-advised funds from which grants over the same period totaled less than 5 percent of each account's average assets. The organization was expected to contact the donors or donor-advisors of these accounts to request that they recommend grants of at least this amount. If the donor/donor advisor does not provide the requisite grant recommendations, the sponsoring organization had to be authorized to transfer amounts up to the 5-percent level from the account to qualified charities selected by the organization.

The sponsoring organization will add language to its promotional materials that states that the organization will investigate allegations of improper use of grant funds for the private benefit of donors and/or donor advisors.

The sponsoring organization will add language to its grantee letters to the effect that grants are to be used by grantees exclusively in furtherance of charitable purposes and cannot be used for the private benefit of donors and donor advisors.

Needless to say, this attempt at regulation by means of CPE texts did not work out for the agency.

MISSING LINK

Conventional wisdom has it that donor-advised funds toodled along in community foundations and were relatively unnoticed until the concept of the nationally focused donor-advised fund emerged. According to one account, that is not true—there is a "missing link."

A fellow by the name of Drummond Pike wrote in an opinion piece that he formed, in 1976 (15 years before the Fidelity Charitable Gift Fund ruling), the Tides Foundation.[200] He stated that he and his colleagues at the Foundation "helped invent

---

[200] Pike, "How I Helped Create the Donor-Advised Fund Monster – Inadvertently," *Chron. of Phil.* (Aug. 22, 2018).

the idea of a charity solely intended to support donor-advised funds" (that is, the idea of a sponsoring organization with the sole function of maintaining donor-advised funds). He portrayed the Foundation as the "first DAF-centric, mission-driven charity in the United States."

Pike continued: "We borrowed a sleepy device deployed by community foundations to attract donors." That is, "[i]nstead of focusing on geography as such funds [community foundations] do, we sought to channel money to groups with progressive values nationally and internationally." The IRS eventually recognized the Tides Foundation as a public charity.

APPEARANCE OF NATIONAL SPONSORING ORGANIZATIONS

Lodged in community foundations and similar charitable entities for decades, it was accepted that donor-advised funds would service *communities*. Thus, a major step occurred when these funds became national in scope.

The first of the national donor-advised funds is the Fidelity Investments Charitable Gift Fund, established in 1991. The Fidelity Fund received a determination letter from the IRS recognizing it as a tax-exempt public charity. The origins of this letter are shrouded in history; not much is known about them today. My recollection is that there was little publicity given this event at the time.

When this Fund sought its recognition of tax exemption, the IRS was organized differently than it is today. Back then, applications for recognition of exemption were filed with what were known as "key districts."[201] The Fund filed for its recognition of exemption with the key district in Baltimore, Maryland. The favorable determination letter was issued by that district office.[202] It is my understanding that the matter was never referred to the IRS's National Office in Washington, D.C.

---

[201] Today, this process is centralized, with all applications for recognition of exemption filed with the IRS in Cincinnati, Ohio.

[202] Paul Streckfus mused that this ruling "was the result of some fuzzy reasoning by the IRS years ago that confused the commercial DAF sponsors with community trusts" (*EO Tax Jour.* 2019-162). I doubt that. The IRS had been ruling on the tax status of discrete funds since at least 1962 (Rev. Rul. 62-113, 1962-1 C.B. 10) (see *infra* note 209) and the *National Foundation* case had been decided about four years earlier (see *supra*, pp. 41-43). The thinking at the IRS on these topics at that time is reflected in Shoemaker and Henchey, "Donor Directed Funds," Topic M in the 1996 Exempt Organizations Continuing Professional Education Text.

The Fidelity Investments Charitable Gift Fund states that its mission is "to grow the American tradition of philanthropy by providing programs that make charitable giving accessible, simple, and effective."[203] As Professor Berman wrote, "as Fidelity programs succeeded in drawing clients to invest in its charitable port-folios, other commercial investment houses followed suit and established their own charitable funds."[204] Thereafter, 1997 brought the Vanguard Charitable Endowment Program, the Schwab Charitable Fund arrived in 1999, the Oppenheimer Funds Legacy Program and the Eaton Vance U.S. Charitable Gift Trust, J.P. Morgan Chase, became operational in 2000, and the Goldman Sachs Philanthropy Fund was rec-ognized as a tax-exempt public charity in 2001. Other national donor-advised funds are being added.

Professor Berman observed that "[h]ad DAFs remained solely an instrument of community foundations and a handful of other public charities, Congress likely would not have felt moved to define their legal terrain or impose excise taxes to prevent abuses."[205] This observation is about two Internal Revenue Code provisions introduced by the Pension Protection Act in 2006.[206]

STATE OF THE LAW PRIOR TO THE STATUTE

Much of the law leading up to codification of the donor-advised fund rules may be found in four IRS revenue rulings. The rulings discuss the concept of a fund[207] and application of the commensurate test.[208]

What appears to be the first focus of the IRS on this matter of charitable funds occurred in 1962. In this ruling, the IRS held that monies contributed to a fund established by a church to support the expenses of missionaries, including the donor's child, were deductible as charitable contributions if the contributions were not ear-marked for the child.[209] The IRS reasoned that a charitable deduction is allowable where it is established that a gift is intended by the donor for the use of the organ-ization and not as a gift to an individual. The test as to that point was whether the

---

[203] Fidelity Charitable 2017 Giving Report at 27.
[204] Berman Paper at 24.
[205] *Id.* at 25.
[206] IRC §§ 4966 and 4967.
[207] See Chapter 1.
[208] *Id.*
[209] Rev. Rul. 62-113, 1962-1 C.B. 10.

charitable organization has full control of the contributed funds, and discretion as to their use, so as to ensure that the funds will be used to carry out its functions and purposes. Even at this stage of law development, the IRS was distinguishing between what would be recognized as a donor-advised fund and a donor-directed fund,[210] by addressing the matter of a fund as a conduit (the reference to *earmarking*) and the charity's control of and discretion as to use of the property in the fund.

The *commensurate test*, as noted,[211] came into being in 1964, when the IRS considered a corporation operated for charitable purposes that derived its income principally from the rental of space in a large commercial office building that it owned, maintained and operated. The charitable purposes of this corporation were carried out by aiding other charitable organizations, selected in the discretion of its governing body, through grants to such organizations for charitable purposes. The IRS held that the corporation satisfied the primary purpose test as to charitability and was tax-exempt as a charitable organization, where it was shown to be carrying on through grants a charitable program commensurate in scope with its financial resources.[212]

Three years later, the IRS held tax-exempt as a charitable entity an organization formed for the purpose of providing financial assistance to several different types of charitable entities.[213] It carried on no operations other than to receive contributions and incidental investment income and to make distributions of income to these charitable entities at periodic intervals.

The IRS held that a community trust that was created by a community chest to hold permanently endowed charitable funds and to distribute income to support local publicly supported charities qualified as a supporting organization,[214] where the supported charities were specified by class.[215]

One of the earliest private letter rulings authored by the IRS concerning donor-advised funds was issued in late 1997. In that case, a private foundation planned on transferring 10 percent of its assets to a community foundation,[216] that was managed by a board of trustees composed of members nominated by various community organizations, who reflect the broad and varied interests of the charity's

---

[210] See Chapter 1.

[211] *Id.*

[212] Rev. Rul. 64-182, 1964-1 C.B. 186.

[213] Rev. Rul. 67-149, 1967-1 C.B. 133.

[214] That is, a charitable organization described in IRC § 509(a)(3). See Chapter 1.

[215] Rev. Rul. 81-43, 1981-1 C.B. 350.

[216] This community foundation was a public charity by virtue of IRC §§ 170(b)(1)(A)(vi) and 509(a)(1). See Chapter 1.

community. The distribution was said to be from principal that is not restricted by the private foundation's donors.

The plan was to use the distribution to establish a donor-advised fund within the public charity. A distribution committee of the foundation was authorized to suggest distributions to specific charities from the fund; the public charity's board, however, had the power to direct the application of the donor-advised fund if, in its judgment, that action was necessary to most effectively accomplish the public charity's purposes.

The IRS, having found that there would not be any material restrictions or conditions on the transfer to the community foundation, ruled that the distribution of principal to a donor-advised fund within the community foundation would be an "acceptable transfer" to a public charity. The IRS also ruled that the transferred assets would be considered a component part of the community foundation and would not be classified as a separate fund that is a private foundation.[217]

Most prescient is an IRS private letter ruling published in 2001, concerning creation by a supporting organization of a "donor-advised charitable gift fund." The supported organization was a business league.[218] The primary activity of this supporting organization was the making of grants to two other charitable organizations that are affiliated with the business league and other similar charitable entities.

The supporting organization, the members of which are the members of the business league, proposed to establish this charitable gift fund to enable its members to make contributions for charitable purposes. This fund was expected to "appeal primarily to members who wish to provide for the long-term charitable needs" of these charitable organizations. The fund was not a "separate legal entity" but rather was to be operated as an "internal division" of the supporting organization. Contributions to the fund, and the resulting earnings, were to be "maintained in separate accounts." The instrument of transfer to the supporting organization for the fund, and descriptive information pertaining to the fund, will provide that "contributions are irrevocable and will thereafter be under the control of [the supporting organization's] board of directors." The supporting organization was to issue a written statement to each donor and distributee organization stating that distributions may be used only for charitable purposes and not for the donors' personal benefit. The supporting organization will verify the public charity (or governmental) status of all distributees prior to distribution.

---

[217] Priv. Ltr. Rul. 9807030 (Nov. 19, 1997).

[218] These are associations that are tax-exempt by reason of description in IRC § 501(c)(6). See *Tax-Exempt Organizations*, Chapter 14.

Donors could direct their contributions, in whole or in part, to two types of accounts. One category of account was a "specific donee account," where one or more charities are named as the "ultimate beneficiaries" of the account. The other type of account was a "donor-advised account," where the donor or designee would be allowed to "consult" with the supporting organization as to the charities to be benefited during the year, with the supporting organization determining the amount, timing, and distributee of each grant. The supporting organization was to make distribution decisions by means of its board of directors or one or more distribution committees.

This ruling states that the supporting organization "contemplates making annual distributions from the [f]und commensurate with its assets." The plan was to distribute from the fund an amount at least equal to 5 percent of the fund's average net assets on a five-year rolling basis.[219] If anticipated grant amounts are not met, recommendations were to be sought with respect to accounts where grants totaled less than the payout policy. If sufficient grant recommendations were not timely received, assets could be transferred to the supporting organization's unrestricted fund for grantmaking.

In this case, the IRS ruled that donors to this proposed charitable gift fund will be entitled to charitable contribution deductions and that the supported organization, once it commences operation of the gift fund, will continue to be classified as a public charity.[220]

The IRS provided this pre-statutory definition of the term *donor-advised fund*, in 2006, as a prelude to a summary of the statutory law enacted in that year[221]: Prior to the Pension Protection Act of 2006, the Internal Revenue Code did not define this term. It was, however, "commonly understood" to refer to the "component funds of certain community trusts."[222] The IRS added that the term was "also commonly understood to refer to an account established by one or more donors but owned and controlled by a public charity to which such donors or other individuals designated by the donors could provide nonbinding recommendations regarding distributions from the account or regarding investment of the assets in the account."[223]

---

[219] This policy of the supporting organization mimicked, of course, the private foundation mandatory payout requirement (IRC § 4942). See *Private Foundations*, Chap. 6.

[220] Priv. Ltr. Rul. 200149045 (Aug. 3, 2001).

[221] See Chapter 4, pp. 86–89.

[222] See *supra*, pp. 46–47.

[223] Notice 2007-109, 2006-51 I.R.B. 1121 § 2.01.

About ten years later, the IRS provided this pre-statutory definition of the term: It "was understood to refer to separate funds or accounts established and maintained by public charities to receive contributions from a single donor or group of donors. The charities had ultimate authority over how the assets in each account were invested and distributed, but the donors, or individuals selected by the donors, were permitted to provide nonbinding recommendations regarding account distributions and/or investments."[224]

CLINTON ADMINISTRATION DAF PROPOSALS

At the close of the Clinton Administration, the Department of the Treasury announced the need for legislation to "encourage the continued growth of donor advised funds by providing clear rules that are easy to administer, while minimizing the potential for misuse of donor advised funds to benefit donors and advisors."[225]

The proposal was that a charitable organization that has, as its primary activity, the operation of one or more donor-advised funds may qualify as a public charity only if (1) there is no material restriction or condition that prevents the organization from freely and effectively employing the assets in the donor-advised funds it maintains, or the income therefrom, in furtherance of its exempt purpose; (2) distributions are made from the funds only as grants to public charities, private operating foundations, or governmental entities; and (3) annual distributions from donor-advised funds equal at least five percent of the net fair market value of the organization's aggregate assets held in donor-advised funds (with a five-year carryforward).

Failure to comply with any of these requirements with respect to a donor-advised fund would have caused the charitable organization maintaining the fund or funds to become classified as a private foundation. Any other charitable organization that operated one or more donor-advised funds, but not as its primary activity, would also be required to comply with these three elements. If this type of organization (such as a college or university) failed to satisfy these requirements with respect to its donor-advised funds, the organization would retain its public charity status but

---

[224] Priv. Ltr. Rul. 201313034 (Dec. 5, 2012).
[225] Department of the Treasury, "General Explanation of the Administration's Fiscal Year 2001 Revenue Proposals" 105 (February 2000).

all assets maintained by the organization in donor-advised funds would have been subject to the private foundation rules, including excise taxes.

As discussed next, when Congress decided to legislate in the donor-advised fund setting, it took a much different approach.

PENSION PROTECTION ACT OF 2006

Enactment of the Pension Protection Act of 2006[226] introduced statutory law concerning donor-advised funds.[227] This law did not substantially alter the preexisting concept of the donor-advised fund. As Professor Berman wrote, "[a]lthough it instituted modest regulations over the funds in 2006, Congress did not substantially change DAFs in spirit."[228] Yet, she also concluded that "[n]othing did more to sanction DAFs and broaden the industry than the passage of the Pension Protection Act of 2006."[229]

Professor Berman offered another conclusion: "Though impossible to prove, we might surmise that by sharpening the legal status of DAFs, Congress helped them grow."[230] She based this observation on the fact that between 2006 and her writing time (2015), the number of DAFs and assets held in them had more than doubled.

2014 DAF "REFORM" LEGISLATIVE PROPOSAL

During 2014, under the leadership of its chairman, Rep. David Camp, the House Ways and Means Committee drafted a proposed Tax Reform Act of 2014.[231] One of the elements of this proposal, which was not enacted, was a mandatory distribution of monies from donor-advised funds within five years of their placement in DAF accounts, sanctioned by a 20 percent excise tax.

The Community Foundation Public Awareness Initiative responded to this legislative proposal by letter to the Ways and Means Committee, observing that the

---

[226] Pub. L. No. 109-280, 109th Cong., 2nd Sess. (2006). See Chapter 4.
[227] See Chapter 4.
[228] Berman Paper at 25.
[229] *Id.*
[230] *Id.*
[231] H.R. 1, 113th Cong., 2nd Sess. (2014).

proposal "seems to promote the perspective that DAFs *by their very nature* are somehow abusive."[232] The letter made these points: (1) if the goal of the Committee is to increase the amount of money "going out the door" from donor-advised funds, the proposal will have "exactly the opposite impact over the medium to long term;" (2) the effect of the proposal is to communicate to the public that the "concept of 'endowment' (building a permanent resource that is there both now and in the future) is reserved only for large institutions and the very wealthy;" (3) the proposal "implies that inactive donor-advised funds are a significant public policy problem that requires attention, but the vast majority of DAF advisors are making grants regularly;" (4) the proposal "sets up a structure where donor-advised funds are treated much more harshly than other forms of endowments, which will be complicated and confusing to donors, as well as create an administrative nightmare for community foundations and other DAF administrators;" (5) the proposal "fails to recognize the important difference between *endowed* and *non-endowed* DAFs, and that the forced five-year spend-down on endowed DAFs would require [community foundations and others] to go to court to undo thousands of legal arrangements and potentially put some community foundations in violation of state law and the donor's intent;" (6) the proposal "seems to imply that DAFs only provide value to the community when money is 'paid out,' but at least where most community foundations are concerned, this is not the case;' and (7) a five-year payout requirement on donor-advised funds would make it "nearly impossible for DAF advisors to engage in the rapidly growing field of 'impact investing' via their DAFs."

Although this Camp proposal has not been enacted into law, the concept underlying it lives on in the hearts of donor-advised fund critics.

DONOR-ADVISED FUND CRITICISMS COMMENCE

Criticism of donor-advised funds began to emerge about 2014. For example, early in that year, law professor Ray Madoff wrote: "I and many other critics of the laws governing the funds are concerned that donors and the people who manage their money have been the primary recipients of benefits from the growth of donor-advised funds, while charities and the people they serve are being starved of resources. Donors get an immediate up-front tax benefit—money that drains the federal treas-

---

[232] CFPAI, letter to House Ways and Means Committee (July 14, 2014).

ury of much-needed revenue for government services—but face no obligations to ensure that the money makes its way out to charities in a timely fashion. Under the law, these funds can be kept in place in perpetuity."[233]

This initial round of criticism, as reflected by the foregoing, is notable for its hyperbole, distortions, and in some instances inaccuracies. Thus, donors and fund managers are seen as the primary beneficiaries of the growth of donor-advised funds, charities are being starved, the U.S. fisc is being drained, and monies in donor-advised funds "can" be kept there in perpetuity (which does not mean that they *are*).

Two of the most outspoken critics of donor-advised funds are law professor Ray Madoff and fundraising consultant Alan Cantor. Their early writings serve as examples for this analysis. They both wrote articles in reaction to publication of the *Chronicle of Philanthropy's* Philanthropy 400.

Alan Cantor reacted to publication of the *Chronicle's* Philanthropy 400 for 2014, which featured Fidelity's, Schwab's, and Vanguard's sponsoring organizations as among the top ten fundraising organizations with an article that led him to his only possible conclusion: the "inexorable takeover of the [U.S.] charitable sector by Wall Street."[234] This "accelerating trend of warehousing philanthropic dollars," he wrote, is a "deeply troubling trend for American philanthropy." As Mr. Cantor sees the situation, "[e]ven as nonprofits are struggling to survive, and even as they are dealing with enormous unmet needs, ever more money is being warehoused for future distribution." He adds that, "because there is no requirement that donor-advised funds spend all their money, there is no guarantee that the money will ever be directed to charitable purposes." After (incorrectly) stating that private foundations "must distribute 5 percent of [their] assets on average each year," he pronounces (without explanation) the foundation payout requirement "inadequate." Then, he (also incorrectly) states that this payout rule "applies to each and every private foundation."

Professor Madoff was moved to write an article critical of donor-advised funds in the aftermath of a "stunning change": Fidelity Charitable became the top charity in 2015 in the ranks of the *Chronicle's* Philanthropy 400.[235] This led to the statement in this article that "there is no evidence that the benefits from these funds are going

---

[233] Madoff, "5 Myths About Payout Rules for Donor-Advised Funds," *Chron. of Phil.* (Jan. 13, 2014)).

[234] Cantor, "A Gain to Commercial Funds Is a Loss to Charities," XXVII *Chron. of Phil.* (No. 2) 29 (Nov. 6, 2014).

[235] Madoff, "Charities and Taxpayers Deserve More From Donor-Advised Funds," 29 *Chron. of Phil.* (Issue 1 (Nov. 2016)).

to the public." No benefits at all? Charitable organizations that are establishing donor-advised fund programs are compared to "Invasion of the Body Snatchers" because they are "victims" of the donor-advised fund boom, "turning around and offering them on their own." Sponsoring organizations are said to be making "side agreements" with donors to "hold these funds and let the contributor[s] have control over the money." When people contribute to donor-advised funds, professor Madoff wrote, "they do so with the understanding that they will be able to direct charitable gifts from their DAFs." The legal documents say "advice," but "everyone understands it is direction." Everyone? Private foundations "must distribute a minimum percentage of assets each year." Except perhaps for the "stunning change" remark, none of the foregoing comments are accurate.

Articles like this set the tone for a great torrent of bluster that would soon appear.

VITRIOL INCREASES

Credit should be given where credit is due. One area where donor-advised fund critics are winning (way ahead) on points is colorful speech. Yes, it is often hyperbole, misleading, and downright inaccurate but the phraseology is also dramatic, striking, and arresting.

And so, enduring criticism never before heaped on a charitable giving vehicle (of all things), donor-advised funds are being called "shams," "loopholes," "black holes" that suck up money, "warehouses" of wealth, "black-box charities," "monsters," "zombies," and purveyors of "moral bankruptcy."[236]

Reaction to these comments has certainly not been equal to their force. One commentator wrote that "[t]his popular giving vehicle [DAFs, obviously] should be celebrated for *broadening* America's base of philanthropists," adding that "[d]ropping down the IRS's hammer on these lightly regulated vehicles would only serve to restrict philanthropy to huge foundations and the ultra-rich."[237] A defense of the

---

[236] See Chapter 1, pp. 3-4; Chapter 5, *passim.* Developments in the law ostensibly imperiling the nonprofit sector in its entirety seem to be the rage (literally) these days. For example, in writing to the IRS about a problem concerning the rules accompanying the tax on excess compensation imposed on certain tax-exempt organizations (IRC § 4960), the Alliance for Charitable Reform wrote that, "[i]f Treasury and the IRS do not resolve this ambiguity favorably, and soon, the nonprofit sector will suffer a major setback" (letter dated June 18, 2019).

[237] Ludwig, "Donor-Advised 'Dark Money'?," *Philanthropy Daily* (Aug. 12, 2019).

donor-advised fund programs sponsored by Jewish Federations across North America, in responses to criticisms of DAFs, was published in mid-2019;[238] it followed a similar analysis published in late 2018.[239] A Harvard University law professor blogged that donor-advised funds should be "applauded," in that "[p]utting money into a DAF is essentially a commitment to give that part of your wealth, plus all future returns. to charity."[240]

NONPROFIT QUARTERLY ARTICLES

Dozens of articles and papers about donor-advised funds have been published (most of them critical of DAFs). *The Nonprofit Quarterly*, however, ran a series of articles that nicely captures contemporary thinking about the policy underlying donor-advised funds and whether more regulation is required.

One of the editions of *The Nonprofit Quarterly* contains three articles about donor-advised funds. The first of these articles, written by Ruth McCambridge, draws a distinction that is found throughout this book: "widespread abuse in donor-advised funds" and existence of the "conditions" (sometimes referenced as the "potential") for widespread abuse.[241] Deprived of the former, donor-advised fund critics rely heavily on the latter. Later in her article, this distinction appears again, this time framed as the "[t]racking the extent of any problem (or whether a problem even exists)."[242] Some DAF critics are encouraging the government to launch a massive donor-advised fund regulatory regime in an effort to determine if any regulation is actually needed.[243]

---

[238] Email from Steven Woolf, Senior Tax Policy Counsel, The Jewish Federations of North America, published in *EO Tax Jour.* 2019-159 (Aug. 15. 2019).

[239] Beckwith and Woolf, "Donor-Advised Funds: Separating Myth from Fact," reproduced in *EO Tax Jour.* 2018-206 (Oct. 19, 2018).

[240] Mankiw, "DAFs Should Be Applauded," blog posted Aug. 5, 2018, reproduced in *EO Tax Jour.* 2018-157 (Aug. 10, 2018).

[241] McCambridge, "Do Donor-Advised Funds Require Regulatory Attention," 25 *Nonprofit Quar.* (Issue 2) 41 (Summer 2018).

[242] *Id.* at 42.

[243] For example, Paul Streckfus wrote in a letter to *Tax Notes*, paraphrasing Donald Rumsfeld, that, when it comes to donor-advised funds, "we don't know what we don't know – his 'unknown unknowns'" (letter reproduced in *EO Tax Jour.* 2019-156 (Aug. 12, 2019)). He added that he "suspects" that "some DAFs are being used in an abusive manner" but "can't prove any of this is going on." Yet Paul wants an "investigation" of donor-advised funds by Congress, the Treasury Department, and/or the IRS. By the way, Paul rhetorically asked: "[H]as a DAF sponsor ever been audited? Probably not." Shortly after Paul wrote this, a sponsoring organization was audited – and had its tax exemption revoked (Priv. Ltr.

The other two articles in this series are written by two well-known critics of donor-advised funds and are discussed elsewhere in this book.[244]

These three articles were quickly followed up by an article, published in *The Nonprofit Quarterly*, written by community foundation leaders who expressed their concern that a "few bad examples" do not "distract from the fact that DAFs are also a vehicle that raises billions in charitable donations to provide critical services and solve important problems in communities across the country."[245] Expressing an understanding that the "recent growth" in the use of donor-advised funds "brings scrutiny," they noted that "some of the most vocal critics of DAFs have not worked directly with donors to understand their motivations and behaviors." They expressed the view that "philanthropy is not a zero-sum game, where giving levels can be assumed to be fixed and transferable, regardless of [the] giving vehicle." They stated that it is "important to make sure we are thoughtful and deliberate and that any changes will not bring unintended consequences in the form of decreased charitable giving." Their concern was said to be to "avoid government overreach, excessive regulation, and bureaucratic waste" that could result from "arbitrary rules and guidelines." They concluded their articles by stating that they "look forward to working with those who want to ensure that DAFs remain a powerful force for good, recognizing the inherent value of community foundations and our goal of continuing to advance philanthropy in communities large and small."

The Fidelity Investments Charitable Gift Fund announced, in mid-2019, that donors to its donor-advised funds "continued to break records in 2019, recommending $4 billion in grants, a 48% increase compared to the same period last year."[246] This level of giving involved 668,000 donor-recommended grants supporting 105,000 charities. This grantmaking record, Fidelity Charitable continued, "follows an unprecedented $5.2 billion in grants in 2018, $700 million more than the pre-

Rul. 201922038 (Mar. 7, 2019)). This case is now docketed in the U.S. Tax Court (National Outreach Foundation, Inc. v. Commissioner (Docket No. 20291-19X (Nov. 14, 2019)).

Somewhat along this same line, a law professor blogged that DAF sponsors know that "we will draw negative inferences from their refusal to release detailed payout information," "yet they persist in hiding it anyway," asking "[h]ow bad must it actually be?" A comparison is then made with President Donald Trump's refusal to make his tax returns public, writing that both of these situations involve "something someone doesn't want you to know." Reproduced in *EO Tax Jour.* 2018-163 (Aug. 20, 2018).

[244] Madoff, "Three Simple Steps to Protect Charities and American Taxpayers from the Rise of Donor-Advised Funds," 25 *Nonprofit Quar.* (Issue 2) 46 (Summer 2018); Zerbe, "DAF Reform – A Chance to Provide Real Benefit to Working Charities," 25 *Nonprofit Quar.* (Issue 2) 52 (Summer 2018)).

[245] Kridler, Philipp, Slutsky, Seleznow, and Williams, "Donor-Advised Funds: How to Make Sure They Strengthen Our Communities," *Nonprofit Quar.* (Aug. 20, 2018).

[246] Fidelity Investment Charitable Gift Fund press release (July 29, 2019).

vious year." Fidelity Charitable added that, overall, it has made more than $35 billion in donor-recommended grants to more than 278,000 charities."

The Giving USA report on the levels of charitable giving in 2018, while featuring overall impressive numbers ($427.71 billion is the second highest level of giving in U.S. history), some disturbing trends stood out.[247] One of these adverse trends was a 1.1 percent drop in the level of charitable giving by individuals, attributed to a number of causes including market volatility at the end of 2018 and tax law changes.[248] But, as an article written by Alfred E. Osborne, Jr., pointed out, "there was one area of individual charitable giving that bucked this worrying trend": "[s]trong grantmaking from donor-advised funds."[249] This article added that this phenomenon "show[s] why growing adoption in recent years of these strategic giving accounts should be counted among most positive developments in philanthropy."

Using Fidelity Charitable as an illustration (and echoing the press release), Mr. Osborne states that Fidelity Charitable's grants to charities increased by 17 percent in 2018 to $5.2 billion. He pointed out that charitable giving by means of its funds is on track for "continued growth" in 2019, with an "incredible" 48 percent in giving in relation to that level in mid-2018.

The article referenced a recent study from the University of Pennsylvania that examined IRS data from nearly 1,000 sponsoring organizations from 2017-2016, finding that grantmaking from donor-advised funds "tends to be resilient during economic downturns." This is because many of these donor-advised grants "are going to charities that donors support steadily year after year." The article concluded that donor-advised funds are "crucial 'rainy day' sources of funding for charities," having "emerged as a stabilizing force in philanthropy."

Another trend this article observed is the increase in the number of donor-advised fund accounts in recent years—more than 200 percent in the past five years. The author wrote of an "ever-broader group of Americans" that are embracing these funds "in order to approach their philanthropy in the kind of thoughtful, strategic way once reserved for only the highest echelon of wealth earners."

The article noted that "[g]iving with a donor-advised fund means removing

---

[247] *Giving USA 2019: The Annual Report on Philanthropy for the Year 2018*, published by the Giving USA Foundation and researched and written by the Indiana University Lilly Family School of Philanthropy. This level of charitable giving is a 1.7 percent decrease from the 2017 amount of $435.1 billion.

[248] E.g., Haynes and Theis, "A Tough Year for Giving," 31 *Chron. of Phil.* (Issue 9) 22 (July 2019).

[249] Osborne, Jr., "Voices from the Field: Fidelity's 2019 DAF Grants Spike – How Donor-Advised Funds Changed Giving for the Better," *Nonprofit Quar.* (July 29, 2019) (online).

the time pressure from the decision, allowing donors the space needed to fully vet their charitable choices." It "also means consolidating not only funds, but also all of the information about giving in a single place, making it possible to easily get a view into impact over time," so that charitable giving "becomes more than just a collection of checks filed away for the accountant—it becomes a fully-fledged program."

"More than ever before," Alfred Osborne concluded, "Americans are turning to donor-advised funds to address and foster their philanthropic needs." He is "convinced that this shift will continue—and it is clearer to me than ever that the nonprofit sector will reap the benefits."

After reading this article, I had several reactions. One was how refreshing it was to read a positive and informative article about donor-advised funds, a nice antidote to the ongoing torrent of criticism of these funds. Another reaction was that, in a period of declining charitable giving, how impressive it is that Fidelity Charitable alone accounted for more than one percent of total giving in 2018; without Fidelity Charitable, it appears, the charitable giving level for 2018 would have been $423 billion rather than $428 billion. A third reaction was—proving how naïve I can be, apparently—that even donor-advised fund critics might tip their hats to Fidelity Charitable for this accomplishment.

Good luck with that last one! One of the first critics out of the box on this was Alan Cantor, who wondered who wrote this "one-sided screed" and labeled the article "self-promoting huffery-puffery of Fidelity Charitable."[250] That quote also gave rise to five reactions on my part, one being that Mr. Cantor is the last individual on the planet to criticize someone for writing one-sided articles[251] and another being that "one-sided screed" is a redundancy.[252] A third reaction was that Alfred Osborne's article was not a "screed" at all, because it is neither a "lengthy discourse" nor a "ranting piece of writing." Fourth, my research does not reveal Al Cantor speaking out in rage over the two one-sided articles severely critical of donor-advised funds that were published in *The Nonprofit Quarterly* in 2018.[253] Fifth, Al

---

[250] Quoted in *EO Tax Jour.* 2019-160 (Aug. 16, 2019).

[251] For a classic of this genre, see Cantor, "A Gain to Commercial Funds Is a Loss to Charities," XXVII *Chron. of Phil.* (No. 2) 29 (Nov. 6, 2014).

[252] Sort of along the line of "one-sided propaganda." In fairness, Mr. Cantor is not alone in this regard. Remarks about the format of the impeachment trial by U.S. Senate Majority Leader Mitch McConnell were dismissed by Senate Minority Leader Chuck Schumer as a "partisan screed" (Stolberg and Fandos, "Pelosi Puts Off Sending Impeachment to Senate, Leaving Trial in Limbo," *New York Times*, A1, A18, Dec. 20, 2019).

[253] See *supra*, pp. 55–56.

Cantor invented a new meaning of the word "screed," which is a "piece of writing the content of which does not match his views."

Paul Streckfus wrote that publication of this article had him "wondering how trusting [he] can be of [*The Nonprofit Quarterly*] as a source of unbiased information."[254] I read Paul's online newsletter religiously and don't recall him being critical of those extremely biased NPQ articles either. This development—the Osborne article—made it clear that nothing short of heavy regulation of, and hence the likely demise of, donor-advised funds will satisfy the hardcore donor-advised fund critics.

INTEGRATED PHILANTHROPY

Recent years have brought new thinking about the best use of existing and emerging charitable and other nonprofit vehicles. In the view of some, traditional grantmaking can no longer sufficiently address societal problems. It is in this context that the role of donor-advised funds can be seen from a different perspective. A phrase that attempts to capture this new mindset is *integrated philanthropy*.

One definition of integrated philanthropy is that it is a model of "philanthropy" that places a premium on the "ability to deploy capital for social purposes in whatever way is most effective under the circumstances."[255] This model is integrated in the sense of its blending of structural options, principally limited liability companies, private grantmaking foundations, private operating foundations, donor-advised funds, "operating" public charities (e.g., research institutions and schools), supporting organizations, and social welfare organizations. Factors at play in determining the choice of these vehicles is the factor of control, availability of charitable contributions deductions, flexibility, use of investments, ease of establishment and management, and the regulatory environment.

For example, a limited liability company, while not enabling deductible contributions, can serve as a holding vehicle for funds that are destined for charitable objectives, facilitating investments for social good (investments that do not qualify as program-related investments or mission-related investments). These companies

---

[254] *EO Tax Jour.* 2019-160 (Aug. 16, 2019).

[255] Roady and Madrigal, "Integrated Philanthropy Using Private Foundations, Private Operating Foundations, Public Charities and Non-Charitable Organizations," presentation at Rocky Mountain Tax Seminar for Private Foundations (Sep. 19, 2019). This section is based on this excellent presentation.

are easy to establish and certainly enable donors to retain control over the money and other property transferred. Private foundations retain roles in this model, of course, generating funds for grantmaking and other charitable operations, permitting donor control, and facilitating (often lesser) charitable deductions. The principal difficulty with foundations is the extensive degree of federal and state regulation, reporting, and disclosure.

In this setting, donor-advised funds provide donors with a vehicle that is simple to create, provides for maximum charitable contributions, and facilitates current and future charitable giving. The principal disadvantages of DAFs are the lack of donor control and an uncertain regulatory environment. Supporting organizations offer donors greater opportunities for participation in decision-making, including service on a governing board, and maximum charitable deductions. The downside to use of supporting organization is the extent of their regulation and ongoing imposition of legal requirements. Social welfare organizations can be injected into this mix when advocacy, particularly lobbying, is required.

Use of these various vehicles, either in-tandem or in succession, offers modern philanthropists the means to apply entrepreneurial strategies and flexibility to achieve charitable objectives, perhaps also taking into consideration their personal financial and estate plans.[256] One analysis, employing a broad definition of the phrase *planned giving*, opened with the observation that "[p]lanned giving, including charitable remainder trusts, charitable gift annuities, remainder interest deeds, donor advised funds, and gifts of appreciated stocks and bonds, can offer substantial benefits to donors and provide needed support to charities."[257]

FIDELITY CHARITABLE IS SUED

Between the time the Treasury Department issued its notice foreshadowing its proposed donor-advised funds regulations and issuance of the proposal itself, a lawsuit that attracted national attention emerged.

---

[256] E.g., Johnson, Sheka, and Weeden, "Give to Get: Magnifying the Impact of Executive Compensation through Charitable Giving," 69 *Jour. of Financial Serv. Professionals* (No. 1) 63 (Jan. 2015) (discussing the use of donor-advised funds in conjunction with gifts of stock options and gifts by means of charitable remainder trusts). In general, Hopkins, *How To Be a Successful Philanthropist: Avoiding the Legal Pitfalls* (Dorrance Pub. Co.: 2018).

[257] James, III, "Describing complex charitable giving instruments: Experimental tests of technical finance terms and tax benefits," 28 *Nonprofit Management and Leadership* (Issue 4) (Summer 2018).

A lawsuit was filed, in late 2018, in a federal district court alleging a variety of misdeeds by the Fidelity Investments Charitable Gift Fund in its administration of two contributions made to one of the donor-advised funds it sponsors and administers.[258] This case is being touted in some quarters as highly damaging to Fidelity Charitable and donor-advised fund vehicles in general. Based on the initial pleadings, that does not appear to be the case. Indeed, this litigation may well have the opposite effect: rebuffing donor-advised fund critics on the control issue and demonstrating (if further proof is needed) that sponsoring organizations clearly have exclusive dominion over money and other property contributed to them.

Fidelity Charitable is the largest of the charitable organizations sponsoring donor-advised funds. At the beginning of its fiscal year ended June 30, 2017, Fidelity Charitable held over $16 billion in assets. Because of its relationship with Fidelity Investments, Fidelity Charitable (and other sponsoring organizations with similar affiliations) are dubbed by some (including the plaintiffs in this case) "commercial" sponsoring organizations.

The plaintiffs in this case are wealthy individuals. They were facing a large income tax liability in 2017. To alleviate their tax exposure, they made a gift of 1.93 million shares in Energous, a publicly traded company, generating a large charitable deduction. This gift was made on December 28 and 29 of that year. On December 29, 2017, Fidelity Charitable sold the stock.

Fidelity Charitable "admitted" in its answer that "donors to [its funds] may advise on the investment of donated assets among a variety of options and that donors may advise [it] on the distribution of those funds to appropriate charities." Fidelity Charitable also admitted that the "funds in Fidelity Charitable DAF accounts are owned and controlled by [it], not by a donor."

The gifts involved what the complaint terms a "large block" of Energous stock. The plaintiffs allege that their account representative at Fidelity Charitable promised them that Fidelity Charitable would (1) employ "sophisticated, state-of-the-art methods" for liquidating this large block of stock, (2) not trade more than 10 percent of the daily trading volume of the shares, (3) allow the Fairbairns to advise on a price limit, and (4) not liquidate any shares until the next year.

They allege that the shares were liquidated "for tens of millions of dollars less" than they would have been if Fidelity Charitable had not promptly sold the stock and thus that this "drastic" reduction of share value reduced their charitable deduc-

---

[258] Fairbairn et al. v. Fidelity Investments Charitable Gift Fund, Case No. 18-cv-04881-JSC (N.D. Cal.).

tion by millions of dollars. The complaint seeks restitution based on, among other claims, misrepresentation, breach of contract, and negligence.

Fidelity Charitable, in its answer to the complaint, denied every allegation, including the alleged four promises. Fidelity Charitable also raised 25 affirmative defenses. One of these defenses (which may prove pivotal if this case is tried) is based on the *duty to read*, that is, the causes of action advanced in the complaint are barred in that the matters about which the plaintiffs complain "were adequately disclosed" to them and/or they "failed to read the documents that were provided to them that disclosed such matters." (The complaint actually quotes Fidelity Charitable's policy guidelines that state that contributed stock will be liquidated "at the earliest date possible.")

Another defense recites that "substantial disclosure" was made "of all material facts and circumstances, including in the donor application, contribution form and letter of intent, program circular and/or other agreements and account documents." Still another affirmative defense is that the "Internal Revenue Code and/or Internal Revenue Service Regulations prohibit or foreclose the recovery Plaintiffs seek." (The basis for this defense is not clear.)

The complaint in this case is rather unusual. It goes on for pages about commercial donor-advised funds and private foundations, competition among sponsoring organizations, and treatment of gifts of "complex assets." (Fidelity Charitable pointed out that publicly traded stock is not a complex asset.) It is florid in its characterizations, referencing "false promises," "egregious" conduct, "stonewalling," "sweet spot," "outrageous mishandling" of the contribution, "big fish" (i.e., wealthy individuals), "outrageous actions," and "incompetence." This complaint must be one of the very few to employ the term "gobsmacking." It even recites an old joke ("liquidating" stock does not mean tossing stock certificates in the ocean).

The complaint contains odd statements. It opens with the observation that "[p]rivate charitable giving is critically important to funding public and social goods in the United States." Goods? (Perhaps the intended word was "groups.") It advises the court that donor-advised funds "fill a gap in the otherwise stark landscape of philanthropic vehicles." Are DAFs really that colorful? Some recitations are just wrong, such as the one stating that gifts of appreciated stock to private foundations are deductible only to the extent of basis.

The complaint states that "it is beyond likely that Fidelity Charitable acted based on improper, self-interested motivations" and "Fidelity Charitable knew when it made these promises that it had no intention of keeping them."

This is not really a donor-advised fund case. Essentially, it involves a breach-of-contract claim. This case (if not settled) will turn more on its facts, rather than law. The documents will probably favor Fidelity Charitable. Did Fidelity Charitable's representative really make the four promises? The Fairbairns say he did; Fidelity Charitable says he didn't. Can these promises (if made) override the written policies? Usually, agreements state they can be amended only by a writing. To the extent this is a donor-advised fund case, it will prove a basic point: sponsoring organizations own and control the property in the donor-advised funds they maintain, not the donors.[259]

Once the complaint and answer were filed in this case, nothing more was heard from the parties about it for months. The case is set for trial in April, 2020.[260] In the interim, the case stands as a reminder that sponsoring organizations do in fact, as well as law, have complete control over the property in the donor-advised funds they maintain.[261]

AS TO FAIRNESS, TWO LOW POINTS

The U.S. Government Accountability Office was asked by the Senate Committee on Finance to review what is known about abusive transactions involving tax-exempt organizations and how the IRS addresses them. The GAO responded with a report, made public in late 2019.[262] The overall purpose of this report is to survey IRS programs that attempt to identify abusive tax schemes involving tax-exempt organizations, such as the agency's Office of Tax Shelter Analysis and the several program that are linked by the IRS-wide Compliance Strategy Executive Steering Committee.

The GAO provided examples of some of these abusive tax schemes. It observed

[259] In an article, a university professor wrote that this lawsuit "may bring some more information to bear about what control donors can and cannot retain when making irrevocable gifts to public charities" (Mittendorf, "Fairbairn vs. Fidelity: The Lawsuit That Reflects Rising Concerns About the DAF Boom," reprinted in *EO Tax Jour.* 2019-114 (June 12, 2019).

[260] This case was discussed by a panel at the October 4, 2019, meeting of the Exempt Organizations Committee, Tax Section, American Bar Association (transcript provided in the *EO Tax Jour.* 2019-223 (Nov. 14, 2019)).

[261] A thorough analysis of the *Fairbairn* case is in Sheppard, "Disciplining Donor-Advised Funds" *Tax Notes* 795 (Aug. 5, 2019). For an inaccurate prediction and portrayal of this litigation, see "Lawsuit Could Cool a Fast-Growing Way of Giving to Charities," *New York Times* (May 31, 2019).

[262] Government Accountability Office, "Tax-Law Enforcement: IRS Could Better Leverage Existing Data to Identify Abusive Schemes Involving Tax-Exempt Entities" (GAO-19-491 (Sep. 2019)).

that "[t]axpayers seeking to reduce their tax liability through charitable donations may participate in legal tax planning strategies that allow them to maximize their deductions while giving to charitable organizations."[263] By contrast, "abusive tax schemes occur when taxpayers conduct transactions that are not supported by established law to improperly claim tax benefits, or that have no economic significance or business purpose other than the avoidance of tax, among other factors."[264] Among the latter category of schemes are, the GAO stated, situations where a donor is "grossly overvaluing a charitable contribution to obtain a larger deduction on his or her filed tax returns."[265] Another such scheme is one in which a tax-exempt organization is "providing benefits" to one or more individuals in their private capacity.[266]

In addition, the GAO posited three examples that "illustrate various ways that an entity's exempt status can be used in transactions that are not supported by law or are inconsistent with the law's intent, and how otherwise legitimate tax-exempt activity can be exploited improperly."[267] Two of these illustrations are the syndication of conservation easements[268] and patient assistance programs.[269] The third illustration is the donor-advised fund.

The GAO said that "[s]ome donors may use the donor-advised funds in ways the IRS considers improper."[270] For example, prior to the statutory law enacted in 2006, the IRS said, according to the GAO, that abusive donor-advised funds are those that "appear to be established to generate questionable charitable deductions, and provide impermissible economic benefits to donors and their families (including tax-sheltered investment income for the donors)."[271] A display shows examples of these ostensible abuses, such as "indefinite" accumulations of monies in a donor-advised fund[272] and situations where donors may retain control over the gifted property by means of "complicated financial transactions" while continuing to enjoy the tax law benefits of their gifts.[273]

---

[263] Id. at 10.
[264] Id.
[265] Id.
[266] Id.
[267] Id. at 11.
[268] Id. at 11-13.
[269] Id. at 16-18.
[270] Id. at 14.
[271] Id. There is no citation in support of that statement.
[272] There is no evidence to support the notion that, just because donors may lawfully accumulate funds in a donor-advised fund, that this is a practice that is so extensive as to rise to the level of an "abuse." See Chapter 5, pp. 134-137.

The Congressional Research Service issued a report on the charitable sector, also late in 2019.[274] This analysis has a short section on donor-advised funds, which the CRS promptly labeled "nonactive charities" (along with foundations, supporting organizations, and college and university endowments).[275] This report had nothing positive to say about donor-advised funds and merely rehashed some of the common criticisms of them.

[273] GAO report, *supra*, note 262, at 15. These are instances where the abuse is *of* the concept of a donor-advised fund. E.g., United States v. Mayer, Case No. 18–cv–60704–BLOOM/Valle (S.D. Fla., April 26, 2019). Selection by the GAO of donor-advised funds as examples of abusive tax schemes appears highly inappropriate.

[274] Congressional Research Service, "Tax Issues Relating to Charitable Contributions and Organizations" (R45922 (Sep. 19, 2019)).

[275] *Id.* at 38.

CHAPTER THREE:
The Donor-Advised Fund Universe

The purpose of this chapter is to present a portrait of the donor-advised funds universe. Statistical analyses can be a tricky business; numbers can be manipulated, deliberately or otherwise. Plus, the most valid statistics are the most current ones. Understanding of the remarkable popularity and growth of donor-advised funds, however, requires a longer perspective. The chapter opens with the current statistical portrait, then discusses some significant earlier analyses that help frame the contours of this universe.

TOPICS DISCUSSED IN THIS CHAPTER:

- Current DAF statistics
- Federal government reports
- Manhattan Institute Peers Into DAF's Future
- Institute for Public Studies report
- Lilly School of Philanthropy study

CHARITABLE GIVING

Charitable giving in the United States hit an all-time high in 2017, reaching $435.1 billion—the first time the giving level moved beyond the $400 billion level.[276] In

---

[276] *Giving USA 2018: The Annual Report on Philanthropy for the Year 2017*, published by the Giving USA Foundation and researched and written at the Indiana University Lilly Family School of Philanthropy.

2018, charitable giving in the U.S. was estimated to have totaled $427.71 billion,[277] a 1.7 percent decrease from the 2017 high-level mark. This dip in giving in 2018 was only the thirteenth inflation -adjusted decline in charitable giving in the past four decades, even though the economy grew 2.7 percent.[278] Causes for this decline include the shrinking base of individuals who itemize deductions and a stock market nosedive in late 2018.

America's Favorite Charities 2019 Ranking

A subsequent report informs that "[d]onations rose significantly at many of the nation's largest nonprofits, outpacing giving to the nonprofit world as a whole by a significant margin."[279] This report, the *Chronicle of Philanthropy*'s ranking of "America's Favorite Charities," states that the 100 charitable organizations that "raise the most in private support,"[280] "chalked up an 11.3 percent increase in donations" in 2018.[281] These 100 public charities raised $49.2 billion in 2018, which represents about 8.7 percent of all giving in 2018.[282]

In this listing of America's Favorite Charities 2019, the public charity in the number one spot is United Way Worldwide, which raised slightly over $3 billion. By contrast, the largest of the sponsoring organizations, Fidelity Charitable Gift Fund, raised $9 billion in 2018.[283] Of the other top five sponsoring organizations, Schwab Charitable Fund raised, in 2018, $3.3 billion, the National Philanthropic Trust raised $2.7 billion, Vanguard Charitable Endowment raised $1.8 billion, and the American Endowment Foundation raised $1.1 billion.[284] These five sponsoring organizations collectively raised $17.9 billion in 2018, which is over four percent of total giving in that year. It is also over one-third of what the 100 public charities raised in 2018.

---

[277] *Giving USA 2019: The Annual Report on Philanthropy for the Year 2018.*
[278] Haynes and Theis, "A Tough Year for Giving," 31 *Chron. of Phil.* (Issue 9) 22 (July 2019).
[279] Stiffman and Haynes, "Can the Boom Times Last?," 32 *Chron. of Phil.* (Issue 1) 8, 9 (Nov. 2019).
[280] This compilation reflects only money given to charities "devoted to a cause"; they are termed "cash-support" charities. Cash giving to donor-advised funds is excluded because DAFs are "just a giving vehicle" and "financial tools to hold and distribute charitable funds." Consequently, there is only one community foundation in this listing – the Greater Kansas City Community Foundation, which raised $315 million in 2018, not including gifts to the Foundation's donor-advised funds.
[281] Stiffman and Haynes, "Can the Boom Times Last?," 32 *Chron. of Phil.* (Issue 1) 8, 9 (Nov. 2019).
[282] 8.7 percent is the *Chronicle*'s number. My calculation is that it is 11.5 percent (49.2 divided by 427.7 = 11.5).
[283] Stiffman and Haynes, "Can the Boom Times Last?," 32 *Chron. of Phil.* (Issue 1) 10 (Nov. 2019). Stock gifts comprised 70.3 percent of Fidelity Charitable's total contributions.
[284] Stiffman and Haynes, "Can the Boom Times Last?," 32 *Chron. of Phil.* (Issue 1) 10 (Nov. 2019).

National Philanthropic Trust 2019 Report

The National Philanthropic Trust, on November 12, issued its 13th annual report on donor-advised funds, examining data for 2014-2018 from 989 sponsoring organizations. In her letter introducing this report, NPT President & CEO Eileen R. Heisman writes that "[o]ver the past decade, donor-advised funds have experienced tremendous growth."

The letter highlights three extraordinary developments. One is that "grantmaking from donor-advised funds to qualified charities has nearly doubled in the past five years." Grants from DAFs in 2018 totaled $23.42 billion. Two, there has been an 86 percent increase in contributions to the funds over the past five years. The number for 2018 is $37.12 billion. Three, for the second year in a row, "there was growth above 50 percent in the number of new donor-advised fund accounts."

Total estimated charitable contributions in the U.S. in 2018 were $427.71 billion.[285] Of this amount, $292.09 billion came from individuals (68 percent). Thus, donors to donor-advised funds accounted for 12.7 percent of individual giving. Contributions to DAFs expressed as a percentage of total annual individual giving have steadily increased during 2010-2018.

There were an estimated 728,563 donor-advised funds in 2018, compared to about 80,000 private foundations (not including corporate foundations). Assets in donor-advised funds in 2018 had an estimated value of $121.42 billion, while at the same time assets in private foundations had an estimated value of $872.65 billion. Yet, grants from donor-advised funds in 2018 (as noted, $23.42 billion) equated to just over 43 percent of the estimated $54.03 billion granted by private foundations during the year.

Contributions to donor-advised funds in 2018 increased by 20.1 percent in relation to the total for 2017. Grants from these funds to charitable entities amounted to an 18.9 percent increase from the total for 2017. Assets under management in donor-advised funds increased by 8.3 percent compared to the value in 2017. The number of these funds "increased sharply," rising by 55.2 percent in 2018. The payout rate for donor-advised funds in 2018 was 20.9 percent.

The average size of a donor-advised fund in 2018 is estimated to be $166,653. This is a 30.2 percent decrease compared to the 2017 number ($238,857). The NPT report states that the "emergence of workplace giving donor-advised fund accounts

---

[285] See text accompanied by *supra* note 277.

and sponsoring organizations that have no or low contribution minimums will continue to drive down the average donor-advised fund size."

The NPT report includes a comparison of donor-advised funds from the standpoint of type of sponsoring organization. Noting that there are about 1.33 million "registered" public charities in the US, the charities tracked in the report comprise less than 1/10th of one percent of these organizations. The report offers this overview: (1) the number of donor-advised funds sponsored by national charities exceeds the number of accounts at the other two types of sponsoring organizations combined, (2) the national charities have higher aggregate charitable asset values and distribute more grant dollars, (3) the average donor-advised fund asset size at community foundations is higher than at the other two types of sponsoring organizations, and (4) single-issue charity sponsors have the highest payout rate.

The NPT report includes data from 54 national charities. These sponsoring organizations had, in 2018, combined 593,356 donor-advised funds (an increase of 75 percent compared to 2017) with total assets of $72.35 billion. The compound annual growth rate of donor-advised funds in this category is 46.4 percent (2014-2018). Contributions to these donor-advised funds reached $23.38 billion in 2018 (a 24.1 percent increase over 2017). Grants from these funds in 2018 totaled $13.1 billion (a 26.8 percent increase). Charitable assets in these funds had a value of $72.35 billion (a 22.6 percent increase). The average fund size of these funds in 2018 is estimated to be $121,937 (a 30 percent decline). The total payout rate from these funds in 2018 is 22.2 percent (down from 23 percent).

The report analyses data from 603 community foundations. These sponsoring organizations had, in 2018, combined 77,234 donor-advised funds (a 2.8 percent increase) and total assets of $33.87 billion. The compound annual growth rate of these funds is 3.9 percent (2014-2018). Contributions to donor-advised funds at community foundations in 2018 totaled $8.38 billion (a 15.4 percent increase). Grants from these funds amounted to $6.59 billion (a 10.2 percent increase). Charitable assets in these funds in 2018 were $33.87 billion (a 14.9 percent decrease). The average account size was $438,561 (a 17.2 percent decrease). The total payout rate from these funds in 2018 is 24.8 percent (an increase from 20 percent).

The 332 single-issue charities reflected in this report held, in 2018, 57,973 donor-advised funds (a 5.1 percent increase), with charitable assets totaling $15.19 billion. The compound annual growth rate (2014-2018) was 5.9 percent. Contributions to these funds totaled $5.36 billion (an 11.7 percent increase). Grants from these funds were $3.73 billion (a 10.3 percent increase). Charitable assets amounted to $15.19 billion (an increase of 14.5 percent). The average account size of these funds in 2018 was $262,075 (a 9 percent increase). The payout rate from these funds was 28.2 percent (a drop from the 2017 rate of 29.6 percent).

The NPT expects that grantmaking from donor-advised "will continue to grow at a consistently high rate." It is noted that, in 2018, the growth in contributions to donor-advised funds outpaced the growth of grants from these funds, reversing a four-year trend. Speculation is that bunching is a major factor in this regard. Another observation is that "emerging models" for donor-advised funds, such as workplace giving using them and low- or no-minimum donor-advised fund accounts "will play a significant role" as to the number of individual accounts and consequently "drive down the average donor-advised fund account size."[286]

Fidelity Charitable 2019 Report

The Fidelity Charitable Gift Fund, in its 2019 Giving Report, announced "record-breaking results" in 2018, despite a year of "uncertainty related to tax reform and volatility in the markets." These results include more than $5.2 billion in grants from the Fund (an increase of 17 percent over 2017), "fueled by the collective generosity of more than 200,000 donors who "remain actively engaged and enthusiastic about philanthropy." Donors used their funds at Fidelity Charitable to recommend nearly 1.3 million grants supporting 142,000 charitable organizations in every state and across the world. Individual grants of $1 million or more grew to 582 in 2018 (an increase of 15 percent).

As of the close of 2018, Fidelity Charitable maintained 123,114 donor-advised funds (termed "giving accounts"). Donors established 15,000 new "giving accounts" in 2018. By contrast, there were 51,918 of these funds/accounts in 2009. Fifty-eight percent of these accounts had an account balance below $25,000; 34 percent of

---

[286] My summary of the NPT report in my newsletter is accompanied by the headline "Stunning Portrait of Donor-Advised Funds Issued" (*Nonprofit Counsel* (No. 1) 1 (Jan. 2020)). Paul Streckfus, in his newsletter, mused that I used the word *stunning* "because of the tremendous growth of DAFs as attested to by increased grants from DAFs, more contributions to DAFs, and many new DAF accounts" (*EO Tax Jour.* 2019-252 (Dec. 31, 2019)). That's basically a correct observation. Then Paul rained on my parade: "I am not against DAFs if they move charitable contributions in timely fashion to working charities and are not being misused. Unfortunately, this cannot be said for sure as a general statement. While commercial and ideological DAF sponsors zealously hide their operations we have reason to suspect that DAF sponsors allow many DAF contributors to stockpile their donations, resulting in little benefit to working charities. We also have reason to believe that not all DAF contributions are being used for charitable purposes." *Id.* Chapter 5 in a nutshell.

these accounts had balances in the range of $25,000-$250,000; 8 percent of the accounts had balances in the amount of $250,000 or more. The median account balance at Fidelity Charitable in 2018 was $17,670.

The "vast majority" of grants (92 percent) from Fidelity Charitable's donor-advised funds in 2018 includes the names and addresses of the donors. A few of these grants (5 percent) share only the name of the fund, while only the balance of these grants (3 percent) are anonymous.

Fidelity Charitable reports that its donors are "actively" recommending grants to charities from their advised funds. Its data shows that, within five years of contributions, 74 percent of the grants is distributed to charities. After 10 years, 88 percent of the money has been granted to charities. The data for 2018 shows that the percentages of grant dollars to the charitable sector's subsectors are as follows: education (29 percent), society benefit (18 percent), religion (15 percent), human services (11 percent), health (8 percent), arts and culture (7 percent), international affairs (5 percent), environment and animals (5 percent), and other (1 percent). Since its Giving report was launched in 2013, education has regularly received the most yearly grant dollars, while religion has received the greatest grant volumes (27 percent).

Fidelity Charitable also reports that its donors "reach beyond charitable giving and embrace charitable planning, which is unmistakable when looking at the types of assets that donors contribute." Noting that most charitable contributions in the U.S. are made by means of cash, checks, or debit and credit cards, more than 60 percent of its donors in 2018 made contributions in the form of "more strategic non-cash assets, including publicly traded securities (stocks, bonds, and mutual funds) and non-publicly traded assets (private stock, restricted stock, limited partnership interests, and cryptocurrency). Many donors, the report adds, contributed assets that were "highly appreciated" in value.

The Fidelity Report observes that, although nonpublicly traded assets (such as private stock, limited partnership interests, real estate, and cryptocurrency) represent a significant portion of wealth in the U.S., assets of this nature have "traditionally been a largely untapped source of philanthropic funding, in part because these assets . . . Can be complicated both for individuals to give and for some nonprofits to accept." Fidelity Charitable states it has expertise in the field of contribution of these assets and "has seen notable growth in these types of contributions in recent years." Since inception, the report states, Fidelity Charitable has converted more than $6 billion in nonpublicly traded assets into "dollars for charity." For example, since Fidelity Charitable began accepting cryptocurrency, including bitcoin, in 2015, donors have made cryptocurrency contributions totaling $106 million.

The Fidelity Charitable report notes the ten years (2009-2018) of "strong and steady economic growth," despite volatility in the market in the final weeks of 2018. Nonetheless, in addition to funds contributed, the Fund has granted $5 billion in investment income to charitable organizations.

FEDERAL GOVERNMENT REPORTS

To date, there are two reports on donor-advised funds prepared by components of the federal government.

Department of Treasury Report

The Department of the Treasury was directed by Congress, in the legislation that codified the concept of the donor-advised fund, to undertake a study on the organization and operation of donor-advised funds, to consider whether (1) the deductions allowed for income, estate, or gift taxes for charitable contributions to sponsoring organizations of donor-advised funds are appropriate in consideration of the use of contributed assets or the use of the assets of such organizations for the benefit of the person making the charitable contribution; (2) donor-advised funds should be required to distribute for charitable purposes a specified amount in order to ensure that the sponsoring organization with respect to the donor-advised fund is operating in a manner consistent with its tax exemption or public charity status; (3) the retention by donors to donor-advised funds of "rights or privileges" with respect to amounts transferred to such organizations (including advisory rights or privileges with respect to the making of grants or the investment of assets) is consistent with the treatment of these transfers as completed gifts; and (4) these issues are also issues with respect to other forms of charitable organizations or charitable contributions.[287]

The Treasury Department issued this report in early December 2011. The report focused on both supporting organizations and donor-advised funds. his report summarized these two bodies of law, including the rules enacted in 2006; provided a statistical analysis of supporting organizations and donor-advised funds; and answered

---

[287] Pension Protection Act of 2006, Pub. L. No. 109-280 § 1226.

questions posed by Congress. Overall, this report concluded that supporting organizations and donor-advised funds "play an important role in the charitable sector."

Statistics

The statistics utilized by the Treasury Department are for 2006, the first year for which complete data were available for use in time for this report. Organizations sponsoring donor-advised funds received, in that year, $59.5 billion, including $9 billion in contributions to the funds. These sponsoring organizations had total expenses of $37.7 billion, including $5.7 billion in grants paid from donor-advised fund assets, $6.8 billion in other grants made, and $20.7 billion in program expenses. These organizations had a net worth of $211.3 billion at the end of the year. The 2,398 organizations sponsoring donor-advised funds had 160,000 of them, entailing assets valued at $31.1 billion as of the end of the year.

The report noted that, beginning with 2006, the annual information return (Form 990) was redesigned, requiring sponsoring organizations to report the aggregate value of assets held in, the aggregate contributions to, and the grants from their donor-advised funds. This data, the report added, will make it possible to calculate aggregate payout rates at the sponsoring organization level and compare the payout rates of these aggregate donor-advised funds with those of private foundations.

The report referenced sponsoring organizations that have a "national reach" and have as their primary role services as "intermediaries between donors and a broad range of charities providing direct charitable services by sponsoring and maintaining donor-advised funds and other similar charitable funds." These were referred to as *national donor-advised funds*. A subset of national donor-advised funds was those that are sponsored by charitable affiliates of financial institutions—accorded the (unfortunate) name of *commercial national donor-advised funds*.

Aggregate donor-advised funds that are commercial national donor-advised funds had an average of $424.5 million in total assets and median assets of $58.9 million. The average payout rate across all aggregate donor-advised funds in 2006 was 9.3 percent. Among the national donor-advised funds, the average payout rate was 14.2 percent. This led the report to conclude that it would be "premature to recommend a distribution requirement for [donor-advised funds] at this point."

OVERALL CONCLUSIONS

The report stated that the Pension Protection Act "appears to have provided a legal structure to address abusive practices and accommodate innovations in the sector without creating undue additional burden or new opportunities for abuse."

As for public comments received by Treasury, the report observed that respondents "generally praised the relative benefits of [supporting organizations] to the supported organizations compared to the benefits that charities derive from [donor-advised funds] and private foundations." Also, "[t]here is a consensus among the respondents that [donor-advised funds] have been a helpful development for donors in the charitable sector."

The final component of this report is a collection of answers to questions posed by Congress. As to the workability of the charitable contribution deduction in these contexts, the report concluded that the charitable deduction rules "for gifts to [donor-advised funds] and [supporting organizations], which are the same as the rules for gifts to other public charities, appear to be appropriate." Concerning distribution requirements, the report stated, as noted, that "it would be premature to make a recommendation regarding distribution requirements for [donor-advised funds] on the basis of this first year of reported data." The report was of the view that "it is consistent to treat donations to [donor-advised funds] and [supporting organizations] that comply with existing legal requirements as completed gifts even if the donor retains non-binding advisory rights."

The report concluded with this: "The [Pension Protection Act] enacted provisions designed to mitigate undue donor influence on [supporting organizations] and [donor-advised fund] sponsoring organizations and to increase the required transparency of these organizations. New reporting requirements will make more data available to federal and state regulators, as well as to researchers, the press, and the general public. As the effects of the [Pension Protection Act] and new regulations become clearer over time, Treasury looks forward to working with Congress to determine whether additional legislation or reporting is necessary."

Congressional Research Service Report

The Congressional Research Service issued a report, dated July 11, 2012, that includes statistics on donor-advised funds, using data derived from Forms 990 for 2008.

Statistics

In 2008, more than 181,000 individual donor-advised fund accounts were maintained. In that year, there were about 1,818 organizations maintaining at least one donor-advised fund account. Approximately one-third of organizations claiming to have donor-advised funds reported that only one fund was maintained. About one-half of all sponsoring organizations reported that five or fewer funds were held.

Thus, according to this report, a small percentage of sponsoring organizations held a large number of donor-advised fund accounts. Fifty-one organizations (about 3 percent of all sponsoring organizations) reported having 500 or more individual donor-advised funds. More than 121,000 of all fund accounts (or two-thirds of them) were maintained by organizations that have at least 500 individual accounts. The report observes that the fact that a large proportion of individual donor-advised fund accounts are maintained by a small number of sponsoring organizations explains why the number of donor-advised funds per organization (100) is "highly skewed." Also: "Since most [donor-advised fund] accounts were held by organizations maintaining multiple [fund] accounts, little is known about the characteristics of the majority of individual [fund] accounts."

For the year, sponsoring organizations reported $29.5 billion in donor-advised fund assets. On average, assets per donor-advised funds had a value of about $162,000. Nearly all donor-advised fund assets (87 percent) were held by sponsoring organizations that maintain 100 or more individual fund accounts.

Total contributions to donor-advised funds in the year were reported to be $7.1 billion. These contributions represented approximately 3.3 percent of total individual giving. On average, sponsoring organizations received $3.9 million in contributions. The average contribution per fund account was $39,103.

Sponsoring organizations reported paying out $7 billion in grants. On average, $38,641 in grants were paid per donor-advised funds. Out of the 1,828 sponsoring organizations included in the sample, an estimated 453 did not pay out any grants. The organizations that sponsored donor-advised funds but did not pay grants held $280.4 million in assets in 2008.

The average payout rate across sponsoring organizations for the year was 13.1 percent. The median payout rate was 6.1 percent; this average was said to be "skewed" by the payout rates of organizations with "unusually large payouts." Forty-three percent of sponsoring organizations had an average payout of less than 5 percent. Twenty-six percent did not report a payout.

This study included a review of 21 "commercial" organizations maintaining donor-advised funds. In 2008, 46.7 percent of individual fund accounts were maintained by these organizations. For the year, 34.3 percent of donor-advised fund assets, 39.2 percent of fund contributions, and 39.7 percent of fund grants involved "commercial" sponsoring organizations.

The average payout rate for commercial donor-advised funds was 26.5 percent. The report observes that, since commercial sponsoring organizations "tend to sponsor a large number of individual accounts (2,720 on average), it is possible that there is substantial variation in payout rates across individual accounts that is masked by the aggregate nature of available payout data."

Policy Considerations

This report extensively addressed the matter of a minimum distribution requirement for donor-advised funds. It noted that the Treasury's position on a minimum payout for donor-advised funds was that it is premature to consider it based on one year of data. Yet, both the 2006 and 2008 data indicate a payout ratio in the aggregate that was higher than that of private foundations (but considerable variability in these ratios across sponsoring organizations).

The Treasury report stated that the payout rates for donor-advised funds in the aggregate in 2006 "appear to be high for most categories of [fund] sponsoring organizations." This statement, said the CRS, "seems to imply that observing an overall payout rate higher than that for foundations is a rationale for not imposing a minimum payout requirement" in the donor-advised fund context. The CRS, however, wrote that "there is ample reason to reject the notion that an aggregate payout ratio higher than that of private foundations provides a good rationale for not imposing such requirements on a per [fund] account basis." Yet, the CRS noted, although for sponsoring organizations maintaining a single fund account the average payout rate was 10.6 percent, over one-half of these organizations did not make any distribution and over 70 percent made a distribution of less than 5 percent. The CRS concluded that "there is likely to be substantial variation in payout rates at the individual account level across all sponsoring organizations."

The CRS report, not so subtly advocating consideration of a minimum payout rate for donor-advised funds on a fund-by-fund basis, stated that a minimum rate imposed on sponsoring organizations would be "relatively meaningless," given the data. This approach, the CRS report stated, "would also create an incentive for donors who wished to accumulate funds and maintain endowments while paying little or nothing in grants to move to the larger [fund] sponsors, including commercial [donor-advised funds]."

This report also recalled that the Treasury report rejected application of private foundation rules to donor-advised funds on the ground that, as a matter of law, control of the fund is in the sponsoring organization (a public charity). The CRS report rejected this, writing that "donors appear to have actual control of grant-making because sponsoring organizations typically follow their advice." The report states that, "[i]n considering this issue, one question is whether the restricted legal rights of the donor or actual practice should determine the appropriate treatment."

The report raised the issue as to whether commercial donor-advised funds and national ones lacked a charitable purpose. It noted that some have suggested "tighter regulations and greater restrictions" for these sponsors. Also referenced was, in the case of commercial donor-advised funds, a "tension" between the "needs of charitable organizations . . . and the incentive to maintain large investment accounts."

Another proposal discussed in the CRS report is the one to restrict the duration of donor-advised funds. This could be done by limiting the life of these accounts or by limiting the period of years that advisory rights would be effective. The report states that this approach "would be an alternative or perhaps addition to a payout requirement to insure that the amounts in [fund] accounts are used for charitable purposes in some reasonable time period."

The CRS report bemoaned the fact that "all reporting is done at the aggregate [donor-advised fund] sponsor level, which means there is information only by inference concerning the shares of accounts that have low or no payout ratios." It stated: "Requiring reporting on individual [fund] accounts is an option that could improve understanding of how [donor-advised funds] operate and provide better oversight."

The report stated: "Useful information that could be provided by [donor-advised fund] sponsors could include the share of their [fund] accounts that made no distributions, the share that made distributions of less than 5 [percent], or a general distribution of accounts across different payout intervals." Also: "Information on investment fees and administrative costs of managing the [donor-advised funds], separated from other costs, could also be useful." Further: "Additional information could help policy makers evaluate whether giving through [donor-advised funds] is achieving charitable giving policy goals."

The CRS report concluded with this: "In some ways, the fundamental policy issue about how freely to allow donors to make contributions that are not immediately used for charitable purposes is whether such arrangements increase charitable giving per dollar of cost or decrease it. Allowing for contributions to accumulate and earn a tax-free return increases the benefit to the donor and thus may increase contributions to funds or foundations, albeit at an additional cost. Such arrangements can also reduce current charitable giving by encouraging fund accumulation, a concern that presumably motivated the minimum distribution rules for private foundations. [Donor-advised funds] differ from foundations in some ways, including the legal technicalities, but in practice, are very similar. One concern that remains for both foundations and [donor-advised funds] is how soon donations are put to charitable use."

MANHATTAN INSTITUTE PEERS INTO DAFS' FUTURE

The Manhattan Institute, in 2015, issued a report on donor-advised funds, in the context of a lament that, although wealth was continuing to increase in the U.S. (among higher-income households), "overall philanthropic giving has, over the past generation, remained roughly constant as a percentage of economic activity."[288] It was noted that a "new generation of not-for-profits, led by young social entrepreneurs, is injecting both greater dynamism and stiffer competition for funds into the charity marketplace." The report mused that donor-advised funds were "becoming a means through which net U.S. charitable giving, along with the funds supporting it, might significantly increase," driven by enactment of the 2006 tax legislation and the "increased marketing" by the national sponsoring organizations. The report concluded that the growth of donor-advised funds "could signal the start of a surge in the volume of total charitable giving" and that these funds "provide the preconditions for significant growth in overall U.S. charitable giving." The report noted, however, that "DAF growth is not inevitable" and that changes in the tax law "could discourage the deposit of funds and assets" into donor-advised funds, "curtailing overall U.S. charitable giving in the process."

---

[288] Husock, "Growing Giving: American Philanthropy and the Potential of Donor-Advised Funds" (Manhattan Institute Civic Report No. 97 (April 2015)) (Manhattan Institute Report).

79

This report ended with these observations ("offer[ing] cause for optimism"):

"Continued growth in appreciated DAF assets will lead to a significant pool of capital that, because gifts to DAF accounts are irrevocable, will be available exclusively for charitable giving."

"Administrative efficiencies enjoyed by the large tax accounting teams and legal compliance departments at [the national sponsoring organizations] facilitate the giving of illiquid assets, thus reducing the effective cost of giving."

"Continued growth in the number of DAF account holders could precipitate increased charitable giving."

The report concluded that the "possibility that new DAF accounts will, over time, merely substitute for traditional check-writing to charities cannot be dismissed, but numerous factors—from convenience to asset appreciation—suggest that [donor-advised funds] housed in [the national sponsoring organizations] and major community foundations could signal a new era in U.S. mass philanthropy (one rivaling, say, the Community Chest/United Way movement of the 1920s). The potential thus exists for a large group of relatively small donors to make a big positive difference in the magnitude of what is already the world's largest charitable giving sector."[289]

INSTITUTE FOR POLICY STUDIES REPORT

Typical of today's criticism of donor-advised funds is a report from the Institute for Policy Studies that appeared in mid-2018.[290] The tone of this report is clearly set at its outset: "At a time of staggering inequality, wealthy individuals are using donor-advised funds ... to claim substantial tax benefits, while often failing to move funds in a timely manner to independent nonprofits addressing urgent social needs." Particular blame for this "often" failing is laid on the national sponsoring organizations or, as the report characterizes them, "DAFs founded by for-profit Wall Street financial corporations that provide incentives for the warehousing of wealth." This report references an "unregulated DAF system."[291]

This report highlights "potential risks," including the absence of any "legal requirement for DAFs to pay out their funds to qualified charities—ever"; encourage-

---

[289] Id. at 12.
[290] Institute for Policy Studies, "Warehousing Wealth: Donor-Advised Charity Funds Sequestering Billions in the Face of Growing Inequality" (July 25, 2018).
[291] See Chapter 4.

ment by donor-advised funds of a "wealth preservation mentality in donors, rather than incentives to move donations to qualified charities"; and the provision by donor-advised funds of "loopholes for both donors and private foundations to get around tax restrictions and significantly reduce transparency and accountability."

The report intones that the "public interest has not been upheld by the regulations addressing DAFs." (At the time of that writing, there were no donor-advised fund regulations, not even proposed ones.) Reference is made to a "broken incentive system," that has "encouraged and enabled ultra-wealthy individuals to use DAFs as a tax avoidance strategy rather than for the greater good of serving charitable needs." The rapid growth of donor-advised funds "has raised questions about their nature as public charities and the degree to which the public is being served by their activities." There are "concerns," it is written, that the "dollars going into DAFs may stay undistributed for years—warehousing dollars that otherwise often would have gone directly to active nonprofits."

Chuck full of "oftens," "mays," "generallys," "frequentlys," this sophomoric report meanders on in this vein for many pages. It concludes with recommendations for "mitigating the risks" of donor-advised funds, including this (predictable) litany: the requirement that all contributions to donor-advised funds be distributed within three years, a delay in the donors' charitable tax deduction until the property in the funds is paid out to "active charity," establishment of a payout rate, a prohibition on private foundation grants to donor-advised funds and vice versa, an increase in scrutiny of rules around donations of non-cash appreciated assets to "ensure public interest and taxpayers are protected," imposition of a cap on management fees for "commercial advisors of" donor-advised funds, and imposition of a rule that a donor-advised fund cannot be managed by the same organization that manages the donor's personal assets.

LILLY SCHOOL OF PHILANTHROPY STUDY

A recent study of the donor-advised fund environment, researched and written at the Lilly School of Philanthropy, based at Indiana University, opens with the conclusion that donor-advised funds "are one of the fastest-growing charitable giving vehicles in the United States."[292] A measurement of this growth is based on a com-

[292] Giving USA, *The Data on Donor-Advised Funds: New Insights You Need to Know* 11 (January

parison to charitable giving in the U.S. generally. In 2016, charitable giving in the U.S. totaled $390 billion, a 2.7 increase in giving compared to 2015.[293] By contrast, in 2016, contributions to donor-advised funds amounted to $23.27 billion, a 7.6 percent increase in giving in relation to the prior year.[294] Thus, charitable giving to donor-advised funds in 2016 was nearly triple the overall charitable giving growth rate. This analysis added that, between 2010 and 2015, contributions to donor-advised funds had an annualized growth rate of 18.3 percent.[295]

The Fidelity Charitable Gift Fund, the largest national sponsoring organization, received contributions in the amount of $4.1 billion in 2016, making it the largest tax-exempt charitable organization in the U.S.[296] National donor-advised fund sponsoring organizations constitute five of the top ten U.S. charitable organizations.[297]

Two analyses of the economics of donor-advised funds are conducted by the Indiana University and the National Philanthropic Trust. Contributions to and aggregate asset value of donor-advised funds experienced "strong growth rated" during 2008-2014.[298] The strongest of these growth years, in terms of dollars contributed to funds, was 2012. The University study shows an increase of 48 percent; the Trust's study pegged the increase at 35 percent. The largest amount contributed to donor-advised funds occurred in 2014, being $22 billion according to the University and $20 billion according to the Trust. Asset values of donor-advised funds also peaked in 2014; the University set that value at $76 billion, while the Trust reported it to be $70 billion.[299]

Donor-advised funds numbered, in 2014, over 250,000, according to the University, and just under 250,000, the Trust estimated.[300] This report observed that, "[g]enerally speaking, the overall number of individual accounts has grown at a comparatively slower pace than the dollar amount contributed or asset value from 2008-2014, never exceeding 11 percent for the estimates" in either of the analyses.[301]

2018). This report (Giving USA 2018 DAF Report) was researched and written by the Lilly Family School of Philanthropy at Indiana University.
[293] Giving USA 2017, *The Annual Report on Charitable Giving.*
[294] Giving USA 2018 DAF Report, at 11.
[295] *Id.*
[296] See, however, *supra* note 280.
[297] Giving USA 2018 DAF Report, at 7.
[298] *Id.* at 18.
[299] *Id.* at 19.
[300] *Id.* at 20.
[301] *Id.* at 18.

The University report found that sponsoring organizations are "more likely to have larger contributions, assets, and investment income," yet have "much lower reported revenue from programs, services, and other activities." This fact was considered unusual, in that charitable organizations with these characteristics typically also have high revenue. Sponsoring organizations "may buck this trend," the report states, "because they do not provide services for a charge, collect rent, or hold fundraising events as many traditional nonprofits do."[302]

The University report also found considerable concentration of sponsoring organizations in relation to grantmaking from donor-advised funds. That is, a few large sponsoring organizations hold the majority of assets held in donor-advised funds and are responsible for most of the grantmaking from the funds. Identification of the top ten sponsoring organizations, in terms of total grants made during 2008-2014, led to the conclusion that the "list was relatively stable," in that only 15 organizations were ever among the top group.[303] These 15 entities held nearly 60 percent of donor-advised fund assets and made over 60 percent of fund grants in 2014.

This report is said to be the "first attempt to track donor-advised fund distribution on a large scale."[304] Most of these grants were made to organizations in the education (28 percent), religion (14 percent), and public benefit (14 percent) subsectors.[305] This is a "slightly different pattern" compared to charitable giving distributions generally, where the top donees and grantees are in the categories of religion (32 percent), education (15 percent), and human services (12 percent).[306] This granting pattern for donor-advised funds is relatively stable year-to-year.[307]

Another finding in the University's report is that granting patterns from donor-advised funds align with some granting patterns of high-net-worth donors. For example, giving to education is the top priority in both instances, with the giving levels to religion being about the same.[308] Yet, "not all high-net-worth donors are using donor-advised funds." Indeed, in 2015, only 3 percent of charitable giving by these donors originated from a donor-advised fund (or similar vehicle) and a mere 4.2 percent of these individuals had a donor-advised fund.[309]

---

[302] *Id.* at 21.
[303] *Id.*
[304] *Id.* at 23. These findings are based on 2012-2015 data.
[305] Giving USA 2018 DAF Report at 24.
[306] *Id.* at 25.
[307] *Id.* at 28.
[308] *Id.* at 30.

Still another of these findings was that there are few differences between large and small sponsoring organizations. During 2012-2014, however, the percentage of grants from smaller donor-advised funds to education, the arts, and community foundations subsectors exceeded the comparable percentages of grants from the larger funds.[310] The report mused that some of these differences "may be a consequence of the type of donor-advised fund sponsors in each category."[311] Also, larger donor-advised funds granted a greater percentage of grants, as compared to smaller funds, to religious and international affairs organizations.[312]

---

[309] *Id.*
[310] *Id.* at 31.
[311] *Id.* at 31-32.
[312] *Id.* at 32.

CHAPTER FOUR:
The Statutory Framework

Enactment of the Pension Protection Act of 2006[313] brought statutory law, in the federal tax context, concerning donor-advised funds.[314] This law did not substantially alter the preexisting concept of the donor-advised fund,[315] although it added several tax law rules, such as those taxing certain distributions and denying a charitable deduction for certain contributions.

TOPICS DISCUSSED IN THIS CHAPTER:

- Definition of *donor-advised fund*
- Exceptions to definition
- Other definitions
- Taxable distributions
- Disqualified supporting organizations
- Private benefit taxes
- More-than-incidental benefits
- Excess business holdings rules
- Nondeductible contributions
- Excess benefit transactions rules
- Disqualified persons

---

[313] Pub. L. No. 109-280, 120 Stat. 780.
[314] Internal Revenue Code of 1986 sections (IRC §§) 4966 and 4967. The IRS published a brief summary of this body of law, in the form of interim guidance (Notice 2006-109, 2006-51 I.R.B. 1121 § 2). This interim guidance was modified but not as to the donor-advised fund law summary (Notice 2014-4, 2014-2 I.R.B. 274).
[315] See Chapter 2, pp. 46-50.

- Excess benefit transactions tax regime
- Substantiation requirements
- Applications for recognition of exemption
- Reporting requirements
- Sponsoring organizations operating policies

DEFINITION OF DONOR-ADVISED FUND

A *donor-advised fund* is a fund or account (1) that is separately identified by reference to contributions of one or more donors, (2) that is owned and controlled by a sponsoring organization, and (3) as to which a donor or a donor advisor has, or reasonably expects to have, advisory privileges with respect to the distribution or investment of amounts held in the fund or account by reason of the donor's status as a donor.[316] The legislative history of this provision states that "[a]ll three prongs of the definition must be met in order for a fund or account to be treated as a donor advised fund."[317]

As to this first prong, a distinct fund or account of a sponsoring organization does not meet this prong of the definition unless the fund or account refers to contributions of a donor or donors, such as by naming the fund after a donor, or by treating a fund on the books of the sponsoring organization as attributable to funds contributed by a specific donor or donors. Although a sponsoring organization's general fund is a "fund or account," it generally will not be treated as a donor-advised fund because the general funds of an organization typically are not separately identified by reference to contributions of a specific donor or donors; rather contributions are pooled anonymously within the general fund. Similarly, a fund or account of a sponsoring organization that is distinct from the organization's general fund and that pools contributions of multiple donors generally will not meet the first prong of the definition unless the contributions of specific donors are in some manner tracked and accounted for within the fund. Accordingly, if a sponsoring organization establishes a fund dedicated to the relief of poverty within a specific community, or a scholarship fund, and the fund attracts contributions from several donors but does not separately identify or refer to contributions of a donor or donors, the

---

[316] IRC § 4966(d)(2)(A).
[317] Staff of the Joint Committee on Taxation, "Technical Explanation of H.R. 4, the 'Pension Protection Act of 2006'" (JCX-38-16 (Aug. 3, 2006)) (Jt. Comm. Technical Explanation), at 342.

fund is not a donor-advised fund even if a donor has advisory privileges with respect to the fund. A fund or account, however, may not avoid treatment as a donor-advised fund even though there is no formal recognition of such separate contributions on the books of the sponsoring organization if the fund or account operates as if contributions of a donor or donors are separately identified. The IRS has the authority to look to the substance of an arrangement, and not merely its form. In addition, a fund or account may be treated as identified by reference to contributions of a donor or donors if the reference is to persons related to a donor. For example, if a husband made contributions to a fund or account that in turn is named after the husband's wife, the fund is treated as being separately identified by reference to contributions of a donor.[318]

The second prong of the definition provides that the fund be owned and controlled by a sponsoring organization. To the extent that a donor or person other than the sponsoring organization owns or controls amounts deposited to a sponsoring organization, a fund or account is not a donor-advised fund. In cases where a donor retains control of an amount provided to a sponsoring organization, there may not be a completed gift for purposes of the charitable contribution deduction.[319]

The third prong of the definition provides that, with respect to a fund or account of a sponsoring organization, a donor or donor advisor has or reasonably expects to have advisory privileges with respect to the distribution or investment of amounts held in the fund or account by reason of a donor's status as a donor. Advisory privileges are distinct from a legal right or obligation. For example, if a donor executes a gift agreement with a sponsoring organization that specifies certain enforceable rights of the donor with respect to a gift, the donor will not be treated as having advisory privileges due to such enforceable rights for purposes of the donor-advised fund definition.[320]

The presence of an advisory privilege may be evident through a written document that describes an arrangement between the donor or donor advisor and the sponsoring organization whereby a donor or donor advisor may provide advice to the sponsoring organization about the investment or distribution of amounts held by a sponsoring organization, even if such privileges are not exercised. The presence of an advisory privilege also may be evident through the conduct of a donor or donor advisor and the sponsoring organization. For example, even in the absence

---

[318] Id., at 342-343.
[319] Id., at 343.
[320] Id.

of a writing, if a donor regularly provides advice to a sponsoring organization and the sponsoring organization regularly considers the advice, the donor has advisory privileges. Even if advisory privileges do not exist at the time of a contribution, later acts by the donor, through the provision of advice, and by the sponsoring organization, through the regular consideration of advice, may establish advisory privileges subsequent to the time of the contribution. For example, if a past donor of $100,000 telephones a sponsoring organization and states that he or she would like the sponsoring organization to distribute $10,000 to a charitable organization, although the mere act of providing advice does not establish an advisory privilege, if the sponsoring organization distributed the $10,000 to the organization specified by the donor in consideration of the donor's advice, and reinforced the donor in some manner that future advice similarly would be considered, advisory privileges (or the reasonable expectation thereof) might be established. The mere provision of advice by a donor or donor advisor, however, does not mean the donor or donor advisor has advisory privileges. For example, a donor's singular belief that he or she has advisory privileges with respect to a contribution does not establish an advisory privilege—there must be some reciprocity on the part of the sponsoring organization.[321]

A person reasonably expects to have advisory privileges if both the donor or donor advisor and the sponsoring organization have reason to believe that the donor or donor advisor will provide advice and that the sponsoring organization generally will consider it. Thus, a person reasonably may expect to have advisory privileges even in the absence of the actual provision of advice. A donor's expectation of advisory privileges is not reasonable, however, unless it is reinforced in some manner by the conduct of the sponsoring organization. If, at the time of the contribution, the sponsoring organization had no knowledge that the donor had an expectation of advisory privileges, or no intention of considering any advice provided by the donor, then the donor does not have a reasonable expectation of advisory privileges. Ultimately, the presence or absence of advisory privileges (or a reasonable expectation thereof) depends on the facts and circumstances, which in turn depend on the conduct (including any agreement) of both the donor or donor advisor and the sponsoring organization with respect to the making and consideration of advice.[322]

A further requirement of the third prong is that the reasonable expectation of advisory privileges is by reason of the donor's status as a donor. Under this requirement,

---

[321] Id., 343-344.
[322] Id., at 344.

if a donor's reasonable expectation of advisory privileges is due solely to the donor's service to the organization, for example, by reason of the donor's position as a director, officer, or employee of the sponsoring organization, the third prong of the definition is not satisfied. For instance, in general, a donor that is a member of the board of directors of the sponsoring organization may provide advice in his or her capacity as a board member with respect to the distribution or investment of amounts in a fund to which the board member contributed. If, however, by reason of the donor's contribution to the fund, the donor secured an appointment on a committee of the sponsoring organization that advises how to distribute or invest amounts in the fund, the donor may have a reasonable expectation of advisory privileges, notwithstanding the fact that the donor is a director, officer, or employee of the sponsoring organization.[323]

The third prong of the definition is applicable to a donor or any person appointed or designated by the donor, that is, the donor advisor. For purposes of this prong, a person appointed or designated by a donor advisor is treated as being appointed or designated by a donor. In addition, for purposes of any exception to the definition of a donor-advised fund, to the extent a donor recommends to a sponsoring organization the selection of members of a committee that will advise as to distributions or investments of amounts in a fund or account of the sponsoring organization, the members are not treated as appointed or designated by the donor if the recommendation of the members by the donor is based on objective criteria related to the expertise of the member. For example, if a donor recommends that a committee of a sponsoring organization that will provide advice regarding scholarship grants for the advancement of science at local secondary schools should consist of persons who are the heads of the science departments of the schools, the donor generally would not be considered to have appointed or designated those persons, that is, they would not be treated as donor advisors.[324]

EXCEPTIONS TO DEFINITION

A fund is not a donor-advised fund if it is a fund that makes distributions only to a single identified organization or governmental entity.[325] For example, an endowment

---

[323] *Id.*
[324] *Id.* at 344–345.
[325] IRC § 4966(d)(2)(B)(i).

fund owned and controlled by a sponsoring organization that is held exclusively for the benefit of the organization is not a donor-advised fund, notwithstanding the fact that the fund is named in honor of its principal donor and the donor has advisory privileges with respect to the distribution of amounts held in the fund to the sponsoring organization. Accordingly, a donor that contributes to a university for purposes of establishing a fund named after the donor that exclusively supports the activities of the university is not a donor-advised fund even if the donor has advisory privileges regarding distribution or investment of amounts in the fund.[326]

Also, a fund is not a donor-advised fund where it is a fund with respect to which a donor or donor advisor advises as to which individuals receive grants for travel, study, or similar purposes.[327] For this second exception to be available, (1) the individual's advisory privileges must be performed exclusively by the individual in the individual's capacity as a member of a committee all of the members of which are appointed by the sponsoring organization; (2) no combination of donors, donor advisors, or individuals related to them controls, directly or indirectly, the committee; (3) all grants from the fund or account are awarded on an objective and nondiscriminatory basis pursuant to a procedure approved in advance by the board of directors of the sponsoring organization; and (4) this procedure is designed to ensure that the grants meet the requirements imposed by the private foundation rules pertaining to grants to individuals.[328] As to this fourth element, the grant must be a (1) a scholarship or fellowship grant that is excludable from the recipient's gross income and used for study at an educational institution; (2) prize or award that is excludable from the recipient's gross income, where the recipient is selected from the public; or (3) a grant the purpose of which is to achieve a specific objective, produce a report or similar project, or improve or enhance a literary, artistic, musical, scientific, teaching, or other similar capacity, skill, or talent of the grantee.[329]

Further, the IRS has the authority to exempt a fund or account from treatment as a donor-advised fund.[330] For this authority to be exercised, the fund or account must be advised by a committee not directly or indirectly controlled by the donor or any person appointed or designated by the donor for the purpose of advising with respect to distributions from the fund (and any related parties).[331] For these

---

[326] Jt. Comm. Technical Explanation, at 345.
[327] IRC § 4966(d)(2)(B)(ii).
[328] Id.
[329] IRC § 4945(g)(1)-(3).
[330] IRC § 4966(d)(2)(C)(i).
[331] Id.

purposes, indirect control includes the ability to exercise effective control. For example, if a donor, a donor advisor, and a lawyer hired by the donor to provide advice regarding the donor's contributions constitute three of the five members of the committee, the committee is treated as controlled indirectly by the donor for purposes of the exception. Board membership alone does not establish direct or indirect control. In general, under this authority, the IRS may establish rules regarding committee-advised funds generally that, if followed, would result in the fund not being treated as a donor-advised fund. The IRS may also establish rules excepting certain types of committee-advised funds, such as a fund established exclusively for disaster relief, from the definition of donor-advised fund.[332]

The IRS also has the authority to exempt a fund or account from treatment as a donor-advised fund where the fund or account benefits a single identified charitable purpose.[333]

OTHER DEFINITIONS

A *sponsoring organization* is a public charity[334] that maintains one or more donor-advised funds.[335] A *donor advisor* is a person appointed or designated by a donor.[336]

TAXABLE DISTRIBUTIONS

A distribution from a donor-advised fund is taxable if it is to (1) a natural person, (2) any other person for a noncharitable purpose, or (3) any person (other than an individual) unless expenditure responsibility is exercised by the sponsoring organization with respect to the distribution.[337] This is termed a *taxable distribution*.

For purposes of the requirement that a distribution be *to* a public charity, in general, the rules similar to the foreign charity equivalency rules, in the taxable ex-

---

[332] Jt. Comm. Technical Explanation, at 345. The Department of the Treasury and the IRS exercised this authority in excluding from the definition of *donor-advised fund* an employer-sponsored disaster relief fund that met certain requirements, including service of a "large or indefinite class" (Notice 2006-109, 2006-51 I.R.B. 1121 § 5.01). This type of class is a "charitable class" (see *Tax-Exempt Organizations* § 6.3(a)).
[333] IRC § 4966(d)(2)(C)(ii).
[334] That is, it is not a private foundation (IRC § 509(a)).
[335] IRC § 4966(d)(1).
[336] IRC § 4966(d)(2)(A)(iii).
[337] IRC § 4966(c)(1).

penditures context, apply.[338] Pursuant to these rules, for purposes of determining whether a grant by a private foundation is to an eligible public charity and thus not a taxable expenditure, a foreign organization that otherwise is not a public charity is considered as such if the private foundation makes a good faith determination that the grantee is such an organization. Similarly, if a sponsoring organization makes a good faith determination (under standards similar to those applicable for private foundations) that a distributee organization is a public charity (other than a disqualified supporting organization), a distribution to such organization is not considered a taxable distribution.[339]

The concept of *expenditure responsibility* is taken from the private foundation rules.[340] A sponsoring organization is considered to be exercising expenditure responsibility in connection with a distribution as long as it exerts all reasonable efforts and establishes adequate procedures to see that the amount distributed is spent solely for the purpose for which it was made, obtains full and complete reports from the distributee on how the funds were spent, and makes full and detailed reports to the IRS with respect to the expenditures.[341]

A taxable distribution does not include a distribution to a public charity (other than a disqualified supporting organization[342]), the sponsoring organization of the donor-advised fund involved, or to another donor-advised fund.[343]

Sponsoring organizations may make grants to individuals from amounts not held in donor-advised funds and may establish scholarship funds that are not donor-advised funds. A donor may choose to make a contribution directly to such a scholarship fund or advise that a distribution from a donor-advised fund be made to such a scholarship fund.[344]

An excise tax of 20 percent of the amount involved is imposed on a taxable distribution by a sponsoring organization.[345] Another excise tax, of 5 percent, not to exceed $10,000 with respect to any one taxable distribution, is imposed on the agreement of a fund manager to the making of a taxable distribution where the manager knew that the distribution was a taxable one.[346] The term *fund manager*

---

[338] Reg. § 53.4945-5(a)(5).
[339] Jt. Comm. Technical Explanation, at 349.
[340] IRC § 4945(d)(4).
[341] IRC § 4945(h); Reg. § 53.4945-5(b)-(d).
[342] See text accompanied by *infra* notes 352-363.
[343] IRC § 4966(c)(2).
[344] Jt. Comm. Technical Explanation at 349, note 527.
[345] IRC § 4966(a)(1).
[346] IRC § 4966(a)(2).

embraces trustees, directors, officers, and executive employees of the sponsoring organization involved.[347] These taxes on taxable distributions are subject to abatement.

The tax on fund management is confined to $10,000 per transaction,[348] and is subject to a joint and several liability requirement.[349] The tax on taxable distributions does not apply to a distribution from a donor-advised fund to most public charities, the fund's sponsoring organization, or another donor-advised fund.[350]

As to the first of the foregoing three exceptions from the concept of a taxable expenditure, the term *public charity* generally refers to the preferred category of tax-exempt charities.[351] These types of charities are churches, conventions or associations of churches, colleges, universities, other schools, hospitals, medical research organizations, agricultural research organizations, fundraising organizations for public colleges and universities, governmental units, publicly supported charities, and certain supporting organizations.

DISQUALIFIED SUPPORTING ORGANIZATIONS

Generally, grants from donor-advised funds are made to public charities.[352] Public charities include supporting organizations. The law concerning supporting organizations,[353] however, was made considerably more complex in 2006.[354] One of the fundamental law changes wreaked in 2006 was classification of supporting organizations into four categories: Type I, Type II, and Type III supporting organizations, with third category divided into functionally integrated and nonfunctionally integrated supporting organizations. The law significantly disfavors the fourth category of supporting organization, including making them ineligible grantees of sponsoring organizations.[355]

---

[347] IRC § 4966(d)(3).
[348] IRC § 4966(b)(2).
[349] IRC § 4966(b)(1).
[350] IRC § 4966(c)(2).
[351] IRC § 170(b)(1)(A).
[352] See Chapter 1, pp. 6–8.
[353] See *Private Foundations* § 15.7.
[354] Some, including this author, believe many of these changes were unnecessary and severely damaged the supporting organization as a charitable management and fundraising vehicle. E.g., Knoepfle, "The Pension Protection Act of 2006: A Misguided Attack on Donor-Advised Funds and Supporting Organizations," 9 *Fla. Tax Rev.* 221 (2009). It is these types of "reforms" that many are fearful will likewise severely harm the use of donor-advised funds. See Chapter 6, pp. 208–209.
[355] The IRS promulgated reliance criteria for sponsoring organizations (and private foundations) in de-

The term eligible *public charity* does not, however, in the donor-advised fund context, include disqualified supporting organizations.[356] There are three categories of *disqualified supporting organizations.* One of these categories encompasses Type III supporting organizations[357] that are not functionally integrated Type III supporting organizations.[358] The second category of disqualified supporting organization embraces Type I and II supporting organizations[359] and functionally integrated Type III supporting organizations[360] where a donor, donor advisor, or related party directly or indirectly controls a supported organization[361] of any of these types of supporting organizations.[362] The third category of disqualified supporting organization entails a Type I supporting organization, a Type II supporting organization, or a functionally integrated Type III supporting organization where the Department of the Treasury determines by regulations that a distribution to one or more of these entities "otherwise is inappropriate."[363]

PRIVATE BENEFIT TAXES

If a donor, donor advisor, or a person related to a donor or a donor advisor with respect to a donor-advised fund provides advice as to a distribution from the fund that results in any of those persons receiving, directly or indirectly, a benefit that is more than incidental, an excise tax equal to 125 percent of the amount of the benefit is imposed on the person who advised as to the distribution and on the recipient of the benefit.[364] More specifically, this tax applies, in addition to a donor or donor advisor,[365] to a member of the family of a donor or a donor advisor[366] and to a 35-percent controlled entity.[367] An individual is determined to be a *member of the family*

termining whether a potential grantee is a public charity, including the types of supporting organizations (Rev. Proc. 2009-32, 2009-28 I.R.B. 142). This guidance was superseded as the IRS upgraded its database on tax-exempt organizations (Rev. Proc. 2011-33, 2011-25 I.R.B. 887, then Rev. Proc. 2018-32, 2018-23 I.R.B. 739).

[356] IRC §§ 4966(c)(2)(A), (d)(4).
[357] IRC § 4943(f)(5)(A).
[358] IRC § 4966(d)(4)(A)(i). Functionally integrated Type III supporting organizations are the subject of IRC § 4943(f)(5)(B).
[359] IRC § 4966(d)(4)(B).
[360] IRC § 4966(d)(4)(C).
[361] IRC § 509(f)(3).
[362] IRC § 4966(d)(4)(A)(ii)(I).
[363] IRC § 4966(d)(4)(A)(ii)(II).
[364] IRC § 4967(a)(1).
[365] IRC § 4966(d)(2)(A)(iii). Also IRC § 4958(f)(7)(A).
[366] IRC §§ 4967(d). 4958(f)(7)(B).

by use of the definition of the phrase in the private foundation setting, which applies to individuals who are, with respect to a donor or donor advisor, the spouse, ancestors, children, grandchildren, great grandchildren, and the spouses of children, grandchildren, and great grandchildren.[368] Also, members of the family include the brothers and sisters (whether by the whole or half blood) of the individual and his or her spouse.[369] The term *35-percent controlled entity* means (1) a corporation in which donors, donor advisors, and members of their families own more than 35 percent of the total combined voting power; (2) a partnership in which these individuals own more than 35 percent of the profits interest; and (3) a trust or estate in which these individuals own more than 35 percent of the beneficial interest.[370] Constructive ownership rules apply in this context;[371] they are similar to those that apply in the private foundation law setting.[372]

If a manager of the sponsoring organization involved agreed to the making of the distribution knowing that the distribution would confer more than an incidental benefit on a donor, donor advisor, or related person, the manager is subject to an excise tax equal to 10 percent of the amount of the benefit.[373] The maximum amount of this tax on fund management per distribution is $10,000[374] and both of these taxes are subject to a joint and several liability requirement.[375] These taxes on more-than-incidental benefits are subject to abatement.

These taxes may not be imposed if a tax with respect to the distribution has been imposed pursuant to the excess benefit transactions rules.[376]

MORE-THAN-INCIDENTAL BENEFITS

In general, there is a more-than-incidental benefit if, as a result of a distribution from a donor-advised fund, a donor, donor advisor, or related person with respect to the fund receives a benefit that would have reduced or eliminated a charitable

---

[367] IRC §§ 4967(d), 4958(f)(7)(C).
[368] IRC §§ 4958(f)(4), 4946(d).
[369] IRC § 4958(f)(4).
[370] IRC § 4958(f)(3)(A).
[371] IRC § 4958(f)(3)(B).
[372] IRC § 4946(a)(3), (4).
[373] IRC § 4967(a)(2).
[374] IRC § 4967(c)(2).
[375] IRC § 4967(c)(1).
[376] IRC § 4967(b).

contribution deduction if the benefit was received as part of the contribution to the sponsoring organization. If, for example, a donor advises that a distribution from the donor's donor-advised fund be made to the Girl Scouts of America, and the donor's daughter is a member of a local unit of the Girl Scouts of America, the indirect benefit the donor received as a result of the contribution is considered incidental, inasmuch as it generally would not have reduced or eliminated the donor's deduction if it had been received as part of a contribution by the donor to the sponsoring organization.[377]

EXCESS BUSINESS HOLDINGS RULES

The private foundation excess business holdings rules apply to donor-advised funds.[378] This means that donor-advised funds are limited as to the extent to which they can own interests in commercial business enterprises. A donor-advised fund and all disqualified persons with respect to it generally are permitted to hold no more than 20 percent of a corporation's voting stock or other interest in a business enterprise; these holdings are termed *permitted holdings*.[379] If effective control of the business can be shown to be elsewhere, a 35 percent limit may be substituted for the 20 percent limit.[380] A donor-advised fund must hold, directly or indirectly, more than 2 percent of the value of a business enterprise before these limitations become applicable.[381]

For this purpose, the term *disqualified person* means, with respect to a donor-advised fund, a donor, a donor advisor, a member of the family of either, or a 35-percent controlled entity of any such person.[382] The family of an individual includes only his or her spouse, ancestors, children, grandchildren, great grandchildren, and the spouses of children, grandchildren, and great grandchildren.[383] A 35-percent controlled entity may be a corporation, partnership, trust, or estate.[384]

---

[377] Jt. Comm. Technical Explanation, at 350. E.g., Rev. Rul. 80-77, 1980-1 C.B. 56; Rev. Proc. 90-12, 1990-1 C.B. 471.

[378] IRC § 4943(e)(1).

[379] IRC § 4943(c)(2)(A), (c)(3).

[380] IRC § 4943(c)(2)(B).

[381] IRC § 4943(c)(2)(C).

[382] IRC § 4943(e)(2).

[383] IRC § 4946(d).

[384] IRC § 4953(f)(3). Transition rules apply to the present holdings of a donor-advised fund similar to those of IRC § 4943(c)(4)-(6) (IRC § 4943(e)(3)).

There are three principal exceptions to these rules. One of the exceptions is for a business at least 95 percent of the gross income of which is derived from passive sources.[385] These sources generally include dividends, interest, annuities, royalties, and capital gain.[386] The section exception is for holdings in a *functionally related business*.[387] This is a business that is substantially related to the achievement of the donor-advised fund's exempt purposes (other than merely providing funds for the fund's grantmaking activity); in which substantially all of the work is performed for the fund without compensation; that is carried on by the fund primarily for the convenience of its employees; that consists of the sales of merchandise, substantially all of which was received by the fund as contributions; or that is carried on within a larger aggregate of similar activities or within a larger complex of other endeavors that is related to the exempt purposes of the fund.[388] The third exception is for program-related investments.[389]

An initial excise tax is imposed on the excess business holdings of a donor-advised fund in a business enterprise for each tax year that ends during the taxable period.[390] The amount of this tax is 10 percent of the total value of all of the fund's excess business holdings in each of its business enterprises.[391]

If the excess business holdings are not disposed of during the taxable period, an additional tax is imposed on the donor-advised fund; the amount of this tax is 200 percent of the value of the excess business holdings.[392]

The termination taxes[393] serve as third-tier taxes.

A supporting organization[394] maintaining donor-advised funds received an IRS private letter ruling holding that its ownership of certain nonvoting stock constitutes permitted holdings and thus that it does not have any excess business holdings, because all disqualified persons do not own more than 20 percent of the voting stock of the corporation.[395]

---

[385] IRC § 4943(d)(3)(B).

[386] Reg. § 53.4943-10(c).

[387] IRC § 4943(d)(3)(A).

[388] IRC § 4942(j)(4); Reg. § 53.4943-10(b).

[389] Reg. § 53.4943-10(b).

[390] IRC § 4943(a)(1). The *taxable period* is the period beginning on the first day on which there are excess business holdings and ending on the earlier of the date of mailing of a notice of deficiency with respect to the initial tax or the date on which the initial tax is assessed (IRC § 4943(d)(2)).

[391] IRC § 4943(a)(1).

[392] IRC § 4943(b).

[393] IRC § 507(a)(2).

[394] See the text accompanied by *supra* note 353.

[395] Priv. Ltr. Rul. 201311035 (Dec. 18, 2012), applying IRC § 4943(c)(2).

NONDEDUCTIBLE CONTRIBUTIONS

Contributions to a sponsoring organization for maintenance in a donor-advised fund are not eligible for a charitable deduction for federal income tax purposes if the sponsoring organization is a tax-exempt fraternal society, cemetery company, or a veterans' organization.[396] Contributions to a sponsoring organization for this type of maintenance are not eligible for a charitable deduction for federal estate or gift tax purposes if the sponsoring organization is an exempt fraternal society or a veterans' organization.[397] Contributions to a sponsoring organization for such maintenance are not eligible for a charitable deduction for federal income, estate, or gift tax purposes if the sponsoring organization is an exempt fraternal society or a veterans' organization.[398]

Contributions to a sponsoring organization for maintenance in a donor-advised fund are not eligible for a charitable deduction for income, gift, or estate tax purposes if the sponsoring organization is a nonfunctionally integrated Type III supporting organization.[399] A functionally integrated Type III supporting organization is a Type III supporting organization that is not required under the federal tax regulations to make payments to supported organizations due to the activities of the organization related to performing the functions of, or carrying out the purposes of, the supported organizations.[400]

EXCESS BENEFIT TRANSACTIONS RULES

Pursuant to the excess benefit transactions rules, an *excess benefit transaction* is any transaction in which an economic benefit is provided by a donor-advised fund directly or indirectly to or for the use of a disqualified person, if the value of the economic benefit provided by the fund exceeds the value of the consideration received

---

[396] IRC § 170(f)(18)(A)(i). See *Tax-Exempt Organizations* §§ 19.4, 19.6, and 19.11(c), respectively.
[397] IRC §§ 2055(e)(5)(A)(i), 2522(c)(5)(A)(i).
[398] IRC §§ 170(f)(18)(A)(ii), 2055(e)(5)(A)(ii), 2522(c)(5)(A)(ii).
[399] IRC § 170(f)(18)(A)(ii).
[400] Reg. § 1.509(a)-4(i)(3)(ii).

for providing the benefit.[401] This type of benefit is known as an *excess benefit*.[402] In other words, where the value of the benefit provided by the fund is reasonable, there is no excess benefit.

An economic benefit may not be treated as consideration for the performance of services unless the organization providing the benefit clearly indicates its intent to treat the benefit as compensation when the benefit is paid.[403] In determining whether payments or transactions of this nature are in fact forms of compensation, the relevant factors include whether (1) the appropriate decision-making body approved the transfer as compensation in accordance with established procedures or (2) the fund provided written substantiation that is contemporaneous with the transfer of the economic benefit at issue.[404] If a fund fails to provide this documentation, any services provided by the disqualified person will not be treated as provided in consideration for the economic benefit for purposes of determining the reasonableness of the transaction.[405] These transactions are thus known as *automatic excess benefit transactions*. A transaction can be an automatic excess benefit transaction even though its terms and conditions show that it is, in fact, reasonable.

A grant, loan, compensation, or other similar payment from a donor-advised fund to a person that, with respect to the fund, is a donor, donor advisor, or person related to a donor or donor advisor is automatically treated as an excess benefit transaction for intermediate sanctions law purposes.[406] This means that the entire amount paid to any of these persons is an excess benefit.

Other similar payments include payments in the nature of a grant, loan, or payment of compensation, such as an expense reimbursement. Other similar payments do not include, for example, a payment pursuant to a bona fide sale or lease of property, which instead are subject to the general intermediate sanctions rules (under the special disqualified person rule described below). Also (as described below), payment by a sponsoring organization of, for example, compensation to a person who both is a donor with respect to a donor-advised fund of the sponsoring organization and a service provider with respect to the sponsoring organization generally, is not subject to this automatic excess benefit transaction rule unless the payment (of a

---

[401] IRC § 4958(c)(1)(A).
[402] IRC § 4958(c)(1)(B).
[403] IRC § 4958(c)(1)(A).
[404] Reg. § 53.4958-4(c)(1).
[405] *Id.*
[406] IRC § 4958(c)(2).

grant, loan, compensation, or other similar payment) properly is viewed as a payment from the donor-advised fund and not from the sponsoring organization.[407]

Any amount repaid as a result of correcting an excess benefit transaction may not be held in a donor-advised fund.[408] A *correction* of an excess benefit transaction occurs when the transaction is undone to the extent possible, and additional measures are taken to place the tax-exempt organization in a financial position not worse than that in which it would be if the disqualified person were dealing under the highest fiduciary standards.[409]

DISQUALIFIED PERSONS

Donors and donor advisors with respect to a donor-advised fund, and related persons, are disqualified persons for intermediate sanctions law purposes with respect to transactions with the donor-advised fund (although not necessarily with respect to transactions with the sponsoring organization generally).[410] For example, if a donor to a donor-advised fund purchased securities from the fund, the purchase is subject to the intermediate sanctions rules because the donor is a disqualified person with respect to the fund. Thus, if as a result of the purchase, the donor receives an excess benefit (as defined under those rules), the donor is subject to tax under the rules. If, as generally would be the case, the purchase was of securities that were contributed by the donor, a factor that may indicate the presence of an excess benefit is if the amount paid by the donor to acquire the securities is less than the amount the donor claimed the securities were worth for purposes of a charitable contribution deduction claimed by the donor. In addition, if a donor-advised fund distributes securities to the sponsoring organization of the fund prior to purchase by the donor, consideration should be given to whether the distribution to the sponsoring organization prior to the purchase was intended to circumvent the disqualified person rule. If so, such a distribution may be disregarded with the result that the purchase is treated as being made from the donor-advised fund and not from the sponsoring organization.[411]

---

[407] Jt. Comm. Technical Explanation, at 347.
[408] *Id.* IRC § 4958(f)(6).
[409] IRC § 4958(f)(6).
[410] IRC § 4958(f)(1)(D), (E).
[411] Jt. Comm. Technical Explanation, at 347-348.

A person who is a donor to a donor-advised fund and thus a disqualified person with respect to the fund also may be a service provider with respect to the sponsoring organization. In general, the sponsoring organization's transactions with the service provider are not subject to the intermediate sanctions rules, unless the service provider is a disqualified person with respect to the sponsoring organization (such as by being a member of its board) or unless the transaction is not properly viewed as a transaction with the sponsoring organization but in substance is a transaction with the service provider's donor-advised fund. If the transaction properly is viewed as a transaction with the donor-advised fund, the transaction is subject to the intermediate sanctions rules and (as described above) if the transaction involves payment of a grant, loan, compensation, or other similar payment, the transaction is subject to the special automatic excess benefit transaction rule. For example, if a sponsoring organization pays an amount as part of a service contract to a service provider (such as a bank) who is also a donor to a donor-advised fund of the sponsoring organization, and the amounts reasonably are charged uniformly in whole or in part as routine fees to all the sponsoring organization's donor-advised funds, the transaction generally is considered to be between the sponsoring organization and the service provider in the service provider's capacity as a service provider. The transaction is not considered to be a transaction between a donor-advised fund and the service provider, notwithstanding the fact that an amount paid under the contract was charged to a donor-advised fund of the service provider.[412]

An investment advisor (and persons related to the investment advisor) is treated as a disqualified person, for purposes of the excess benefit transactions rules, with respect to the sponsoring organization.[413] The term *investment advisor* means, in this context, any person (other than an employee of the sponsoring organization) compensated by the sponsoring organization for managing the investment of, or providing investment advice with respect to, assets maintained in donor-advised funds (including pools of assets all or part of which are attributed to donor-advised funds) owned by the sponsoring organization.[414]

---

[412] *Id.*, at 348.
[413] IRC § 4958(f)(1)(F), (8)(A).
[414] IRC § 4948(f)(8)(B).

EXCESS BENEFIT TRANSACTION TAX REGIME

A disqualified person who benefited from an excess benefit transaction is subject to and must pay an excise tax—termed the *initial tax*—equal to 25 percent of the amount of the excess benefit.[415]

A fund manager who participated in an excess benefit transaction, knowing that it was such a transaction, is subject to and must pay an excise tax of 10 percent of the excess benefit (subject to a maximum amount of tax as to a transaction of $20,000[416]), where an initial tax is imposed on a disqualified person and if there was no correction of the excess benefit transaction within the taxable period.[417] This tax is not imposed, however, where participation in the transaction was not willful and was due to reasonable cause.[418]

Another excise tax—the *additional tax*—may be imposed on a disqualified person where the initial tax was imposed and if there was no correction of the excess benefit within the taxable period. In this situation, the disqualified person is subject to and must pay a tax equal to 200 percent of the excess benefit involved.[419]

If more than one fund manager or other disqualified person is liable for an excise tax, all such persons and jointly and severally liable for the tax.[420]

The IRS has the authority to abate an intermediate sanctions excise tax penalty if it is established that the violation was due to reasonable cause and not due to willful neglect, and that the transaction was corrected within the appropriate taxable period.[421]

The term *correction* means undoing the excess benefit transaction to the extent possible and taking any additional measures necessary to place the donor-advised fund involved in the transaction in a financial position that is not worse than the position it would be in if the disqualified person were dealing under the highest fiduciary standards.[422] This phraseology is taken from the private foundation self-deal-

---

[415] IRC § 4958(a)(1).
[416] IRC § 4958(d)(2).
[417] IRC § 4958(a)(2).
[418] *Id.*
[419] IRC § 4958(b).
[420] IRC § 4958(d)(1).
[421] IRC § 4962.
[422] IRC § 4958(f)(6). The lawyers for the IRS wrote that the primary purpose of the intermediate sanctions rules is to "require insiders who are receiving excess benefits to make their exempt organizations whole, with the goal of keeping them operating for the benefit of the public" (Chief Couns. Adv. Mem. 200431023 (July 13, 2004)).

ing rules.[423] There is almost no law on this point. Phrases such as *to the extent possible* and *additional measures* remain unexamined. Presumably they are applied in the context of the facts and circumstances of each case. The phrase *highest fiduciary standards* is the subject of an appellate court analysis, with the court concluding that these standards were not adhered to in the correction process.[424] .

SUBSTANTIATION REQUIREMENTS

The federal tax law is replete with charitable gift substantiation requirements.

A donor must obtain, with respect to each charitable contribution to a sponsoring organization to be maintained in a donor-advised fund, a contemporaneous written acknowledgement from the organization that the organization has exclusive legal control over the funds or assets contributed.[425] (This fact should be reflected in the donor-advised fund agreement.)

This requirement is in addition to other charitable gift substantiation requirements.

The federal tax law contains several charitable gift substantiation rules. Under one of these bodies of law, donors who make a separate charitable contribution of $250 or more in a year, for which they claim a charitable contribution deduction, must obtain written substantiation from the donee charitable organization.

More specifically, the rule is that the charitable deduction is not allowed for a separate contribution of $250 or more unless the donor has written substantiation from the charitable donee of the contribution in the form of a contemporaneous written acknowledgment. Thus, donors cannot rely solely on a canceled check as substantiation for a gift of $250 or more.

An acknowledgment meets this requirement if it includes the following information: (1) the amount of money and a description (but not value) of any property other than money that was contributed; (2) whether the donee organization provided any goods or services in consideration, in whole or in part, for any money or property contributed; and (3) a description and good-faith estimate of the value of any goods or services involved or, if the goods or services consist solely of intangible

---

[423] IRC § 4941(e)(3).
[424] Oliff v. Exchange International Corp., 669 F.2d 1162 (7th Cir. 1980), *cert. den.*, 450 U.S. 915 (1981).
[425] IRC §§ 170(f)(18)(B), 2055(e)(5)(B), 2522(c)(5)(B).

religious benefits, a statement to that effect. The phrase *intangible religious benefit* means "any intangible religious benefit which is provided by an organization organized exclusively for religious purposes and which generally is not sold in a commercial transaction outside the donative context." An acknowledgment is *contemporaneous* if the contributor obtains the acknowledgment on or before the earlier of (1) the date on which the donor filed a tax return for the taxable year in which the contribution was made or (2) the due date (including extensions) for filing the return.

Other technical terms abound. The phrase *goods or services* means money, property, services, benefits, and privileges. Certain goods or services, however, are disregarded for these purposes: (1) those that have insubstantial value and (2) certain annual membership benefits offered to an individual in exchange for a payment of $75 or less per year. A charitable organization provides goods or services *in consideration* for a donor's transfer if, at the time the donor makes the payment to the charity, the donor receives or expects to receive goods or services in exchange for the payment. Goods or services a charitable organization provides in consideration for a payment by a donor include goods or services provided in a year other than the year in which the payment was made. A *good-faith estimate* means a charitable organization's estimate of the fair market value of any goods or services, without regard to the manner in which the organization in fact made the estimate.

These rules are taken quite seriously in court, where often charitable deductions involving millions of dollars are eradicated, solely because the acknowledgement document was incomplete or (worse) misleading. In one case, for example, the U.S. Tax Court voided charitable deductions valued at $4.5 million, where the preparers of the document, in reciting elements of consideration provided to the donors, deliberately omitted reference to a variety of additional material elements.

As noted, the substantiation rule applies in respect to separate payments. Separate payments are generally treated as separate contributions and are not aggregated for the purpose of applying the $250 threshold. In cases of contributions paid by withholdings from wages, the deduction from each paycheck is treated as a separate payment. Congress has provided the IRS with authorization to issue antiabuse rules in this area (addressing practices such as the writing of multiple checks to the same charity on the same date).

The written acknowledgment of a separate gift is not required to take any particular form. Thus, acknowledgments may be made by letter, postcard, e-mail, or computer-generated form. A donee charitable organization may prepare a separate acknowledgment for each contribution or may provide donors with periodic (e.g., annual) acknowledgments that set forth the required information for each contribution of $250 or more made by the donor during the period.

The U.S. Tax Court held that the requisite substantiation language can be found in a gift agreement. A series of documents evidencing a bargain sale was ruled to adequately satisfy these substantiation rules. This court has also held that a deed, in this case a conservation easement deed, may satisfy the substantiation requirements. The easiest way to satisfy the requirements in this fashion, of course, is where the deed contains the requisite language. The court has also held, however, that, when a deed does not include the explicit statement, the deed as a whole may determine if the donee provided goods or services in exchange for the contribution. Factors that support this compliance are that the deed recites no consideration other than preservation of the property and that the deed states that it constitutes the entire agreement of the parties. The properly executed deed in another case did not contain the requisite language nor did it meet the *as a whole* test. Suitable substantiation was found in a letter signed by a government official. It has been held, however, that a settlement agreement between a donor and a donee cannot serve as an appropriate substantiation document.

The Tax Court has made the administration of this area of the law much more difficult. This is because it held that these rules apply with respect to verbal (unwritten) *expectations* or *understandings* a donor may have with respect to the charitable recipient when making a contribution. This court thus equated, for this purpose, expectations with goods or services. How representatives of charitable organizations are supposed to divine their donors' inner thoughts when giving is not clear.

It is the responsibility of a donor to obtain the substantiation and maintain it in his or her records. (Again, the charitable contribution deduction is dependent on compliance with these rules.) A charitable organization that knowingly provides a false written substantiation to a donor may be subject to a penalty for aiding and abetting an understatement of tax liability.

These substantiation rules do not apply to transfers of property to charitable remainder trusts or to charitable lead trusts. The requirements are, however, applicable to transfers to pooled income funds. In the case of these funds, the contemporaneous written acknowledgement must state that the contribution was transferred to the charitable organization's pooled fund and indicate whether any goods or services (in addition to the income interest) were provided in exchange for the transfer. The contemporaneous written acknowledgement, however, need not include a good-faith estimate of the income interest.

The substantiation requirements add other documentation obligations when the gift amounts exceed $500,[426] $5,000,[427] and $500,000.[428]

APPLICATIONS FOR RECOGNITION OF EXEMPTION

Nearly all organizations that desire federal income tax exemption must file an application for recognition of exemption with the IRS and receive a favorable determination as to that status.[429] This application asks the applicant organization, among many questions, whether it does or will "maintain separate accounts for any contributor under which the contributor has the right to advise on the use or distribution of funds."[430] The organization is required to check a "yes" box "if the donor may provide advice on the types of investments, distributions from the types of investments, or the distribution from the donor's contribution account." Also, if the answer is "yes," the applicant is to "describe this program, including the type of advice that may be provided [,] and submit copies of any written materials provided to donors."

A sponsoring organization is expected, when seeking recognition of its tax-exempt status, to provide information regarding its planned operation of donor-advised funds, including a description of the procedures it intends to use to (1) communicate to donors and donor advisors that assets held in donor-advised funds are the property of the sponsoring organization and (2) ensure that distributions from donor-advised funds do not result in more than incidental benefit to any person.

REPORTING REQUIREMENTS

Nearly all tax-exempt organizations, that are charitable entities under the federal tax law, are required to file annual information returns or submit an annual report

---

[426] IRC § 170(f)(11)(A)(i), (B).
[427] IRC § 170(f)(11)(C).
[428] IRC § 170(f)(11)(D).
[429] IRC § 508(a).
[430] Form 1023, Part VIII, question 4e

to the IRS. Organizations with gross receipts that are normally less than $50,000 annually are required to submit a short annual report (informally known as the *e-postcard*).[431] Organizations with gross receipts normally less than $200,000 annually and with assets less than $500,000 are required to file a short annual information return.[432] Other organizations file a more extensive annual information return.[433] Sponsoring organizations with donor-advised funds, however, are required to file the more extensive annual information return, irrespective of size.[434]

The more extensive annual information return is accompanied by a host of schedules. The return includes a checklist of required schedules.[435] One of the questions in this checklist is: "Did the organization maintain any donor advised funds or similar funds or accounts for which donors have the right to provide advice on the distribution or investment of amounts in such funds or accounts?"[436] If the answer to this question is "yes," the organization is required to attach a schedule to its return.[437]

This schedule bears the euphemistic title of "supplemental financial statements." The schedule requires the organization to report the (1) total number of donor-advised funds and other "similar" funds it owns as of the end of the reporting year, (2) aggregate value of contributions made to them during the year (separately reported), (3) aggregate value of grants made from them during the year (separately reported), and aggregate value of the assets in the funds at the end of the year (separately reported).[438]

The schedule also contains a question asking the filing sponsoring organization whether it "inform[ed] all donors and donor advisors in writing that the assets held in donor advised funds are the organization's property, subject to the organization's exclusive legal control"[439] and a question inquiring as to whether the organization "inform[ed] all grantees, donors, and donor advisors in writing that grant funds can be used only for charitable purposes and not for the benefit of the donor or donor advisor, or for any other purpose conferring impermissible private benefit." These two questions are to be answered by checking "yes" or "no" boxes; explanatory statements are not requested.

---

[431] IRC § 6033(i). The report is on Form 990-N.
[432] This return is Form 990-EZ.
[433] This return is Form 990.
[434] IRC § 6033(k).
[435] Form 990, Part IV.
[436] Form 990, Part IV, question 6.
[437] Form 990, Schedule D, Part I.
[438] Form 990, Schedule D, Part I, questions 1–4
[439] Form 990, Schedule D, Part I, question 5. See the text accompanied by *supra* note 425.

The more extensive annual information return also inquires as to whether a donor-advised fund maintained by the filing sponsoring organization had any excess business holdings at any time during the year.[440] The return includes a question as to whether the sponsoring organization made any taxable distributions.[441] Further, the return asks if the sponsoring organization made any distribution to a donor, donor advisor, or related person.[442]

TEMPORARY DISASTER RELIEF LAW

Congress, by an enactment signed into law at the close of 2019, temporarily suspended the limitations on deductibility of cash gifts by individuals (60 percent) and corporations (10 percent) to public charities[443] for disaster relief efforts.[444] To be eligible for this enhanced (full) deduction, a gift must have been made in 2018 or 2019, or by February 18, 2020. The donor must obtain substantiation of the gift, including an acknowledgement that the contribution was used, or is to be used, for disaster relief efforts.[445] The donee, however, may not be a supporting organization or a sponsoring organization (for the establishment or maintenance of a donor-advised fund).

SPONSORING ORGANIZATIONS OPERATING POLICIES

Organizations sponsoring donor-advised funds frequently have written policies concerning their administration of the funds' program. These documents obviously are not statements of law (although they often reflect provisions of law).[446]

---

[440] Form 990, Part V, question 8.

[441] Form 990, Part V, question 9a.

[442] Form 990, Part V, question 9b.

[443] See *Charitable Giving*, Chapter 7.

[444] Further Consolidated Appropriations Act, 2020, signed into law on Dec. 20, 2019 (Pùb. L. No. 116-94, 116th Cong., 1st Sess. (2019)). Division Q of this act, concerning revenue provisions, is the Taxpayer Certainty and Disaster Relief Act.

[445] IRC § 170(f)(8). See this chapter, pp. 103–106.

[446] One commentator, having referenced comments by the New York State Bar Association that donor-advised funds are no longer charitable giving vehicles but have become income tax avoidance vehicles, stated that "[a]t issue is whether the minimums established by sponsoring organizations is [sic] enough or whether there should be some minimum established by law for all donor advised funds" (Hussey, "Avoiding Misuse of Donor Advised Funds," 58 *Clev. St. L. Rev.* 59, 75 (2010)).

Nonetheless, donors to donor-advised funds and lawyers advising them should consult these policies, in addition to the law, in determining which sponsoring organization(s) should be the donee. These policies, of course, cannot be inconsistent with the law but contain useful information, and additional requirements, in connection with the making and management of these gifts.

Here are some of the topics addressed in these policies.

Governance

The matter of governance of sponsoring organizations is particularly acute in connection with the national sponsors. This is certainly the case with respect to the sponsor that are affiliated with investment firms.

For example, the policies of the Vanguard Charitable Endowment Program state that Vanguard Charitable was "founded" by The Vanguard Group, Inc. Vanguard Charitable casts itself as an "independent, nonprofit, public charity." Although the Vanguard Group provides investment management and administrative services to Vanguard Charitable pursuant to a service agreement, the Vanguard Charitable policies state that it is "not a program or activity of Vanguard [Group]." The policies note that a majority of Vanguard Charitable's trustees are "independent" of the Vanguard Group. To cement the point, the policies add that these two organizations are "separate entities."[447]

Schwab Charitable, likewise a public charity, notes that it was established by Charles Schwab & Co. but "is governed by an independent board of directors."[448] Fidelity Charitable states simply that it is an "independent, section 501(c)(3) public charity" (no mention of Fidelity Investments in connection with its origin).[449]

Control Over Gifts

As required by law,[450] once accepted by Vanguard Charitable, contributions are "unconditional and irrevocable." Contributions and any related earnings "are no longer the property of the donor"; "they are owned by Vanguard Charitable and will be used solely for charitable purposes." When contributing, a donor "cannot impose any restrictions or conditions that prevent Vanguard Charitable from freely and effectively using the gift to further its mission."[451]

---

[447] Vanguard Charitable, *Policies and guidelines*, at 1.
[448] Schwab Charitable, *Program Policies*, at 3.
[449] Fidelity Charitable, *Program Guidelines*, at 1.
[450] See Chapter 5, pp. 132–133.

Schwab Charitable observes that it "must maintain exclusive legal authority and control over all donated funds and assets as to their use and distribution." For this reason, this sponsoring organization states, "all contributions to [it], both initial and subsequent, are "irrevocable and unconditional." Once contributions to Schwab Charitable are accepted by it, "they are no longer counted among the donor's personal investments."[452]

Fidelity Charitable states that, once it accepts a contribution, it is "irrevocable" and is "owned and controlled" by its board of trustees, which has "exclusive legal control over all contributed assets," adding that contributions to it are "not refundable."[453] This organization states that it may terminate any advisory privileges with respect to a donor-advised fund or amounts held in a fund on 60 days' notice provided to the donor(s) involved.[454]

The Greater Kansas City Community Foundation[455] offers a variety of funds, including donor-advised funds. These funds are "considered part of (and legally controlled by) the Community Foundation and shall be governed by its Articles of Incorporation, Bylaws and by these Procedures." The Community Foundation is "vested with ultimate authority and control over the principal and income of each Fund."[456]

Account Minimums

Account minimums vary. At Fidelity Charitable, the initial account minimum is $5,000 for individuals, trusts, and estates; it is $25,000 for business entities. Its policies state that account holders may make additional contributions; there is no mention of minimums in that context.[457]

At Vanguard Charitable, the initial account minimum is $25,000;[458] additional contributions of at least $5,000 may thereafter be made by the donor. A group of donors may open an account with multiple contributions of at least $5,000 that together total at least $25,000. A group may also make additional contributions that together total $5,000 or more.[459]

[451] Vanguard Charitable, *Policies and guidelines*, at 7.
[452] Schwab Charitable, *Program Policies*, at 4, 22.
[453] Fidelity Charitable, *Program Guidelines*, at 4.
[454] Fidelity Charitable, *Program Guidelines*, at 28.
[455] See Chapter 3, note 5.
[456] Greater Kansas City Community Foundation, *Procedures for Establishment and Operation of Funds and Supporting Organizations* (Kansas City Community Foundation, *Funds Procedures*), at 6.
[457] Fidelity Charitable, *Program Guidelines*, at 2, 4.
[458] Vanguard Charitable, *Policies and guidelines*, at 3, 7.

Schwab Charitable offers two account options. One is a "core account," which requires an initial $5,000 minimum contribution in instances of cash, cash equivalents, or publicly traded securities, with subsequent contributions of at least $500; contributions of more complex assets may be subject to higher minimum contribution requirements.[460] A "professionally managed account" requires a minimum contribution of $250,000.[461]

Fund Names

At Vanguard Charitable, the name of each donor-advised fund must begin with "The" and end with "Fund." Account names may not include the words *trust, foundation*, or *endowment* (because they are terms for other charitable giving options).[462]

Schwab Charitable states that donors to its advised funds can "recommend a name for their donor-advised fund account to honor an individual or a family, to cultivate a legacy of charitable giving, or for another charitable purpose." With this sponsoring organization, names may include words like *foundation, fund*, or *account* but not *trust* (as this word denotes a different type of charitable giving vehicle).[463]

Fidelity Charitable's policy observes that, "[t]pically," donors to its donor-advised funds "choose a name in honor of themselves, their families, relatives, or friends," noting that it "reserves the right not to approve a name for" a fund.[464]

At the Kansas City Community Foundation, "[e]ach Fund will be named as the Donor wishes," although the Foundation reserves the right to reject names that it finds "objectionable."[465]

Donors

The Vanguard Charitable policies state that donors to its donor-advised funds "may include individuals, corporations, private foundations, partnerships, trusts, and other charitable organizations."[466] At Fidelity Charitable, individuals, corporations and other business entities, trusts, and estates are eligible donors but not charitable organizations such as private foundations.[467]

---

[459] *Id.* at 7.
[460] Schwab Charitable, *Program Policies*, at 9.
[461] Schwab Charitable, *Program Policies*, at 4.
[462] Vanguard Charitable, *Policies and guidelines*, at 3.
[463] Schwab Charitable, *Program Policies*, at 4.
[464] Fidelity Charitable, *Program Guidelines*, at 2.
[465] Kansas City Community Foundation, *Funds Procedures*, at 6.
[466] Vanguard Charitable, *Policies and guidelines*, at 3.
[467] Fidelity Charitable, *Program Guidelines*, at 2.

Donor-Advisors

When a donor opens a donor-advised fund account at Vanguard Charitable, the person receives the privilege of identifying a maximum of two account advisors, and nominating successor-advisors.[468] Account holders at Schwab Charitable can "authorize up to four individuals as additional account users, such as certified public accountants, family members, assistants, or authorized investment advisors."[469] At Fidelity Charitable, primary account holders may name up to three other persons, as "additional account holders, who will have "full and equal privileges to recommend grants."[470]

Fundraising in General

Once a donor-advised fund is established at Vanguard Charitable, additional donors may contribute to the fund.[471] This policy embraces matching contributions from employers.[472]

Fidelity Charitable states that third parties may make charitable contributions to it. Account holders, however, "may not solicit third-party contributions on behalf of a specific charitable organization or on their own behalf, and may not guarantee to contributors that intended grant recommendations will be approved."[473] The Fidelity Charitable policy also is that a grant will not be made in support of an account holder's "own fundraising commitment, such as a walk, bike ride, or run, unless the full obligation has been satisfied," although an account holder "can express his or her intention to recommend a grant—for example, when sponsoring someone else in a walk, bike ride, or run."[474]

Schwab Charitable accepts third-party contributions—contributions made to an account from an entity or individual with no active role on the account." In general, however, "[d]ue to significant regulatory and administrative complexities, account holders may not solicit third-party contributions to their accounts; fundraising is not permitted in Schwab Charitable accounts." Nonetheless, donor-advised fund holders may use their accounts to receive "third-party donations in memory of a loved one or in honor of a loved one's significant life event such as a graduation,

---

[468] Vanguard Charitable, *Policies and guidelines*, at 3.
[469] Schwab Charitable, *Program Policies*, at 5. Nothing said about lawyers; perhaps we are covered by *assistants*.
[470] Fidelity Charitable, *Program Guidelines*, at 3.
[471] Vanguard Charitable, *Policies and guidelines*, at 4.
[472] *Id.* at 10.
[473] Fidelity Charitable, *Program Guidelines*, at 5.
[474] *Id.* at 15.

birthday, or wedding."[475]

The Kansas City Community Foundation "will not sponsor or assist with any fundraising or other events" for any of its funds, and "will not process event registrations or tickets or be responsible for any funds collected by a third-party or crowdfunding source."[476]

Charitable Deductions

Fidelity Charitable, in its policy document, includes an extensive summary of the federal income tax charitable contribution deduction rules, including the amount giving rise to the deduction for various types of gifts and application of the percentage limitations applicable to individuals.[477] Fidelity Charitable provides, for donors who contribute at least $500 in publicly traded securities, an IRS Form 8283[478] showing an estimate of the fair market value of the contributions.[479]

The Vanguard Charitable policy expressly states that amounts in its donor-advised funds that reflect growth due to market fluctuation do not give rise to any additional charitable contribution deduction.[480]

Grant Advice Due Diligence

Fidelity Charitable states that it "approves only those grants that are used exclusively in furtherance of charitable purposes." It reserves the right to "perform additional due diligence and to decline to make a recommended grant to a charitable organization" in a variety of circumstances, including (1) where the grant would confer a more-than-incidental benefit on an account holder, a donor advisor, or other third party; (2) where the grant would be used for lobbying or political campaign purposes; (3) where the grant would be used for "improper purposes"; (4) where the account holder and related persons control the prospective grantee; and (5) for "other reasons in accordance with Fidelity Charitable policies." (Other reasons why Fidelity Charitable may decline to make a grant are referenced below.) Remedial actions may include "requiring that the grant be returned or that the Account Holder make an additional nondeductible contribution."[481]

---

[475] Schwab Charitable, *Program Policies*, at 9.

[476] Kansas City Community Foundation, *Funds Procedures*, at 9.

[477] See *Charitable Giving*, Chapters 7, 9.

[478] *Id.* § 21.4.

[479] Fidelity Charitable, *Program Guidelines*, at 8.

[480] Vanguard Charitable, *Policies and guidelines*, at 13.

[481] Fidelity Charitable, *Program Guidelines*, at 14.

As to Fidelity Charitable's policy to not make grants where more-than-incidental benefits are involved, examples of these types include (1) goods or service provided by the grantee, unless the items are of de minimis value, such as a logo-bearing keychain, coffee mug, or calendar; (2) raffle tickets or goods or services purchased at a charity's auction; (3) membership benefits, if any portion of the membership fee is not tax-deductible, unless the account holder waives the benefits; (4) benefits in connection with athletic events, such as where the account holder is eligible to receive benefits, e.g., preferred seating at sporting events; and (5) school tuition and other required fees, such as enrollment fees and deposits.[482] (Other benefits of this nature are referenced below.)

Vanguard Charitable states that, before approving a grant, it follows a "strict review and approval process" in order to "protect the charitable tax deductions and philanthropic intentions" of its donors, avoid any federal tax penalties, protect its "standing with the IRS," and ensure that all grant dollars are distributed only for qualified charitable purposes.[483] In the event that a grant recommendation violates these guidelines, Vanguard Charitable reserves the right to transfer account assets to its Philanthropic Impact Fund.[484]

The Kansas City Community Foundation will not make a grant that provides a "financial benefit" to a donor, donor advisor, or any related party, although it will make such grants in circumstances where the IRS has recognized that the benefit is no more than an incidental one, such as name recognition.[485]

It appears that the Renaissance Charitable Foundation has the most extensive grantmaking due diligence policy, although its policy extends to its grants made from sources other than donor-advised funds. In accordance with its policy, the Foundation "exercises full authority and control over the making of every donor-advised fund grant," with the policy "designed to ensure that each grant recipient organization is qualified to receive a grant including grants connected with a specific DAF and that the grant is not made for a disqualifying charitable purpose."[486] In general, the Foundation's policies for grant due diligence are designed to "assess the risk" associated with the identity of the grant recipient, the amount of a proposed grant, and the charitable purpose of a proposed grant.

---

[482] *Id.*, at 14–15.
[483] Vanguard Charitable, *Policies and guidelines*, at 19.
[484] *Id.*
[485] Kansas City Community Foundation, *Funds Procedures*, at 6.
[486] Renaissance Charitable Foundation, Inc., *Grantmaking Due Diligence Policy* (Renaissance, *Due Diligence Policy*), at 1.

As to the matter the identity of a prospective grant recipient, the Foundation differentiates between U.S. charities the activities of which are predominantly U.S.-based, U.S. charities with pass-through operations in connection with foreign charities, and foreign charities. Disqualified grant recipients are noncharitable tax-exempt organizations, standard grantmaking private foundations, nonfunctionally integrated Type III supporting organizations, organizations not yet recognized by the IRS, organizations that "otherwise fail" the Foundation's procedures, and organizations that appear on a watchlist such as the one maintained by the Office of Foreign Asset Control.[487]

The Foundation, in 2018, granted more than $311 million across more than 54,000 grants to over 21,000 charities, with an average grant amount of $5,700 and a median grant amount of $525. If a prospective grant is in excess of $100,000, one of the Foundation's officers must personally review the grant due diligence paperwork for that grant and personally authorize the grant.[488]

Concerning the charitable purposes requirement, the Foundation's policies allow for anonymous grants, grants in honor or in memory of a loved one, or to support specific programs maintained by a qualified charity. Grants may not, however, be made to benefit a donor advisor or family member, ;pay for dues, membership fees, tuition, goods from a charitable auction, or other goods and services; support a political campaign or lobbying activity; or to fulfill an existing, binding pledge.[489]

Grant Minimums

At Vanguard Charitable, the grant minimum is $500.[490] Fidelity Charitable will consider grant recommendations of at least $50 (or the fund balance).[491] Schwab Charitable does not appear to have a policy in this regard.

Fidelity Charitable allows unlimited grants from a donor-advised fund.[492] The policy at the Greater Kansas City Community Foundation confers on the Foundation's board of directors the authority to designate a minimum grant amount for its donor-advised funds.[493]

---

[487] Id.
[488] Id., at 2.
[489] Id.
[490] Vanguard Charitable, Policies and guidelines, at 19.
[491] Fidelity Charitable, Program Guidelines, at 16.
[492] Fidelity Charitable, Program Guidelines, at 16.
[493] Kansas City Community Foundation, Funds Procedures, at 10.

Minimum Account Activity

At Vanguard Charitable, if after 30 months there has not been a grant from a donor-advised fund, the sponsoring organization will attempt to contact account advisors to initiate at least one $500 grant. If this attempt are unsuccessful after six months, the sponsoring organization reserves the right to take action, depending on the balance size of the fund. If the balance is $15,000 or less, the sponsor will invoke an account succession plan and close the account or transfer the funds to The Philanthropic Impact Fund. If the balance is larger, Vanguard Charitable will initiate an annual policy of making grants equal to 5 percent of the account balance to public charities or its Philanthropic Impact Fund.[494]

Schwab Charitable's policies state that its mission is to "increase charitable giving in the U.S. and [thus] account holders are expected to be actively involved in recommending grants to eligible charitable organizations." If account holders do not recommend grants during a 30-month period, the account involved will be considered inactive and Schwab Charitable will request that the primary account holder make a grant recommendation. If that does not happen, Schwab Charitable will make a grant from the fund to an eligible public charity in accordance with the fund's succession plan or granting history or otherwise to the sponsoring organization's Philanthropy Fund. If nothing happens within a subsequent two-year period, the account will be considered dormant and Schwab Charitable will make grants to eligible charities or its Philanthropy Fund. Extensions of time may be granted.[495]

Schwab Charitable requires that its total annual grants in the aggregate be an amount equal to at least 5 percent of the average net assets of all donor-advised funds, on a fiscal five-year rolling average basis. If this requirement is not met, account holders with funds that have not granted above this 5 percent threshold may be requested to make the requisite additional grants. If that approach is not successful within 90 days, Schwab Charitable may elect to distribute the amounts in the fund to charities in accordance with the account's recent grant history or to its Philanthropy Fund.[496]

Fidelity Charitable states that "[a]ctive charitable grantmaking is required" for each of its donor-advised funds. It reports that it historically "has made grants of

---

[494] Vanguard Charitable, *Policies and guidelines*, at 20.
[495] Schwab Charitable, *Program Policies*, at 23-24.
[496] Schwab Charitable's policies state that, since inception, its annual aggregate grant distributions have "consistently far exceeded" 5 percent (at 24).

about 20% of average net total assets to charities each year." Its "formal" grantmaking policy requires that minimum annual grants, on an overall basis, be greater than 5 percent of average net assets on a fiscal five-year rolling basis. If this requirement is not met, it will ask for make-up grant recommendations. Absent a response within 60 days, Fidelity Charitable will make grants of the required amounts. It makes "every effort" to encourage grant recommendations in the case of a fund where there has not been a distribution in three years. After four years, it will make grants on its own. After five years, Fidelity Charitable will consider the fund abandoned and grant the funds from it.[497]

The Greater Kansas City Community Foundation assumes responsibility for ensuring the funds in its donor-advised funds are used for grantmaking for charitable purposes. It works with donors and donor advisors to determine when grants will be made from these funds. To that end, it "monitors the use of donor advised funds to ensure their activity leads to charitable distributions." A fund is considered *active* when "there is regular communication between a [d]onor, [d]onor {a]dvisor(s) (or named successors) and the Community Foundation regarding the existence and purpose of that [f]und." Examples of activities that deem a fund active include recommendations of charitable grants at least annually; a substantial contribution to a fund, with the donor refraining from advising as to grants for a period during which the donor determines what types of grants will best serve community needs or the donor's philanthropic goals; development of a long-term grant plan; development of a plan for project grants made to a specific charitable organization over a period of years; and accumulation of funds to be able to make substantial grants in the community (a "starter fund").[498]

Qualified Grantees

Vanguard Charitable inventories the types of public charities to which grants will be made from its donor-advised funds. Particular attention is accorded supporting organizations. Grants will not be made to Type III nonfunctionally integrated supporting organizations[499] or to supporting organization that support organizations controlled directly or indirectly by disqualified persons.[500] This policy states that grants from Vanguard Charitable "should not be made for the purpose of enabling

---

[497] Fidelity Charitable, *Program Guidelines*, at 16.
[498] Kansas City Community Foundation, *Funds Procedures*, at 10–11.
[499] See *supra* p. 94.
[500] *Id.*

an organization that is controlled by a [d]isqualified [p]erson to avoid classification as a private non-operating foundation."[501] Vanguard Charitable has various processing times in connection with grants to Type I, Type II, and Type III functionally integrated supporting organizations.[502]

At Schwab Charitable, once a grant has been recommended, it performs due diligence designed to ensure that all grant dollars are issued for qualified charitable purposes, comply with the federal tax law's "deductibility rules and protect philanthropic intentions" of account holders, avoid federal taxes and penalties, protect Schwab Charitable's tax-exempt status. It, too, differentiates among types of supporting organizations.[503]

The policy followed at Fidelity Charitable is that eligible grantees "include the full range of charitable organizations, including hospitals, scientific and medical research organizations, religious organizations and places of worship, environmental and educational organizations, museums and arts organizations, and any other organizations or institutions formed and operated for charitable purposes." Ineligible grant recipients are private non-operating foundations, nonfunctionally integrated Type III supporting organizations, and not formed under the laws of the U.S. and its territories.[504]

The Greater Kansas City Community Foundation will not make a grant, loan, compensation or similar payment (including expense reimbursement) to a donor, donor advisor, or related party from any of its funds. It also generally will not make any grant directly to an individual or to an organization for the benefit of a specified individual. If a distribution is proposed from a donor-advised fund to a noncharitable entity or to a nonfunctionally integrated Type III supporting organization, it will not be allowed until it has been reviewed by a senior management officer of the Foundation and, if required by law, procedures are put in place to enable the Foundation to exercise expenditure responsibility[505] over the distribution.[506]

An emerging issue is whether sponsoring organizations should permit grants from their donor-advised funds to public charities that are under investigation by the IRS or another government agency.[507] Schwab Charitable's policy on the point

---

[501] As to this topic, see Chapter 6, pp. 156-169.
[502] Vanguard Charitable, *Policies and procedures*, at 22.
[503] Schwab Charitable, *Program Policies*, at 19.
[504] Fidelity Charitable, *Program Guidelines*, at 13-14.
[505] See Chapter 4, text accompanied by notes 28, 29.
[506] Kansas City Community Foundation, *Funds Procedures*, at 7, 10.
[507] E.g., Theis, "Fidelity and Schwab Ban Gifts from Donor-advised Funds to NRA-Affiliated Charities,"

is that it "follows IRS guidance and suspends grants to 501(c)(3) organizations that are under investigation, until the investigation concludes and the organization retains its 501(c)(3) status."[508] By contrast, the policy at the Renaissance Charitable Foundation is "to not police possibilities or maybes," adding that "[i]f a legitimate charitable organization is registered and current with the IRS (and the tax code set by Congress), then that organization can receive grants from our DAFs."[509]

Conditional Gifts

Pursuant to Schwab Charitable's policy, contributions to donor-advised funds may not be subject to a "material restriction or condition as defined in the tax laws,"[510] including the account holder's reservation of a right to control or direct distributions from a particular account,[511] a requirement that assets be retained, and any other condition that would prevent this sponsoring organization from "exercising exclusive legal control over the use of contributed assets to further its exempt purposes." Schwab Charitable has the power to modify or disregard any restriction or condition on any contribution held by it if it, in its sole discretion and without the need for approval by any person, determines that a restriction or condition has become "obsolete or impractical or otherwise violates the terms of" its policies.[512]

Anonymous Grants

At Fidelity Charitable, a donor, in the process of recommending a grant, may choose to be identified by name, address, and fund name, identified by fund name only, or be anonymous. It may in its judgment choose to "limit anonymity" but promises to not release a donor's name and contact information without the account holder's explicit consent.[513]

Restricted Grants

Pursuant to Fidelity Charitable's policies, an account holder "may recommend that a grant be used by the charitable organization for a 'special purpose,' such as a building fund, research project, or in honor of a person." It will review the grant rec-

---

Chron. of Phil. (Dec. 4, 2019).
[508] Id.
[509] Id.
[510] See Chapter 1, pp. 12-15.
[511] This type of reservation would cause the fund to be a donor-directed fund. See Chapter 1, pp. 16-17.
[512] Schwab Charitable, Program Policies, at 12.
[513] Fidelity Charitable, Program Guidelines, at 15.

ommendation, including the special purpose, and, if approved, will convey to the charitable organization the recommended special purpose. Fidelity Charitable reserves the right to modify the special purpose as it deems necessary.[514]

Schwab Charitable's policies allow for the "stating of common, specific, and custom purposes" in connection with the recommending of grants. These purposes include "alumni funds, annual funds, capital campaigns, endowment funds, operating expenses, scholarship programs, and holiday giving." Account holders may also recommend that a grant be used for a purpose such as a building fund or research project.[515]

Scholarship Programs

At Vanguard Charitable, grants in support of scholarship programs may be approved as long as donors, donor advisors, interested parties, and their family members cannot participate in the selection process and family members are ineligible to receive the scholarship. Nonetheless, account advisors "may generally set the criteria for determining the recipient[s], provided that the criteria is sufficiently broad and not otherwise illegal or objectionable."[516]

The policy at Fidelity Charitable is that it will not make grants for scholarships where the account holder and/or related persons have "sole or majority discretion regarding the recipients."[517]

Charitable Pledges

It is Vanguard Charitable's policy that grants from its donor-advised funds cannot be used to pay any legal obligation that a disqualified person owes to a charity. Examples of such an obligation are an existing grant agreement or legally binding pledge to make a gift between a donor and a charitable organization. Vanguard Charitable considers that type of grant to constitute an "impermissible benefit" to the individual involved.[518] Alternatively, advisors may express an "intent to recommend" and make nonbinding grant recommendations from their accounts.[519]

Pursuant to Schwab Charitable's policies, "[n]o grant may be used to discharge or satisfy a charitable pledge or obligation that is legally enforceable."[520] Likewise,

---

[514] Fidelity Charitable, *Program Guidelines*, at 15.
[515] *Id.* at 21.
[516] Vanguard Charitable, *Policies and guidelines*, at 24.
[517] Fidelity Charitable, *Program Guidelines*, at 15.
[518] See Chapter 6, pp. 170-176.
[519] Vanguard Charitable, *Policies and guidelines*, at 24.
[520] Schwab Charitable, *Program Policies*, at 21.

the policy at Fidelity Charitable is that a grant will not be made to satisfy a "financial obligation, such as an enforceable pledge, that the Account Holder has made as a legally binding obligation."[521]

The policy at the Greater Kansas City Community Foundation is that a distribution from its donor-advised funds "shall not reference the existence of a charitable pledge."[522]

Fundraising Events

Vanguard Charitable's policy states that "[a]ccount advisors may support fundraising events as long as the funds do not cover event registration fees." In addition, "[t]o maintain good standing with the IRS, and to avoid the risk of fines to account advisors and interested parties, Vanguard Charitable will not approve grants that are intended to cover any portion of a gift that would result in anything more than an incidental benefit accruing to an individual, including benefits associated with fundraising events." This policy means that donors cannot engage in the practice of bifurcation, where the grant from the sponsoring organization is for the deductible portion of the admission amount,[523] because, in Vanguard Charitable's view, the grant "still enables the advisor to receive benefits that would not be available without the grant." Advisors may support fundraising events "by recommending a grant to support only the general underwriting or fundraising efforts of the event."[524]

At Schwab Charitable, "[g]rants may not be used to support any charitable event or membership for which the account holder would receive a quid pro quo benefit, such as the benefit of being able to attend a fundraising dinner, concert, auction, sporting athletic event, or any other benefit." In addition, "[n]o grants may be used to pay for any portion of a split—or bifurcated—disbursement to a charity where there is a deductible portion and a nondeductible portion," adding that "[i]f attendance at an event (or the receipt of any other benefit) is contingent on a grant from an account, Schwab Charitable will not approve the grant."[525]

The Fidelity Charitable policy is that, while a grant "can be recommended for general support/recognition for an event," a donor "may not recommend a grant to be used to purchase a ticket to attend a charitable event, or to cover the tax deductible portion of a ticket to attend the event."[526]

---

[521] Fidelity Charitable, *Program Guidelines*, at 15.

[522] Kansas City Community Foundation, *Funds Procedures*, at 10.

[523] See Chapter 6, pp. 176-182.

[524] Vanguard Charitable, *Policies and procedures*, at 24.

[525] Schwab Charitable, *Program Policies*, at 21.

[526] Fidelity Charitable, *Program Guidelines*, at 14.

The policy at the Greater Kansas City Community Foundation is that distributions from it "may not be used in whole or in part for any private benefit such as tickets or tables at charitable events, goods and services bought at charitable auctions, or priority seating at athletic events, ticket rights or points."[527]

Excess Business Holdings

Schwab Charitable's policy addresses the matter of excess business holdings.[528] It states that a donor-advised fund "cannot, under any circumstances, hold an interest in any operating business that represents greater than 20% of the ownership of the business—either alone or when taken together with the holdings of the primary account holder, any secondary account holders, any successors, any additional account users (other than investment advisors), and/or certain family members or affiliates of such people."[529] Preapproval is required for the contribution of securities representing greater than 2 percent ownership of any operating business and for any contribution of a single security interest representing greater than 2 percent of Schwab Charitable assets under management.[530]

Other Topics

These policies often address other topics, such as the types of property that may be contributed to donor-advised funds, contribution processing times, fees, investment options, reporting and disclosures, and the federal charitable giving rules in general.

---

[527] Kansas City Community Foundation, *Funds Procedures*, at 6.
[528] See this chapter, pp. 96-97.
[529] This policy thus does not allow for use of the 35 percent alternative test. See text accompanied by *supra* note 68.
[530] Schwab Charitable, *Program Policies*, at 12.

CHAPTER 5:
Criticisms and Rebuttals

Donor-advised funds are one of nonprofit law's hottest topics.[531] Although these charitable giving vehicles have been in existence for decades and controversial for years, the level of contentiousness is intensifying as the amount of giving to donor-advised funds continues to rapidly rise, the so-called "national" sponsoring organizations increase their prominence, private foundations make greater use of these funds, and the federal government's regulatory apparatus begins to seriously focus on them. This increase in disputation is sparking growth in the ranks of donor-advised funds' advocates and critics, which stokes still more dissension.

Every statistic demonstrates the dramatic increase in utilization of donor-advised funds: the sheer number of these funds, the amount of giving to them, the amounts of grants from them, and the size of the larger sponsoring organizations.[532] There are record-breaking analyses of donor-advised funds, growing numbers of articles about them, and more presentations about them at nonprofit law conferences.

For the most part, as noted, critics of donor-advised funds have framed and dominated the debate about the worthiness of these funds—or, from their perspective, the absence of worthiness.[533] Donor-advised fund supporters and advocates have largely kept silent.[534] Matters began to change slightly in this regard, in the aftermath of the notice published in late 2017 by the Department of the Treas-

---

[531] See Chapter 1, p. 2.

[532] See Chapter 3.

[533] See Chapter 2, pp. 52-55; this chapter, *passim*.

[534] In one of many illustrations of this phenomenon, the *Nonprofit Quarterly*, in assembling its Summer 2018 issue, decided to publish articles about donor-advised funds, inviting two critics of them to contribute. As Ruth McCambridge, the magazine's editor in chief, wrote, the publication "also invited others to write about why . . . broad-based congressional attention was not now needed and to speak up about what additional, but more limited, regulations were needed, but we mostly got demurrals" (McCambridge, "Do Donor-Advised Funds Require Regulatory Attention?," 25 *Nonprofit Quar.* (Issue 2) 41, 42-43 (Summer 2018)).

ury and the IRS, in advance of issuance of proposed regulations concerning donor-advised funds.[535]

PARADE OF CRITICISMS

The case against donor-advised funds entails the following 17 criticisms. (There is some overlap of assertions here.) Donor-advised funds:

1. Are nefarious and illegitimate, to the point that they are shams;
2. Are a legal fiction;
3. Are a loophole;
4. Involve transfers that are not really gifts;
5. Are vehicles involving merely the warehousing (or stockpiling) of money or other forms of property;
6. Are not authentic charitable programs;
7. Are merely fundraising vehicles, precluded from tax exemption by reason of the commensurate test.
8. Are diverting monies from truly charitable ends;
9. Do not pay out sufficient funds to real (or "working") charities;
10. Are a sidestepping (or "evasion") of the private foundation rules;
11. By using the services of related investment companies, are violating the private inurement or private benefit doctrines;
12. That are national are inherently evil;
13. Unduly cater to the wealthy;
14. Amount to a hijacking of philanthropy by Wall Street;
15. Lack transparency; and/or
16. Are immoral and fraudulent, and contribute to charities' corruption.

Before commencing an analysis of these criticisms, there is one criticism that needs to be dispensed with at the outset: the matter of overvaluation of gifts of property to donor-advised funds. An analysis of the dispute over donor-advised funds observed: "There are two categories of concern that some advocates would like to see answered with regulation: the first has to do with the establishment of systems of

---

[535] See Chapter 6.

accountability that look into the transactions of individual funds, and the second is what such a sight line might reveal—for example, overvaluation of noncash contributions, inactivity in disbursement of funds, and transfers of funds from private foundations in an attempt to bypass their payout rates."[536]

Overvaluations of property gifted to charity is a subject that cuts across every mode of charitable giving. Overvaluation in this context is a major problem—indeed, it is a problem far larger than consideration of these funds themselves.[537] This matter of property overvaluation is certainly is not confined to gifts to donor-advised funds. Thus, it is inappropriate to criticize donor-advised funds and their sponsoring organizations on this basis; overvaluation of contributed property, therefore, is not on the above list.[538]

Six issues of law involving donor-advised funds are being debated alongside these criticisms:

- Whether grants from these funds should constitute, in their entirety, public support.
- Whether monies in these funds should be used to fulfill charitable pledges.
- Whether these funds should be used to make grants to charitable fundraising events.
- Whether private foundations should be able to utilize donor-advised funds.
- Whether donor-advised funds should be subject to some form of mandatory payout.
- Whether donors to donor-advised funds should have their charitable deduction deferred.[539]

---

[536] McCambridge, "Do Donor-Advised Funds Require Regulatory Attention?," 25 *Nonprofit Quar.* (No. 2) 41 (Summer 2018).

[537] For example, one of the contemporary controversies in the realm of charitable giving is the abuse of the conservation easement rules (IRC § 170(h)) by promoters of syndicated easement arrangements. This matter has become so severe that the Department of the Treasury and the IRS have cast these syndications as tax-avoidance transactions, so that they and substantially similar transactions are now identified as listed transactions under the tax shelter rules (Notice 2017-10, 2017-4 I.R.B. 544). The government is particularly troubled by the promotions that offer charitable deductions that are worth substantially more than the original investment (e.g., IR-2019-182 (Nov. 12, 2019)). Yet, the abuse element in these schemes does not lie in the syndication feature per se. The outsized charitable deductions arising out of these promotions is attributable to the overvaluation of the eased property.

[538] Another example of unfair dragging of donor-advised funds into a legal controversy where the DAF involvement is beside the point is the case involving a public charity (that happens to be a sponsoring organization) that may be engaging in tax shelter activities (National Outreach Foundation, Inc. v. Commissioner, docketed in the U.S. Tax Court on Nov. 14, 2019 (Docket No. 20291-19X)). See *EO Tax Jour.* 2019-245, 2019-247.

[539] See Chapter 6.

CRITICISM # 1: DONOR-ADVISED FUNDS ARE SHAMS

A frequent technique employed in public policy discussions (particularly these days) is bombast. Pejorative labels are thoughtlessly tossed about, untethered to the law, data, or common sense. In this context, and from this perspective, the word *sham* is sometimes employed.[540] Thus, in some quarters, donor-advised funds are portrayed as shams.[541]

Inasmuch as the concept of the donor-advised fund is now codified,[542] with the statutory definition not that much different from the common-law one,[543] the contention that donor-advised funds are shams, loopholes, or legal fictions is not, as a matter of law, credible. This fact is underscored by the gift substantiation requirement.[544]

To select from these observations, the starkest may be that of the law professor who wrote that "you must begin [an analysis of donor-advised funds] with the self-evidently true factual proposition that the independence of the DAF from the donor is a sham."[545]

One dictionary defines a *sham* as a "trick that deludes," in the nature of a "hoax," or "cheap falseness," as in "hypocrisy."[546] Another dictionary defines the word as "something that is not what it purports to be; a spurious imitation; fraud or hoax."[547]

---

[540] It is particularly painful to read and hear lawyers and law professors loosely invoke words such as *sham, loophole*, and *legal fiction*; as to the latter two terms, see criticism # 2 and # 3. As an appellate court stated, a transaction is a sham when it has no "practicable economic effects other than the creation of income tax losses" (Dow Chemical Co. v. United States (435 F.3d 594, 599 (6th Cir. 2006)). Obviously, the donor-advised fund is not a sham using this definition.

[541] The word *sham* is generally tossed around by someone criticizing something. For example, Paul Streckfus, in his online newsletter, proclaimed the IRS procedures for processing applications for recognition of tax exemption (which are now numbering close to 100,000 annually) are a "sham" because, in a particular week only one private letter ruling denying recognition was made public (*EO Tax Jour.* 2019-236 (Dec. 5, 2019)). About two weeks later, a batch of private letter rulings came tumbling out.

[542] See Chapter 4.

[543] E.g., National Foundation, Inc. v. United States, 87-2 U.S.T.C. ¶ 9602 (Ct. Cl. 1987); Priv. Ltr. Ruls. 200149045 (referencing a "charitable gift fund" with "donor-advised account[s]") (Aug. 3, 2001), 9807030 (Nov. 19, 1997).

[544] See Chapter 4, pp. 103-106.

[545] Kleinbard, TaxProf Blog Op-Ed, Aug. 10, 2018 (reproduced in *EO Tax Jour.* 2018-158 (Aug. 13, 2018)). It may be noted that something cannot be "true factual" (which has overtones of redundancy) and a "proposition."

[546] Merriam-Webster Dictionary (online).

[547] Dictionary.com.

Donor-advised fund critics get agitated—and thus deploy the word *sham*—when coping with the concept of *advice*. They insist that, in reality, the donor to a donor-advised fund retains control over the contributed money or other property. This ostensible retention of control is rested on the fact that sponsoring organizations almost always follow the recommendations of the donors.[548] Thus, a law professor stated that the "DAF is the donor's agent, not an independent actor that happens to get along with the donor."[549]

One abject critic of the donor-advised fund concept opened his analysis in this regard by stating that the "role of the donor in this arrangement has always been treated with a wink and a nod."[550] He wrote that donors "technically give up absolute control of the funds once they establish their DAFs, which is why they can claim a full charitable tax deduction."[551] He added that donors "understand that they can essentially distribute the funds to any charitable causes they choose and the sponsors will almost always accede to their wishes."[552] This was referred to as "de facto control over the charitable distribution."[553]

Thus, the argument goes, in its harshest form, that this matter of *advice* is really a sham, because the sponsoring organizations nearly always follow the donors' recommendations, so that in substance the donors *direct* the ultimate distribution of the assets in their donor-advised funds, rather than merely *recommend*. Another way to state this criticism is that donor-advised funds are, in reality, donor-directed funds.[554]

The fundamental flaw in this criticism is that there are federal statutes that directly deflect this criticism. One of the elements of the statutory definition of the phrase *donor-advised fund* is that the fund is "owned and controlled" by the sponsoring organization involved.[555] This definition includes the concept that the donor or donor-advisor "has, or reasonably expects to have, advisory privileges with respect to the distribution or investment of amounts held in the fund."[556] Indeed, a donor

---

[548] The word *fact* is used, although I am unaware of an objective study or report on the point. For purposes of this criticism, it is assumed that this statement is true (or true factual).
[549] TaxProf Blog Op-Ed, *supra* note 14. As discussed, this statement is, as a matter of law, false.
[550] Cantor, "A Gain to Commercial Funds Is a Loss to Charities," XXVII *Chron. of Phil.* (No. 2) 29 (Nov. 6, 2014).
[551] *Id.* The key word in this quote is *technically*. It is not merely a technicality. The giving up of control of the gift property is a major legal concept, enshrined in the Internal Revenue Code (see Chapter 4, pp. 103–106).
[552] Cantor, *supra* note 550, at 29.
[553] *Id.*
[554] See Chapter 1, pp. 16–17.
[555] See Chapter 4, p. 103.
[556] *Id.* This element of the definition suggests that it is unreasonable for a donor or donor-advisor to

is not entitled to a charitable contribution deduction for a transfer to a donor-advised fund unless the donor receives a contemporaneous written acknowledgment from the sponsoring organization stating that the organization has "exclusive legal control" over the funds or other assets contributed.[557] Consequently, it is crystal clear, as a matter of law, that the assets in a donor-advised fund are completely owned and controlled by the sponsoring organization and the most the donor has with respect to the assets is the advisory privilege. This body of law is not properly dismissible as amounting to a mere technicality—or a sham.

Thus, when critics contend that donor-advised funds are shams, they are essentially asserting that Congress has legislated, or provided the legislative basis for, a fraud or hoax. Congress, they are arguing, has perpetrated a trick that deludes, engaged in cheap falseness, and has concocted a spurious imitation. The absurdity of this position is, to use a law professor's terminology, self-evident.

This argument that donors to donor-advised funds in reality maintain control over the transferred property has been made since creation of these funds. It is an assertion that has been rejected by courts, Congress, and (eventually) by the IRS.

As to the courts, for example, the Supreme Court of Nevada considered a case where a donor made a contribution to a public charity pursuant to a written agreement that the charity would place the donor's gift in a donor-advised fund. The charity breached the agreement by not establishing the fund. The donor sued for return of the gift. The state Supreme Court ruled that the district court was correct in holding that this donor was not entitled to return of the gift proceeds because, in accordance with the agreement's terms, the donor "gave up any interest in the money when he made the unrestricted gift" to the charity, "allowing [the charity] the discretion to reject any of his recommendations for the donation's use."[558] The court noted that this donor claimed a charitable contribution deduction for the gift.[559] The Supreme Court also affirmed the district court's conclusion that this donor "suffered no damages [in this regard] because once he made the unrestricted gift, he no longer had any interest in or control over the donation."[560]

---

have an expectation that he, she, or it has a privilege that goes beyond advisory.

[557] See Chapter 4, p. 103 This fact is usually also stated in the donor-advised fund agreement executed between the donor(s) and the sponsoring organization.

[558] Styles v. Friends of Fiji, 373 P. 3d 965 (Sup. Ct. Nev. 2011).

[559] The court cited a federal appellate court decision stating that a "donor must have surrendered dominion and control over the gift for it to qualify as a charitable contribution" and that an "expectation of a 'quid pro quo' defeats deductibility of [the] contribution" (U.S. v. Estate Preservation Services, 202 F.3d 1093, 1102 (9th Cir. 2000)).

[560] Styles v. Friends of Fiji, 373 P.3d 965 (Sup. Ct. Nev. 2011).

The American Bar Association Tax Section observed that, "once a donor makes a contribution to a donor advised fund, that donor has relinquished control of the contributed funds, which become the legal property of the sponsoring organization of the donor advised fund."[561] The Section continued: "While a Donor/Advisor may retain advisory privileges over such amounts, the sponsoring organization is under no obligation to heed the Donor/Advisor's advice with respect to a particular recommended grantee."[562] Thus: "Should a sponsoring organization, in its diligence process with respect to a grant recommendation, determine that a Donor/Advisor is attempting to utilize his or her donor advised fund to circumvent the 2% Limitation, the sponsoring organization could decline the grant recommendation."[563] The nation's tax lawyers have spoken—correctly.

It is now clear that, as a matter of law, when a donor contributes to a legitimate donor-advised fund, he, she, or it forfeits control of the money or other property transferred. That is, these transfers are bona fide gifts, with the donors relinquishing their title to and rights in the property to the donee sponsoring organization. The retention of the right to advise does not detract from the undeniable fact that the money or other property, immediately following the contribution, is wholly owned by the sponsoring organization and is subject to its complete discretion and control.[564] Congress has not created a sham arrangement.

CRITICISM # 2: DONOR-ADVISED FUNDS ARE A LEGAL FICTION

This criticism that donor-advised funds are a legal fiction is a polite restatement of criticism # 1.

The term *legal fiction* has taken on various meanings over the decades. Today, it is usually used as a derogatory classification. That is certainly the case when it comes to donor-advised funds. This is unfortunate, in part because the word *fiction* does not connote falsehood; it means merely that the item involved is conjured by the writer.

Donor-advised fund critics, as noted, get agitated when confronted with the concept of *advice*. They say that the statement that a sponsoring organization owns and controls the money or other property contributed to donor-advised funds is a legal fiction (meaning, in this setting, that the statement is false) because in reality the donor retains

---

[561] ABA Tax Section comments in response to Notice 2017-73 (April 19, 2018).
[562] *Id.*
[563] *Id.*
[564] See Chapter 4, p. 103.

control over the property. This ostensible retention of control is rested on the assertion that the sponsoring organization always (or almost always) follows the recommendation of the donor.[565] As will be discussed, this matter of sponsoring organization ownership is not a legal fiction at all. Indeed, Congress, a court, and the IRS have said so.[566]

The phrase *legal fiction* is defined as an "assumption that something occurred or someone or something exists which, in fact, is not the case, but that is made in the law to enable a court to equitably resolve a matter before it." That is, "[i]n order to do justice, the law will permit or create a legal fiction."[567]

Contemplate the notion that it is assumed that something exists when in fact that is not the case. What is *existence*? Presumably, something really exists when it has objective reality, that is, it is tangible and can be perceived as a physical thing; it is material, that is, a form of matter. Thus, if something does not truly exist, but someone in authority (such as a legislature or a court) says that it does, that something is a legal fiction. In some quarters, that means that the something is something to be scorned. Those are the quarters where donor-advised fund critics dwell.

Think about the legal fictions that are central to the lives of lawyers—and many other types of humans: corporations, partnerships, limited liability companies, trusts, estates, sole proprietorships. And those are only types of entities recognized in the law. There are all sorts of intangible properties, such as shares of stock and interests in real estate. Contracts are legal fictions. These legal fictions are usually evidenced by documents; the substance, however, is intangible.

These and like concepts, all inventions of the law, are used daily. Rarely are these entities or relationships disparaged because they are legal fictions. Somehow, donor-advised fund critics have managed to make the phrase legal fiction—in the donor-advised fund context—mean the same as a lie or fake news.

When a donor-advised fund critic employs the phrase legal fiction, it should be recognized for what it is—a misapplication of a concept, a little bomb thrown to create a diversion to make these funds look nefarious and illegitimate when, in fact, they are not. Ownership of and control over contributed funds, by sponsoring organizations, is real, in law and fact—not, in any event, fiction, legal or otherwise.

---

[565] Typical of this view is the one stating the "formal requirement of legal control is a legal fiction, since DAF sponsors are in essence conduits, almost uniformly following the directions of donors" (*EO Tax Jour.* 2018-50 (Mar. 12, 2018). Likewise, "donor-advised funds offer the particular advantage – control – available from private foundations" (Jones, "Regulating Donor Advised Funds," 75 *Florida Bar Jour.* (Issue 5 (May 2001)).

[566] See Chapter 2, pp. 41-43, 46-50; Chapter 4, p. 103.

[567] The online Free Legal Dictionary.

CRITICISM # 3: DONOR-ADVISED FUNDS ARE A LOOPHOLE

This use of the term *loophole* essentially is a rehash of criticisms ## 1 and 2. This word, however, is more clearly understood in the tax law than the terms sham and legal fiction. Yet critics of donor-advised funds frequently toss the term *loophole* around in the donor-advised fund context, obviously to impugn the concept.[568] Thus, *The New York Times* published an article with this glaring (and jarring) title: "How Tech Billionaires Hack Their Taxes With a Philanthropic Loophole."[569]

Here, for example, is a writer for the Bloomberg BNA *Daily Tax Report* (except for commentaries, a collection of supposedly objective articles) about the matter of grants from donor-advised funds constituting public support. He wrote that an objective of Treasury's and the IRS's proposed guidance is "aimed towards a potential loophole using donor-advised funds to circumvent limitations on public support."[570] Within a few paragraphs, this writer used the word loophole in two additional places and, for good measure, included the word "workaround."

As another example, one commentator raised the question as to whether donor-advised funds are "substitutes for private foundations" and thus a "loophole that avoids the private foundation anti-abuse rules?"[571] (A former IRS official answered that question by declaring that classifying "DAF sponsors as public charities is best viewed as a loophole providing donors a way around the private foundation rules.[572]) In a third instance, another commentator observed that donor-advised

---

[568] This phenomenon is by no means confined to the realm of donor-advised funds. Commentators frequently use the word *loophole* to describe something they have just discovered and do not understand or something they are trying to discredit. The word *loophole* as used in the donor-advised fund context is inaccurate, as evidenced by private letter rulings from the IRS approving their use (see Chapter 2, pp. 41-43). For example, an article about adoption of the Eighteenth Amendment noted, that while the amendment prohibited the purchase or transport of alcohol, it said nothing about drinking alcohol one already had; this article then proclaimed that "[b]oozehounds quickly seized upon this loophole" (Harlan, "A Splashy Start to Prohibition, 100 Not-So-Dry Januaries Ago," *New York Times*, A16 (Jan. 8, 2020)). I suspect this not to be a loophole at all but quite intentional.

[569] Article by David Gelles (Aug. 3, 2018).

[570] Lee, "Regulating Donor-Advised Funds: Not Everyone's a Fan of IRS Plans," Bloomberg BNA, *Daily Tax Report* (April 4, 2018).

[571] Colinvaux, "Donor Advised Funds: Charitable Spending Vehicles for 21st Century Philanthropy," 92 *Wash. L. Rev.* 39, 41 (2017).

[572] Comments of Marvin Friedlander, in *EO Tax Jour.* 2018-50 (Mar. 12, 2018). His "solution": "[T]hrow out both community trusts and donor-advised funds from qualifying as public charities" and "[t]reat [DAF] accounts as separate private foundations."

funds "are too often seen by tax planners as a work-around for the anti-abuse rules of private foundations."[573]

Here is an illustration of the proper use of the word *loophole*. Individuals are not allowed a federal tax deduction for contributions to political organizations. They are allowed, however, a deduction for a debt that becomes worthless in a tax year.[574] Some crafty tax lawyer devised the idea of individuals making loans to political entities; the political organization thereafter dissolves without payment of the loan and the lender claims the bad debt deduction, which obviously is an end run around the prohibition on deductions for gifts for political purposes. So, Congress enacted a statute to deny a deduction for the worthlessness of any debt that is owed by a political entity.[575] As the IRS observed, this was a closing of a "loophole that allowed supporters of political parties to claim a bad debt deduction for otherwise disallowed political contributions by disguising them as loans."[576]

The subject of donor-advised funds does not involve a loophole in the slightest. The definition of the word *loophole* proves the point. A loophole is an ambiguity or omission in a text by means of which the intent of a statute, contract provision, and the like may be evaded. Here, the statutory text is (as far as tax law provisions go) quite clear. The law as to loopholes is straightforward: "If Congress sees . . . [a type of transaction or arrangement] as unwise or creating an improper loophole, it should fix the problem."[577] Unless critics are prepared to contend that three Internal Revenue Code sections,[578] plus accompanying case law,[579] constitute one giant loophole, they should drop this argument.[580]

CRITICISM # 4: TRANSFERS TO DONOR-ADVISED FUNDS ARE NOT REALLY GIFTS.

As to the notion that transfers to sponsoring organizations, to be deposited in donor-advised funds, are not authentic gifts, that battle has been fought and its advocates van-

[573] Zerbe, "DAF Reform – A Chance to Provide Real Benefit to Working Charities," 25 *Nonprofit Quar.* (No. 2) 52, 55 (Summer 2018).
[574] IRC § 166(a)(1).
[575] IRC § 271.
[576] Chief Counsel Advice Memorandum 201842006 (Sep. 17, 2018).
[577] Summa Holdings, Inc. v. Commissioner, 848 F.3d 779, 790 (6th Cir. 2017).
[578] See Chapter 4, pp. 86-89, 103-106.
[579] See Chapter 2, pp. 41-43.
[580] One law professor wrote that "of all the tax 'loopholes' to get angry about, I would rank this one [donor-advised funds] quite low on my list" (quoted in the *EO Tax Jour.* 2018-158 (Aug. 13, 2018).

quished.[581] Again, every donor to a sponsoring organization must, if a charitable deduction is desired, by statute, be provided a notice by the organization that it has "exclusive legal control" over the funds or assets contributed,[582] a hallmark characteristic of a gift.

Yet, critics still invoke the argument, apparently of the view that mere repetition of a statement makes the statement true. For example, one critic wrote that the "role of the donor in this arrangement has always been treated with a wink and a nod."[583] Another critic wrote that private foundations make grants to donor-advised funds to satisfy the mandatory payout rules "while still retaining ongoing control over the distributed property."[584] Still another critic was moved to state that, "while donors part ways with their money, they don't give up control."[585] And Ray D. Madoff also wrote that donor-advised funds "enable donors to obtain current tax benefits of charitable giving while maintaining functional control over the investment and distribution of the donated property."[586] Still another commentator referenced the "concept that[,] although legal tide might rest with [donor-advised funds], implicit control over the contributed funds rests with the donors."[587]

Of course, this assertion of donor control ties in with the criticism that donor-advised funds are one great big legal fiction (criticism # 2). Sometimes the commentators in this context struggle so much with this topic that they contradict themselves in their same writing. For example, Ruth McCambridge wrote, in one of the more thoughtful and grounded articles about donor-advised funds, that (1) as these funds were formulated, there was an "understanding that the funds would be segregated and the donor would retain functional control over the distribution . . . of the funds,"[588] and (2) the way donor-advised funds operate, the "grant is finally made by the DAF sponsor, which retains real ownership/stewardship over funds that have been transferred to the DAF."[589] The first observation is incorrect; the second is spot on.[590]

---

[581] See Chapter 2, pp. 41–43.

[582] See Chapter 4, p. 103.

[583] Cantor, "A Gain to Commercial Funds Is a Loss to Charities," XXVII *Chron. of Phil.* (No. 2) 29 (Nov. 6, 2014).

[584] Madoff, "Three Simple Steps to Protect Charities and American Taxpayers from the Rise of Donor-Advised Funds," 25 *Nonprofit Quar.* (No. 2) 46, 47 (Summer 2018).

[585] Gelles, "How Tech Billionaires Hack Their Taxes With a Philanthropic Loophole," *New York Times* (Aug. 2, 2018). How can someone "part ways" with something and continue to "control" it?

[586] Madoff, *supra* note 584, at 47.

[587] Hussey, "Avoiding Misuse of Donor-Advised Funds," 58 *Clev. St. L. Rev.* 59, 64 (2010).

[588] McCambridge, "Do Donor-Advised Funds Require Regulatory Attention?," 25 *Nonprofit Quar.* (Issue 2) 41–42 (Summer 2018).

[589] *Id.* at 42.

CRITICISM # 5: DONOR-ADVISED FUNDS ARE VEHICLES INVOLVING MERELY THE

"WAREHOUSING" (OR STOCKPILING) OF MONEY OR OTHER FORMS OF PROPERTY.

Undoubtedly, one of the biggest raps against donor-advised funds is that the money (and perhaps other property) in them, having been contributed by donors who obtained charitable deductions for their gifts, is now trapped, reposing in the fund and not being used for charitable purposes.[591] To some degree (but not to the extent the critics take it), this charge is true. Usually, the bombast is overdone. One critic wrote that "while donors enjoy immediate tax benefits, charities can wait for funds indefinitely, and maybe forever."[592]

It is not clear why this concept of an intermediary between a donor and the ultimate donee is any different than the comparable use of private foundations, supporting organizations, charitable remainder trusts, and endowment funds. Many donors are "institutionalizing" their charitable giving these days, rather than simply making gifts without any further involvement; that appears to be a positive trend. It appears that this approach is attracting charitable gifts that would not otherwise be made, with donor-advised funds the driver of this type of philanthropic funding.[593] (Related to this contention is the criticism that donor-advised funds are not really engaged in charitable undertakings, such as the argument that they are to be differentiated from "working charities."[594]

[590] Although use of the word "finally" is suggestive of sympathy for the views of those who hurl charges of "warehousing" and "stockpiling" (see criticism # 5).

[591] E.g., Woolley, "The Super-Rich Are Stockpiling Wealth in Black-Box Charities," Bloomberg BNA (Oct. 3, 2018); Institute for Policy Studies, "Warehousing Wealth: Donor-Advised Charity Funds Sequestering Billions in the Face of Growing Inequality" (July 2018). By contrast, one commentator referred to donor-advised funds as "charitable spending vehicles" (see *supra* note 40). The community foundation sector stated that it does "not concur in the view that DAFs are used for 'asset parking' and are thus inherently suspect," adding that "[w]hile it may be mathematically possible for a small percentage of DAFs with very high payouts to skew an overall payout rate, that's not how things work at community foundations" (Community Foundation Public Awareness Initiative submission to House Committee on Ways and Means (July 14, 2014) (CFPAI 2014 Submission)).

[592] Gelles, "How Tech Billionaires Hack Their Taxes With a Philanthropic Loophole," *New York Times* (Aug. 3, 2018).

[593] Gifts to donor-advised funds constituted 10 percent of individual giving in 2017 (see Chapter 3, p. 68). An analysis of the donor-advised fund landscape from the community foundation subsector stated that these foundations want to convert donors "from *charitable givers* to *philanthropists*" (Kridler, Philipp, Slutsky, Seleznow, and Williams, "Donor-Advised Funds: How to Make Sure They Strengthen Our Communities," *Nonprofit Quar.* (Aug. 20, 2018) (Kridler et al. Analysis)).

[594] See criticism # 9.

Nonetheless, one donor-advised fund critic intoned that the "accelerating trend of warehousing philanthropic dollars is a deeply troubling trend for American philanthropy."[595] Another writer, discussing contributions to the Goldman Sachs Philanthropy Fund, which maintains donor-advised funds, proclaimed that the donors to the funds are "stockpiling" cash and other assets.[596]

Admission: Monies contributed to donor-advised funds are not necessarily monies that are devoted immediately and directly to charitable programmatic ends. That statement is undeniable. What is the point of having a donor-advised fund if, after establishing it and making the contribution, all of the money is, a few days later, distributed to one or more charities?[597]

Intermediaries are frequently used in the world of philanthropy. Not every charitable contribution is made to organizations directly operating charitable programs. Thus, this fact hardly reflects an unusual or nefarious set of circumstances. Private foundations, supporting organizations, charitable remainder trusts, and funds such as those for scholarships, research, or endowments are intermediaries. These entities are, at the most, infrequently accused of warehousing or stockpiling money.

Some of these entities are subject to mandatory (law-imposed) payout requirements; they are still intermediaries. Certain of these entities may spend their income for charitable ends but retain (and grow) principal; they too are intermediaries.

A donor-advised fund is an intermediary. That is, the funds contributed to it usually remain in the fund for a period of time before being distributed for the funding of charitable programs. Thus, just because an entity is a form of intermediary does not mean it is not furthering charitable ends.

Critics deride the view of "DAF advocates" that giving to donor-advised funds represents a "long-term commitment to the community."[598] One critic does not see matters this way, charging that giving to these funds is "exacerbating the chronic underfinancing of today's critical needs."[599] This is the same argument being advanced by those who want to immediately deplete college and university endowments by giving the money to students. That approach would be an economic boon

---

[595] Cantor, *supra* note 583, at 29.

[596] Metcalf, "Billionaires Funding a Goldman Charity Unmasked by IRS Snafu," Bloomberg BNA, *Daily Tax Report* (No. 51) 8 (Mar. 15, 2018).

[597] For motives to establish a donor-advised fund, see Chapter 1, pp. 29-32.

[598] Cantor, *supra* note 583, at 31. One such advocate (a law professor) blogged that "[p]utting money into a DAF is essentially a commitment to give that part of your wealth, plus all future returns on it, to charity," adding that, "[a]s such, DAFs should be applauded" (quoted in the *EO Jour.* 2018-157 (Aug. 10, 2018).

[599] Cantor, *supra* note 583, at 31.

to those receiving the windfall but then what about the students that follow, not to mention the state of the capital-deprived institutions of higher education?

Critics' favorite proposal in this connection is the mandatory payout.[600] Some see a payout requirement for donor-advised funds on an account-by-account basis as the "easy solution."[601] Others would confine a payout rule to the "national" sponsoring organizations, contending that, as one commentator observed, "[i]t should be within the competence of these sophisticated financial intermediaries to track subaccount balances and payouts over time, without creating an undue burden."[602]

If there were to be a mandatory payout, applicable to each donor-advised fund, what would it be? Some advocate using the private foundation 5 percent mechanism.[603] Then the question becomes, why have such a payout obligation in this context? The data shows that the payout rate for "national charities" is 22.9 percent, for community foundations is 19.2 percent, and for "single-issue" charities is 26.2 percent.[604] Also, it is one thing to impose a payout on organizations; it is another matter to mandate a payout for nearly 500,000 accounts.[605]

One analysis of a mandatory payout in this context raised seven points. One, if the objective of a payout requirement is to increase the amount of money dispensed from donor-advised funds, a payout rule would "have exactly the opposite impact over the medium to long term." Two, the effect of this type of proposal would be communication to the public that the concept of an endowment is reserved "only for large institutions and the very wealthy." Three, such a proposal "implies that inactive donor-advised funds are a significant public policy problem that requires attention, but the vast majority of DAF advisors are making grants regularly." Four, the proposal would establish a "structure where donor-advised funds are treated more harshly than other forms of endowments, which will be complicated and confusing to donors, as well as create an administrative nightmare for community foundations and other DAF administrators." Five, a forced payout (or spend down) would require sponsoring organizations to "go to court to undo thousands of legal arrangements and potentially put some community foundations in violation of state law and the donor's intent." Six, the proposal "seems to imply that DAFs only provide value to the community when money is 'paid out,' but at least where most community foun-

---

[600] "Payout is the cornerstone of DAF reforms" (Zerbe, *supra* note 573, at 53). See Chapter 6, pp. 194–206.
[601] *Id.*
[602] Colinvaux, *supra* note 571, at 70.
[603] See Chapter 6, pp. 195–197.
[604] See Chapter 3, pp. 69–70.
[605] See *id.*, pp. 70–71.

dations are concerned, that is not the case." Seven, a payout on donor-advised funds would "make it nearly impossible for DAF advisors to engage in the rapidly growing field of 'impact investing via their DAFs.'"[606]

CRITICISM # 6: DONOR-ADVISED FUNDS ARE NOT AUTHENTIC CHARITABLE PROGRAMS.

This criticism and criticism # 7 are related; there are, however, some relatively technical distinctions between the two. The two types of criticisms have one common feature, however, and that is that both are unfounded.

One of the raps on donor-advised funds these days is that they are to be differentiated from "working" charities (or, as one critic put it, "active" charities[607]). Loosely defined, a working charity is one that provides charitable (or educational, religious, or scientific) services directly to individuals, such as the poor, distressed, or those otherwise who are members of a charitable class. Thus, donor-advised funds are denigrated, with this approach, because the contributed money or other property goes into a fund, where it reposes for a period of time until the money is granted, usually to a charity that directly provides services. The argument, therefore, is that if an entity is not a "working" one, it is not really charitable.

This is merely a lame argument, one that lacks any substance from a legal viewpoint. Were there such a law, by which only working charities are true charities, there would not be any tax-exempt private foundations, endowment funds, or charitable remainder trusts, as well as fewer supporting organizations. (It is not known why critics pick on donor-advised funds in this regard, and not these other types of entities. Perhaps it is merely a manifestation of the "piling on" phenomenon.) The fact is that these intermediary entities have status as charities just as fully as those that are service providers.[608] For the most part, these types of tax-exempt intermediate charities are codified;[609] the IRS formally recognizes categories of endowment funds in its principal annual information return.[610]

---

[606] CFPAI 2014 Submission.

[607] Colinvaux, *supra* note 571, at 67.

[608] See Chapter 1, p. 7.

[609] Supporting organizations (IRC § 509(a)(3)); charitable remainder trusts (IRC § 664), private foundations (IRC § 509(a)), and donor-advised funds (IRC § 4966).

[610] Form 990, Schedule D, Part V.

CRITICISM # 7: DONOR-ADVISED FUNDS ARE MERELY FUNDRAISING VEHICLES, GENERALLY PRECLUDED FROM TAX EXEMPTION BY REASON OF THE COMMENSURATE TEST.

This criticism, as far as is known, has only been leveled at the "national" sponsoring organizations[611] by only one commentator. Thus, this critic wrote that "[a]s an intermediary or conduit between donor and other 501(c)(3) organizations, NSOs in effect are no more than fundraising organizations."[612] This disparagement notwithstanding, organizations that engage in fundraising and grantmaking can qualify for tax exemption as charitable entities as long as the amounts paid out are commensurate in scope with their financial resources.[613] The type of fundraising involved is essentially irrelevant. For example, the IRS ruled that an organization that conducts bingo games may be exempt as a charitable entity "if it uses the proceeds from bingo to conduct a charitable program, commensurate in scope with its financial resources, of making grants to other charitable organizations."[614]

There have not been many applications of the commensurate test. In one instance, a public charity had its tax exemption revoked by application of the commensurate test, because, in the two years under examination, although its bingo income was 73 percent and 92 percent of total gross income, only a small amount of this money was distributed for charitable purposes.[615] An organization making "minimal distributions" suffered the same outcome.[616]

Notwithstanding this line of law, this commentator observed that, "when considering the NSO as a fundraising organization, it is important to recognize that the case for 501(c)(3) status is qualitatively weak" and that the "501(c)(3) fundraising organization stands at the edge of legitimacy."[617] And why is that? "Charity is accomplished in the doing."[618] So, now we are back to the concept of the "working

---

[611] See Chapter 1, pp. 45–46.

[612] Colinvaux, *supra* note 571, at 62.

[613] This commensurate test was first articulated by the IRS in 1964, in Rev. Rul. 64-182, 1964-1 (Part 1) C.B. 186. Shortly thereafter, the IRS recognized tax exemption for an organization that carried "on no operations other than to receive contributions and incidental investment income and to make distributions of income to such exempt organizations [charitable entities] at periodic intervals" (Rev. Rul. 67-149, 1967-1 C.B. 133). In general, see Chapter 1, pp. 22–26.

[614] Priv. Ltr. Rul. 201103057 (Oct. 25, 2010).

[615] Priv. Ltr. Rul. 200825046 (Mar. 11, 2008).

[616] Priv. Ltr. Rul. 201415003 (Dec. 19, 2013).

[617] Colinvaux, *supra* note 571, at 64.

[618] *Id.*

charity," which has been discredited.[619] Moreover, fundraising and grantmaking is the "doing"—that is the essence of compliance with the commensurate test.

Thus, calling sponsoring organizations fundraising organizations does not inexorably lead to the conclusion that they do not qualify as tax-exempt charitable organizations. In fact, the opposite is true—they are exempt charitable organizations as long as the commensurate test is met.

This argument that sponsoring organizations ought not be tax-exempt because they are merely fundraising entities (and thus not "doing" anything charitable) leads to an anomaly. Any critic of donor-advised funds must—to maintain creditability as that type of critic—steadfastly insist that there be a payout requirement, preferably on an account-by-account basis.[620] Insistence on application of the commensurate test in the donor-advised fund setting means that there is a payout requirement already in place. True, this payout rule is not as precise as the one imposed on private foundations and nonfunctionally integrated Type III supporting organizations but it is nonetheless a payout rule.

CRITICISM # 8: DONOR-ADVISED FUNDS ARE DIVERTING MONIES FROM TRULY CHARITABLE ENDS.

The contention that monies contributed to donor-advised funds are in actuality monies diverted from truly charitable ends is, of course, directly related to, and largely a rehash of, criticisms ## 6 and 7. Thus, one critic declared that "[m]oney is flowing into advised funds, rather than to nonprofits that provide actual services."[621]

This argument is premised on the incorrect proposition that, if donor-advised funds did not exist, donors would be giving the same amount of their money and other property directly for charitable programmatic ends. Ruth McCambridge wrote, in her thoughtful article, when discussing the matter of imposition of a payout requirement on donor-advised fund sponsors, the "one issue that is most talked about as in need of policy change is the issue of payout rates, which has compared very favorably to foundation payouts—but not so favorably, of course, to direct giving, if you assume that the same amount would have been given elsewhere."[622]

---

[619] See the discussion of criticism # 9.
[620] See Chapter 6, pp. 194–206.
[621] Cantor. *supra* note 583, at 29.
[622] McCambridge, *supra* note 588, at 44. I have no idea as to what the middle portion of that sentence means but the quote is used because of its reference to that assumption, which is, I believe, a faulty one.

It is true that some money flowing into donor-advised funds would be contributed directly to charitable program ends if donor-advised funds did not exist. But the flip side is also true: Money being contributed to donor-advised funds is sometimes money that that otherwise would not be contributed for charitable ends. It is preferable that these monies be in donor-advised funds— and ultimately be destined for charitable purposes—than not be available for charity at all.

Thus, a critic wrote that this state of affairs is "largely a zero-sum game," in that "[m]oney going into DAFs is essentially subtracted from other charitable giving."[623] That assertion does not seem supported by current data.

CRITICISM # 9: DONOR-ADVISED FUNDS DO NOT PAY OUT SUFFICIENT FUNDS TO REAL (OR "WORKING") CHARITIES.

This criticism is, of course, criticism # 8 clothed in different phraseology.

CRITICISM # 10: DONOR-ADVISED FUNDS ARE BEING USED TO SIDESTEP THE PRIVATE FOUNDATION RULES.

There are two aspects of this criticism. One of these aspects is that donor-advised funds are being used instead of private foundations.

As to the first of these aspects, this may be said: Guilty as charged—sort of. It is perfectly obvious that donor-advised funds are an alternative to private foundations. The individual or individuals involved as donors may wish to avoid the responsibilities imposed by law (including annual reporting to the IRS and other foundation regulatory requirements[624]) of operating a private foundation. Use of a private foundation entails procurement of recognition of tax exemption and obtaining state and local tax exemptions, With the donor-advised fund, as opposed to a private foundation, there is no need to form an organization (no governing instruments or policies), construct a governing board (with the

---

[623] Cantor, *supra* note 583, at 31.
[624] See *Private Foundations*, Chapters 5-10.

140

concomitant requirements of board meetings, maintenance of meeting minutes, election and supervision of officers and employees, and personal liability). The donor-advised fund approach accords automatic public charity status. Contributions to these funds are deductible pursuant to the rules concerning public charities, not private foundations. Another factor may be that the amount of money or property involved is too small to warrant the costs of establishment of a private foundation. Use of a donor-advised fund leaves the founder free to see to grant-making and, perhaps, fundraising.

Critics of donor-advised funds, however, reject these considerations. They choose instead to regard use of donor-advised funds as a means of sidestepping, avoiding, or evading the private foundation rules.[625] It is incontrovertible that use of a donor-advised fund amounts to avoidance of the private foundation strictures. (*Evasion* seems too harsh, particularly in the tax law setting.) Indeed, it can be said that every public charity is a mechanism for sidestepping these rules. The point is that this is an avoidance of a set of rules in a lawful manner.[626]

The other aspect of this criticism is that private foundations are using donor-advised funds to avoid the mandatory payout rules imposed on foundations. For example, one commentator made reference to "transfers of funds from private foundations in an attempt to bypass their payout rates."[627] Private foundations make grants to donor-advised funds for many legitimate reasons;[628] there is no data to support the allegation that this type of "bypassing" is occurring.

---

[625] For example, a law professor, not mincing words, blogged that the "DAF is an evasion of the regulatory scheme that Congress intended" (quoted in the *EO Tax Jour.* 2018-158 (Aug. 13, 2018)).

[626] The U.S. Supreme Court long ago observed that the "legal right of a taxpayer to decrease the amount of what otherwise would be his taxes, or altogether to avoid them, by means which the law permits, cannot be doubted" (Gregory v. Helvering, 293 U.S. 465, 469 (1935)). An appellate court wrote that "[w]e recognize that it is axiomatic that taxpayers lawfully may arrange their affairs to keep taxes as low as possible" (Neonatology Associates P.A. v. Commissioner, 299 F.3d 221, 232 (3rd Cir. 2002)). Another appellate court stated that when it "find[s] that the transaction does not violate the plain intent of the relevant statutes," it cannot change the outcome by statutory interpretation (Benenson v. Commissioner, 887 F.3d 511, 523 (1st Cir. 2018)). A court of appeals earlier stated that "[i]f Congress sees . . . [a type of transaction or arrangement] as unwise or creating an improper loophole, it should fix the problem" (Summa Holdings, Inc. v. Commissioner, 848 F.3d 779, 790 (6th Cir. 2017)). Indeed, an appellate court wrote that if "taxpayers have found a hole in the dike, we believe it is one that calls for the application of the Congressional thumb, not the court's" (Fabreeka Products Co. v. Commissioner, 294 F.2d 876, 879 (1st Cir. 1961)).

[627] McCambridge, *supra* note 588, at 41.

[628] See Chapter 6, pp. 183-187.

CRITICISM # 1 1: DONOR-ADVISED FUNDS THAT ARE USING THE SERVICES OF RELATED INVEST-

MENT COMPANIES ARE VIOLATING THE PRIVATE INUREMENT OR PRIVATE BENEFIT DOCTRINES.

Some in the world of philanthropy profess to be highly offended at the prospect of operational relationships between tax-exempt charitable organizations and for-profit companies. Yet these in-tandem operations occur all the time. Most of the major for-profit corporations have related "foundations," nearly all of which are private foundations. Many types of exempt organizations have related, often wholly owned, for-profit subsidiaries. Exempt organizations and for-profit entities co-exist in limited liability companies, partnerships, and other forms of joint ventures. Even when services between or among them are provided for fees, there is no private inurement where the charges are reasonable. These types of relationships usually do not trigger violations of the private inurement or private benefit doctrines.

Still, as critics flail about, conjuring up every criticism of donor-advised funds they can muster, they complain about the relationship between the "national" (and, inevitably, "commercial") sponsoring organizations and the investment companies that spawned them. The rules in the donor-advised fund setting are the same as those in the corporate foundation context: this is not a matter of automatic violations of the private inurement and/or private benefit rules. For the most part, as noted, the test is whether the terms of the transactions or arrangements involved are reasonable.

There are no examples of unreasonable fee arrangements, for example. Nothing about inappropriate board overlaps or self-dealing. The very existence of the relationship is deemed offensive. But that is not the state of the law.

One critic finds this type of relationship "existential."[629] That is an interesting notion but this conception does not make the relationship illegal, corrupting, or infected with private inurement. This critic proclaims that "[p]rivate benefit concerns have long dogged NSOs," then relegates to a footnote the observation that "[p]rivate benefit concerns were rife at the time sponsoring organizations were seeking exemption, though eventually turned out not to be a bar."[630]

The misinformation in this context is regrettable, particularly when authored by lawyers. One wrote that the commercial investment firms that are affiliated with spon-

---

[629] Colivaux, *supra* note 571, at 66.
[630] *Id.*

soring organizations "benefit" from the investment management fees they earn.[631] Yes, they do but that is not private benefit. Human beings benefit every time an exempt charity pays a salary, or rent, or interest on a loan, or the fees charged by a lawyer, accountant, or fundraising consultant. There is no tax or other law violation here.

When reliance on the private inurement or private benefit doctrine fails, as it usually does, critics dredge up a somewhat alternative contention: the "conflict of interest."[632] (Conflicts of interest are not inherently unlawful.) Thus, one critic writes of the "tension" between the need of the sponsoring organization to distribute funds and the mission of the for-profit entity to hold and invest funds. This is not news. In the settings of private foundations, supporting organizations, and endowment funds, for example, that "tension" is always present—with, there, the tension being in the same entity. In any event, just because a relationship causes tension does not mean a conflict of interest is created.

CRITICISM # 12: DONOR-ADVISED FUNDS THAT ARE NATIONAL (OR "COMMERCIAL") IN NATURE ARE INHERENTLY EVIL.

The use of the term *commercial* in the donor-advised fund context is of two forms. The second application is imposed when discussing donor-advised funds that have been established by and continue to be affiliated with financial firms, such as Fidelity Investments, Schwab, and Vanguard. One of the criticisms in this context, which is addressed in criticism # 11, is that the money in the donor-advised funds is invested with these financial houses. Despite the potential for private inurement or private benefit concerns, these in-tandem arrangements have been approved by the IRS.

Perhaps the most searing indictment of this nature came from the founder of the Tides Foundation who wrote that the IRS's determination in 1991 to recognize the Fidelity Investment Charitable Gift Fund as a tax-exempt charitable organization "was a highly damaging mistake that has undermined the entire nonprofit world."[633] (That tops the hyperbole referenced in the next criticism.) These "commercial" funds are, he added, "essentially an asset-accumulation strategy dressed up as charities."[634]

[631] *Id.*
[632] *Id.*
[633] Drummond, "How I Helped Create the Donor-Advised Fund Monster – Inadvertently," *Chron. of Phil.* (Aug. 22, 2018).
[634] *Id.*

Ray Madoff even grumbled that the sponsoring organizations that are affiliated with financial firms "sound[] more like commercial financial institutions than traditional charities,"[635] presumably because of the similarity of names—a silly charge, one never leveled at corporate-related private foundations.

Some critics of donor-advised funds are engaging in "splitting"—advocating law changes only for sponsoring organizations that are affiliated with financial firms. Even Dean Zerbe concedes that "[m]any charities that manage DAFs provide important and valuable support—especially those located at a number of community foundations."[636]

CRITICISM # 13: DONOR-ADVISED FUNDS UNDULY CATER TO THE WEALTHY.

A critic summed up this criticism rather nicely: "[T]o critics, [donor-advised funds] represent the worst of philanthropy today—a system of guaranteed perks for the rich and uncertainty for the rest."[637] In this writing, this critic quoted another critic (a tax law professor) as saying that donor-advised funds are "a way for the affluent to have their cake and eat it, too."

One of the events in the evolution of donor-advised funds that generated great interest in the tax law community, including its media, occurred in early 2018, when Form 990, Schedule B information concerning a major sponsoring organization was inadvertently (?) sent to and published by GuideStar until the mistake was detected and the information deleted. This development was reported in the tax law press.[638] The article reported that "[t]hree of America's most discreet billionaire philanthropists have emerged as the biggest donors to the Goldman Sachs Philanthropy Fund after the IRS accidently revealed their identities." One of these donors "poured" $1.9 billion into the donor-advised fund involved, while the other two contributed $526 million and $114 million. This development helped fuel the contention that donor-advised funds serve only at the behest and benefit of the wealthy. This article concludes that "[s]tockpiling [see criticism # 5] $2.5 billion in cash and

[635] Madoff, "Three Simple Steps to Protect Charities and American Taxpayers from the Rise of Donor-Advised Funds," 25 *Nonprofit Quar.* (no. 2) 46, 47 (Summer 2018).
[636] Zerbe, "DAF Reform – A Chance to Provide Real Benefit to Working Charities," 25 *Nonprofit Quar.* (Issue 2) 52, 56 (Summer 2018).
[637] Gelles, *supra* note 585.
[638] E.g., Lee, "Billionaires Funding a Goldman Philanthropy Charity Unmasked by IRS Snafu," Bloomberg BNA, *Daily Tax Report* (Mar. 14, 2018).

144

assets with the Goldman DAF lets the money grow there until they decide to allo-cate it to charities."

Not that long thereafter, another article concerning donor-advised funds ap-peared, this one focused on contributions by hedge fund managers (another reviled group).[639] The author of this piece stated: "In the world of philanthropy and tax-deductible charitable giving, the explosion of donor-advised funds has touched off intense debate. Now there is evidence that the DAF boom is being further fueled by hedge fund foundation money."

Three aspects of this phenomenon that critics do not mention are that (1) pri-vate foundations are created under these conditions and for the same reasons and no one complains about that, (2) these billions of dollars are destined for charitable use, and (3) often these are funds and assets that would not have otherwise been contributed.

CRITICISM # 14: THE RISE OF THE LARGER DONOR-ADVISED FUNDS AMOUNTS TO A HIJACKING OF PHILANTHROPY BY WALL STREET.

This criticism is a restatement of criticism # 12 and to an extent criticism # 11.

In the aftermath of publication by the *Chronicle of Philanthropy* of its Philan-thropy 400 in 2014, which featured the donor-advised funds associated with Fidelity, Schwab, and Vanguard in the top ten, the *Chronicle* published two side-by-side ar-ticles on opposite views of donor-advised funds.[640]

In one of these articles, a donor-advised fund critic stated that the *Chronicle's* survey "sadly confirms what many of us have feared for the last several years: an in-exorable takeover of the charitable sector by Wall Street."[641] Such a comment seems more a bemusing example of hyperbole than rational analysis. Yet, the criticism en-dures: "The fact that [donor-advised funds] have become a profit center for Wall Street firms is a perversion of the philanthropic system, critics say."[642]

---

[639] "Foundations of Hedge Fund Managers Gave Big to Controversial Donor-Advised Funds," *Forbes* (May 17, 2018).
[640] "2 Views on Donor-Advised Funds," XXVII *Chronicle of Philanthropy* (No. 2) 29 (Nov. 6, 2014).
[641] Cantor, *supra* note 583, at 29.
[642] Gelles, *supra* note 585.

CRITICISM # 15: DONOR-ADVISED FUNDS LACK TRANSPARENCY.

Of all the trendy buzzwords casually tossed around in the nonprofit community these days, the one at the top of the list is *transparency*. When a critic wants to fault some aspect of tax-exempt organizations' operations, the first volley is likely to be "lack of transparency." Thus, for example, some sponsoring organizations are dubbed "black-box" charities.[643] One commentator wrote of the "establishment of systems of accountability,"[644] which perhaps initially sounds quite proper. Often, however, the time and money required to be sufficiently "accountable" is overwhelming. Plus, this gargantuan push for "transparency" shoves other values and principles, such as privacy and free speech rights, aside.[645] As a relatively minor example, anonymous gifts are commonplace and unremarkable throughout the realm of philanthropy[646] but the practice is singled out as being nefarious when done in the context of donor-advised funds.[647]

This matter of touting transparency becomes most important (to the critics) when advocating a mandatory payout for donor-advised funds.[648] At the beginning, there was clamor for payout rules on sponsoring organizations, along the lines of the mandatory payout rules for private foundations. Then, when data showed that payout rates are quite high at the sponsoring organization level, the critics shifted position and started demanding payout obligations on an account-by-account basis.

Ruth McCambridge spent much of her article's focus on this matter of transparency, comparing donor-advised funds "that aren't fluid" to endowment funds "that do not accrue properly to the benefit of the public."[649] These vehicles are there said to "pose a threat to the entire [nonprofit] field by providing rich soil and a veil for misbehavior in that sweet spot of congressional attention."[650] She adds that, "in the absence of transparency, one could assume that none of the proposals [for law changes] have merit or almost all of the proposals have merit."[651] In other words,

---

[643] See Chapter 1, p. 4.

[644] McCambridge, *supra* note 588, at 41

[645] See text accompanied by *infra* notes 649-664.

[646] A law professor blogged that "charitable giving need not be public," adding "[t]here is no law against anonymous giving to charities" (quoted in *EO Jour.* 2018-157 (Aug. 10, 2018)).

[647] For example, the *San Francisco Chronicle*, in a December 12, 2018, article, reported that donor-advised funds "allow[] wealthy individuals to avoid any transparency around their giving – how much they have dedicated to philanthropy, how much they have given away" (reprinted in the *EO Tax Jour.* 2018-242 (Dec. 13, 2018)).

[648] See Chapter 6, pp. 194-206.

[649] McCambridge, *supra* note 588, at 44. That remark about endowments reflects a point of view, not fact.

[650] McCambridge, *supra* note 588, at 44. What "misbehavior"?

sponsoring organizations are to be subjected to enormous and costly disclosure and reporting burdens and monies that would otherwise flow to charitable ends are to be spent on lawyers and accountants, all to the end of discerning whether there is a problem to begin with.[652]

There is a parallel to all of this. Some states, as part of their charitable fundraising regulation, require soliciting charities to file with them copies of their annual information returns, including the schedule that identifies, by name, address, and gift amount, most of their donors.[653] This recently enforced disclosure requirement has spawned litigation, most of which is in favor of the states, on constitutional law and privacy grounds.

The most prominent of this litigation is unfolding in California. For example, the U.S. Court of Appeals for the Ninth Circuit held that this disclosure requirement is substantially related to an important state interest in policing charitable organizations, looking for instances of fraud.[654] This appellate court addressed the issue of whether this disclosure requirement violates the charitable organizations' free speech right to freedom of association. The court wrote that the charities' evidence "shows that some individuals who have or would support [them] may be deterred from contributing if the [charities] are required to submit their [schedules] to the Attorney General," but that that evidence is insufficient to establish a substantial burden on First Amendment rights.[655] Also, the court of appeals conceded the "possibility that the [charities'] contributors would face threats, harassment or reprisals if their information were to become public" but ruled that the charities failed to establish a "reasonable probability of retaliation."[656]

These charities sought a rehearing in this case before the full complement of Ninth Circuit judges; the petition for the hearing en banc was denied.[657] This

[651] McCambridge, *supra* note 588, at 44. She repeated this proposal when she wrote that "access [to all of this newfound information] could provide the robust research and data that would allay regulators' concerns – if no cause for concerns exists" (*id*). Note "could."

[652] McCambridge writes of this utopia: "the whole field would benefit from independent research that examines a number of key questions, identifying patterns that violate standards already in law or regulations" (*id*). What "patterns"? If existing "standards" are being violated, that law can be applied to rectify the problem; more law is not required. Fund-by-fund reporting is not likely to be required by federal law anytime soon. But it may be a matter of law in some states. E.g., Chronicle of Philanthropy, "California Bill Would Require Greater Disclosure of Donor-Advised-Fund Activity" (Jan. 14, 2020).

[653] Form 990 or 990-EZ, Schedule B.

[654] Americans for Prosperity Foundation v. Becerra; Thomas More Law Center v. Becerra, 903 F.3d 1000 (9th Cir. 2018).

[655] *Id.* at 1014.

[656] *Id.* at 1019.

[657] Americans for Prosperity Foundation v. Becerra; Thomas More Law Center v. Becerra, Nos. 16-

denial of a rehearing, however, sparked a vigorous dissent from five of the appellate court's judges, asserting that the panel committed "crucial legal errors."[658] The panel's approach in this case will, the dissent stated, "ensure that individuals affiliated with controversial organizations effectively have little or no protection from compelled disclosure."[659] The dissent surveyed U.S. Supreme Court jurisprudence on the point, writing that the Court "has not wavered from the principle that the First Amendment affords organizations and individuals substantial protection where the government tries to force disclosure of ties that could impact their freedom of association."[660] The dissent observed that because disclosure requirements such as these "can abridge First Amendment associational rights, the Supreme Court has held that these requirements are subject to heightened scrutiny."[661]

One parallel aspect of this case lies with the schedule itself. The Ninth Circuit panel referenced the importance of disclosure in detecting "self-dealing," "illegal activity," and "other unfair business practices."[662] The fact is that the information on the schedule is of almost no help in this regard. Also, the district court in this case found that the state's attorney general's office rarely looked at these schedules when conducting its investigations (a finding that the appellate court ignored).[663] The court wrote that it heard "ample evidence establishing that [the charity], its employees, supporters and donors face public threats, harassment, intimidation, and retaliation once their support for and affiliation with the organization becomes publicly known."[664] The court found that this charity's supporters have been subjected to "abuses that warrant relief," adding that it is "not prepared to wait until an opponent [of the charity] carries out one of the numerous death threats made against its members."[665]

In the aftermath of the rejection by the U.S. Court of Appeals for the Ninth Circuit of First Amendment challenges to California's charitable organization donor disclosure regime and the vigorous dissent in the appellate court's decision to not

---

56855, 16–56902 (9th Cir., Mar. 29, 2019).

[658] *Id.*, 919 F.3d 1177, 1178 (9th Cir. 2019).

[659] *Id.* at 1179.

[660] *Id.*

[661] *Id.*

[662] Americans for Prosperity Foundation v. Becerra; Thomas More Law Center, 903 F.3d 1000–1009 (9th Cir. 2018).

[663] Americans for Prosperity Foundation v. Harris, 182 F. Supp. 3d 1049, 1055 (C.D. Cal. 2016).

[664] *Id.*

[665] *Id.* at 1056.

allow the full panel to review the case, the public charity principally involved in the dispute petitioned the U.S. Supreme Court for review of the case.[666]

As stated in the petition, the California Attorney General is demanding that "thousands of registered charities annually disclose to the State the individual names and addresses of their major donors." Essentially, the appellate court is being faulted for not adhering to decades of precedent by which laws like this are tested against an "exacting scrutiny" standard. The decision, according to the petition "cannot be squared with well-settled constitutional protection for private association." "[A]mple means exist," the petition states, "for California to achieve its claimed law-enforcement interests" without exercising its "blanket demand for donor-identity lists."

The petition states that the Supreme Court "should now determine whether government may compel across-the-board identification of donors, where that practice so clearly stands to chill speech, association, and donor contributions around the country." Unless the Court intercedes, the petition continues, the Ninth Circuit "has opened the door for the major donors of thousands of charities to be exposed and chilled through California's dragnet." If the Court declines review, the "resulting chill will be profound and lasting."

Acceptance of this case would enable the Court to revisit its pronouncement of First Amendment guarantees of the right to associate in its 1958 decision, where the Court struck down the Alabama Attorney General's demand that the organization involved divulge the names of its members. In that case, the Court recognized that "privacy in group association" is "indispensable to preservation of freedom of association," holding that this type of compelled disclosure must satisfying exacting scrutiny to pass constitutional law muster.

The petition makes the case that the Ninth Circuit's holding creates a circuit split, in that the First, Second, Third, Fourth, Fifth, Sixth, Tenth, and D.C. Circuits "have all agreed, in applying exacting scrutiny outside the election context, that any compelled disclosure of a group's supporters must be narrowly tailored to or [be] the least-restrictive means of achieving the asserted governmental interest."

In addition, the petition asserts that the Ninth Circuit's decision "warrants review because it threatens grave harm to vital First Amendment interests on a national basis." The appellate court's holding "condones compelled disclosures from tens of thousands of charities across the country, merely because they operate and register

---

[666] Americans for Prosperity Foundation v. Becerra, Petition for Writ of Certiorari, No. 19-251 (filed Aug. 26, 2019).

in California." The petition states that the "resulting chill will be felt nation-wide as numerous organizations and their donors grapple with disclosure requirements and the attendant threats to confidentiality."

The petition concludes that this case "affords an excellent opportunity [for the Court] to clarify the framework governing compelled disclosure of group affiliations outside of the election context." The petition ends with this: "Unless reversed, the Ninth Circuit's decision may make it difficult for would-be challengers going forward to demonstrate that a charity and its donors face dangers comparable to those demonstrated on the record here—or that disclosure demands confronted elsewhere in the country appreciably surpass those already incurred and condoned in California. If the decision below stands, subsequent challengers will be hard pressed to secure the relief necessary to ward off a governmental demand for donor identities while a case winds its way to this Court. These potential problems afford additional reasons why this Court should use this case to take up and decide the Question Presented."

The question presented by the petition is "[w]hether the exacting scrutiny this Court has long required of laws that abridge the freedoms of speech and association outside the election context—as called for by [the Court's 1958 opinion] and its progeny—can be satisfied absent any showing that a blanket governmental demand for the individual identities and addresses of major donors to private nonprofit organizations is narrowly tailored to an asserted law-enforcements interest."

Paul Streckfus "find[s] the commercial DAF sponsors . . . to be secretive."[667] A law professor blogs that sponsoring organizations are "hiding" payout information, wondering "[h]ow bad must it actually be?"[668] There is no evidence of unwarranted secrecy, of course, just conclusions and presumptions (and not of innocence).

The point is that some semblance of balance needs to be struck. Unchecked "transparency" can trample other values, such as rights of free speech and to privacy. This is particularly true when there is little reason to know if such "robust research" is even needed or if it is worth the cost in terms of time and money.

---

[667] *EO Tax Jour.* 2019-162 (Aug. 20, 2019).
[668] *EO Tax Jour.* 2018-163 (Aug. 20, 2018).

CRITICISM # 16: DONOR-ADVISED FUNDS ARE IMMORAL

AND FRAUDULENT, AND CONTRIBUTE TO CHARITIES' CORRUPTION.

The editor of the *EO Tax Journal*, Paul Streckfus, has been the most outspoken of the critics on this matter of donor-advised funds and morality and the like. On one occasion, he wrote that "DAFs raise a moral issue—the billionaire class is using DAFs as massive tax shelters while depriving working charities the money needed to do their important work," adding that the tax code provision providing the federal in-come tax charitable contribution deduction[669] "has now been transformed from a provision mostly benefiting the needy and good causes to a provision mainly bene-fiting the wealthy."[670] Earlier, he wrote: "We've reached the point where the operation of donor-advised funds is not only a legal and tax issue but also a moral issue. People in need remain in desperate circumstances while the charity dollars that should be going to help them are being warehoused or misdirected for the benefit of DAF contributors and sponsors."[671] He has also written that "all of us need to keep beating the drums and demanding legislative action because the alternative is moral bank-ruptcy for the entire nonprofit sector."[672] Most recently, Paul wrote of the "powerful interests defending the misuse of DAFs and [private foundations],which allows and encourages the corruption of the charitable sector."[673]

As one tax law professor put the matter, donor-advised funds are a "fraud on the American taxpayer."[674] So there you have it: in the minds of some, Congress, in legislating three bodies of law, has created a sham, a legal fiction, a loophole, and a fraud. And this is from lawyers and law professors.

INJECTIONS OF OBJECTIVITY

One of the few objective reviews of this matter of the ostensible need for additional regulation of donor-advised funds concluded that the reviewer "is by no means con-vinced that there is widespread abuse in donor-advised funds" but adds that "con-

---

[669] IRC § 170.
[670] *EO Tax Jour.* 2018-153 (Aug. 6, 2018).
[671] *EO Tax Jour.* 2018-97 (May 16, 2018).
[672] *EO Tax Jour.* 2018-155 (Aug. 8, 2018).
[673] *EO Tax Jour.* 2019-217 (Nov. 6, 2019).
[674] Quoted in Gelles, *supra* note 585.

ditions" exist for "widespread abuse."[675] This analysis stated: "There are two categories of concern that some advocates would like to see answered with regulation: the first has to do with the establishment of systems of accountability that look into the transactions of individual funds, and the second is what such a sight line might reveal—for example, overvaluation of noncash contributions, inactivity in disbursement of funds, and transfers of funds from private foundations in an attempt to bypass their payout rates."[676]

Another review of this subject attempted to separate myths from fact. To those who assert that donor-advised funds merely accumulate charitable gifts and are a barrier to direct support of operating charities, this analysis pointed out that "[a] number of sponsoring organizations themselves are operating public charities, offering significant social service and educational programs." In response to the charge that sponsoring organizations do not interact with donors or adequately supervise grants, the review's response was that "philanthropic professionals engage in ongoing conversations with DAF funders to learn about the donors' philanthropic passions and to provide information about grant opportunities and emerging charitable programs" and "adhere to guidelines regarding permissible grants that ensure that such distributions further" charitable objectives. To those who assert that donor-advised funds stymy philanthropic innovations, this review stated that "[m]any DAFs have existed for decades and have been characterized by regular donations as well as charitable grants from such accounts." Regarding the notion that donor-advised funds are "cloaked in anonymity," the review observed that "[s]ome donors prefer grants from DAFs to remain anonymous, but such grants are rare and are based on personal values and legitimate concerns." As to the myth that donor-advised funds divert monies from operating charities, the response was that, "[f]or many mission-based public charities, DAFs provide a ready reserve to sustain charitable activities during times of need."[677]

Community foundations—the entities that launched the donor-advised fund movement[678]—are understandably concerned about proposed "reforms" in this area,

---

[675] McCambridge, *supra* note 588, at 41.

[676] *Id.* As noted, overvaluations of gifted property is a subject that cuts across every mode of charitable giving; it certainly is not confined to gifts to donor-advised funds (see this chapter, pp. 124–125). Private foundations make grants to donor-advised funds for many reasons other than an effort to "bypass" their payout obligation (see Chapter 6, pp. 183–187). In any event, in life, "conditions" for abuse exist everywhere.

[677] Beckwith and Woolf, "Donor-Advised Funds: Separating Myth from Fact," reproduced in the *EO Tax Jour.* (Oct. 19, 2018).

[678] See the introduction to this chapter.

inasmuch as these funds are "vehicle[s] that raise[] billions in charitable donations to provide critical services and solve important problems in communities across the country."[679] From the standpoint of community foundations, donor-advised funds "are not standalone entities, but one important arrow in the quiver to accomplish [their] work."[680] These foundations are "concerned that some of the most vocal critics of DAFs have not worked directly with donors to understand their motivations and behaviors."[681] They issued this plea: "[I]t's important to make sure we are thoughtful and deliberate and that any changes will not bring unintended consequences in the form of decreased charitable giving."[682] Other potential unwanted consequences in this regard are "government overreach, excessive regulation, and bureaucratic waste."[683]

Another consideration in this regard is that the emergence of donor-advised funds at sponsoring organizations such as Fidelity and Schwab has, in the view of one commentator, "made it easier for financial, tax, and legal advisers to talk to their clients about philanthropy—and that is leading to more giving now and in the future."[684] What this observer is saying is that the advent of donor-advised funds has facilitated discussions about charitable giving in the financial planning and estate planning context, often leading to charitable giving arrangements that do not involve use of these funds. He also observed that the availability of donor-advised funds is making donors aware that they can make charitable gifts of property other than money and publicly traded securities, such as privately held stock, real estate, collectibles, and "other complex assets that many charities aren't equipped to handle." This fact is enabling charities to "receive a larger share of a donor's wealth [,] in many cases from the donor's DAF account, without adding the burdens of new administrative expenses."[685]

This commentator also wrote that charities should be doing more to encourage contributions to them from donor-advised funds, noting that this approach "can open the door to even bigger contributions than the nonprofit would have otherwise received." He stated that charitable organizations "should view DAFs as friends,

---

[679] Kridler et al. Analysis.

[680] Id.

[681] Id.

[682] Id

[683] Id. A look at the statutory law and accompanying regulations concerning Type III supporting organizations (see *Tax-Exempt Organizations* § 15.7(g)) results in confirmation of the validity of these fears.

[684] Nopar, "Savvy Nonprofits Can Reap Big Benefits," XXVII *Chron. of Phil.* (No. 2) 29 (Nov. 6, 2014).

[685] Id., at 32.

not enemies," particularly as the number of donor-advised funds increases. He noted that these funds are being established by donors "at many levels of wealth for multiple reasons, including their desire to distribute more of their assets to charities." Nopar concluded that "[e]verybody in the nonprofit world should support any technique that creates more opportunities for charitable giving."[686]

As noted at the outset, critics of donor-advised funds have, so far, dominated the debate over donor-advised funds. This phenomenon has had unfortunate consequences. One of these consequences is an overlooking of the fact that donor-advised funds are one of many charitable giving vehicles, sharing several of the same characteristics (as intermediaries), principally private foundations, supporting organizations, charitable remainder trusts, and endowment funds.[687] Another of these consequences is a general failure of public charities to adequately integrate donor-advised funds into their fundraising program. One of the few analyses of this point observed that the existence of these funds enhances the "charitable conversation between advisers and [donor] clients," helps "donors make wise giving decisions," and facilitates "even bigger contributions than the nonprofit [organizations] would have otherwise received."[688] This analysis concluded: "Everybody in the nonprofit world should support any technique that creates more opportunities for charitable giving."[689]

An analysis of donor-advised fund issues concludes that "[t]here's a strong case to be made that DAFs are a net good for philanthropy, despite their flaws," adding that "[t]hat's not to say there are *no* good changes to be made to DAFs—only that avoiding unintended consequences must be central to any DAF reform."[690]

Another analysis of donor-advised funds posits the amply reasonable assumption that "interest in these giving vehicles will continue, as will debates about how they should be regulated."[691] This report concluded: "Donor-advised funds are here to stay for the foreseeable future."[692]

---

[686] *Id.*

[687] See the text accompanied by *supra* note 605. These vehicles are compared and contrasted in Hopkins, *How To Be a Successful Philanthropist: Avoiding the Legal Pitfalls* (Dorrance Pub. Co.; Pittsburgh, PA: 2018).

[688] Nopar, *supra* note 684, at 32.

[689] *Id.*

[690] Ludwig and Hartmann, "How Much Regulation of Donor-Advised Funds Is Enough?," *Philanthropy Daily* (Sep. 23, 2019), reprinted in *EO Tax Jour.* 2019-187 (Sep. 25, 2019).

[691] Giving USA, "The Data on Donor-Advised Funds: New Insights You Need to Know" (2018), at 36.
[692] *Id.*

CHAPTER SIX:
Six Major Legal Issues

Six major legal issues are percolating in the donor-advised fund realm. They are:

1. Should grants from donor-advised funds continue to be regarded as forms of public support for the grantee public charities?
2. Should charitable pledges made by donors and donor advisors be able to be satisfied by grants from donor-advised funds?
3. Should distributions from donor-advised funds be part of payments enabling donors and donor advisors to attend or participate in charity-sponsored events?
4. Should private foundations be allowed to utilize donor-advised funds in conducting their programs and meeting their mandatory payout requirements?
5. Should donor-advised funds be subject to a mandatory payout requirement?
6. Should donors' charitable deduction for gifts to donor-advised funds be deferred until corresponding grants are made from the funds?

The first four of these legal issues will be addressed in the forthcoming proposed regulations.[693] The fifth and sixth legal issues, the matters of a mandatory payout imposed on donor-advised funds and a delayed charitable contribution deduction, entail law changes requiring action by Congress.[694]

These five legal issues are discussed below, along with existing law on the topics where applicable. On December 15, 2017, the IRS published a notice indicating its thinking, and that of the Treasury Department, on four of these law issues involving

---

[693] See Notice 2017-73, 2017-51 I.R.B. 562.

[694] Each of these six legal issues can, of course, be addressed by Congress. There is no reason, however, to expect legislation on the donor-advised front any time soon. Conceptually, the Department of the Treasury could, by tax regulation, craft a form of DAF payout as an application of the commensurate test (see Chapter 1, pp. 26-27) but there seems little likelihood that Treasury will attempt such a bold move.

donor-advised funds.[695] These discussions are followed by summaries of comments submitted in response to this notice by the Tax Section of the American Bar Association,[696] the National Philanthropic Trust,[697] the Council on Foundations,[698] the Community Foundation Public Awareness Initiative,[699] the American Association of Certified Public Accountants,[700] the New York State Bar Association,[701] and the Fidelity Investments Charitable Gift Fund,[702] along with comments from the author.

LEGAL ISSUE # 1: SHOULD GRANTS FROM DONOR-ADVISED FUNDS CONTINUE TO BE REGARDED AS FORMS OF PUBLIC SUPPORT FOR THE GRANTEE PUBLIC CHARITIES?

One of these issues pertains to the fact that, under present law, a grant from a donor-advised fund can constitute, in its entirety, "public support" for the benefit of the recipient charity. A summary of this existing law follows.

CURRENT LAW

Pursuant to the federal tax law, a tax-exempt charitable organization[703] is either a public charity or a private foundation.[704] Tax-exempt charitable organizations can

---

[695] Notice 2017-73, 2017-51 I.R.B. 562. A straightforward summary of this notice (despite the article's title) is in Schlesinger & Goodman, "Advance Peek at Proposed Regs. for Donor-Advised Funds," 45 *Estate Planning* (No. 8) 45 (Aug. 2018).

[696] Letter from the American Bar Association, Tax Section, to the IRS commenting on Notice 2017-73 (April 19, 2018) (ABA Notice Comments).

[697] Letter from the National Philanthropic Trust to the Department of the Treasury and the IRS commenting on Notice 2017-73 (Mar. 5, 2018) (NPT Notice Comments).

[698] Letter from the Council on Foundations to the IRS commenting on Notice 2017-73 (Mar. 5, 2018) (COF Notice Comments).

[699] Letter from the Community Foundation Public Awareness Initiative to the IRS commenting on Notice 2017-73 (Mar. 5, 2018) (CFPAI Notice Comments). This group consists of 115 community foundations in 45 states.

[700] Letter from the American Association of Certified Public Accountants to the IRS commenting on Notice 2017-73 (July 24, 2019) (AICPA Notice Comments).

[701] Letter from the New York State Bar Association to the Department of the Treasury and the IRS commenting on Notice 2017-73 (Feb. 28, 2018) (NYSBA Notice Comments).

[702] Letter from the Fidelity Investments Charitable Gift Fund to the IRS commenting on Notice 2017-73 (Mar. 2, 2018) (Fidelity Charitable Notice Comments).

[703] That is, an IRC § 501(c)(3) organization.

[704] IRC § 509(a). Exempt charitable entities are presumed to be private foundations; this presumption may be rebutted by a showing that the entity is a public charity (IRC § 509(b)).

qualify as public charities in several ways.[705] Public charities are of three basic types: the institutions, publicly supported charities, and supporting organizations. These institutions are charitable entities such as churches, schools, and hospitals.[706] Supporting organizations are essentially charitable subsidiaries of public charitable organizations.[707]

There are two basic types of publicly supported organizations.[708] The federal tax statutory law defines the types of revenue that is considered public support and the amount of public support that is required to enable a charitable organization to consider itself publicly supported The so-called "service provider" organization has public support primarily in the form of fee-for-service revenue.[709] This type of publicly supported charity is not particularly relevant to this analysis.[710]

The more pertinent type of publicly supported charity is the "donative" organization; here, public support must principally be in the form of contributions and grants.[711] But not all gifts and grants qualify; they must be from the *public*. The amount of a gift or grant generally is public support only if it does not exceed an amount equal to two percent of the total gifts and grants received by the charity during its most recent five years.[712] Generally, the organization must receive at least one-third of its financial support in the form of public gifts and grants.[713]

This body of law requires the donative publicly supported charity to calculate, on an ongoing basis, a public support fraction. Thus, for example, a contribution by an individual is included in full in the denominator of the fraction but is included in the fraction's numerator only to the extent that the contribution amount does not exceed two percent of the amount of the fraction's denominator.[714]

Pursuant to this statutory regime, charities receive *direct contributions* and *indirect contributions*. Most contributions are of the direct type; the donor gives directly to the charity. An indirect contribution (grant) takes place when a donative publicly supported charity makes a grant to another charity, which is either a donative pub-

---

[705] E.g., *Private Foundations*, Chapter 15.

[706] IRC § 509(a)(1), by reference to IRC § 170(b)(1)(A)(i)-(v), (x).

[707] IRC § 509(a)(3).

[708] *Private Foundations* §§ 15.4-15.6.

[709] IRC § 509(a)(2).

[710] Service provider charities can, however, be sponsoring organizations.

[711] IRC §§ 170(b)(1)(A)(vi), 509(a)(1).

[712] Reg. § 1.170A-9(f)(6)(i).

[713] Reg. § 1.170A-9(f)(2).

[714] Reg. § 1.170A-9(f)(6)(i). In making this calculation, contributions made by a donor and by a related person (i.e., a person with a relationship to the donor that is described in IRC § 4946(a)(1)(C)-(G) – the private foundation disqualified person rules) is treated as made by one person (*id.*).

licly supported charity or is attempting to qualify as such. An indirect contribution is not subject to the two percent limitation;[715] that is, this type of grant is public support in its entirety. A donor contributing directly to the grantor charity is considered to be an indirect donor to the grantee charity.

The term *indirect contribution* is not defined in the Internal Revenue Code. Yet, the foregoing definition of the term is generally understood to be its sole definition.[716] Indeed, this definition is the only definition of the term currently in the tax regulations and has been since their inception.[717]

Sponsoring organizations are almost always donative publicly supported charitable organizations.[718] This means that, under existing law, grants from donor-advised funds are, in their entirety, public support when made to another donative publicly supported charity. That is, these grants are not subject to the two-percent limitation.[719]

This law outcome, however, can be abused. This abuse of the donor-advised fund structure (and law) arises where a donor to a donor-advised fund expressly or impliedly designates the charity that is to be the ultimate recipient of the grant. This is a form of "earmarking."

This type of abuse is contemplated by the existing tax regulations.[720] Where this form of earmarking occurs, the donor-advised fund involved is considered to be a mere "conduit." In this instance, the grant is not public support in full. This is because the grant is considered to not be from a true donor-advised fund; the fund is considered to be a "donor-directed fund."[721]

This body of law may be illustrated as follows. M, a national organization for the encouragement of the musical arts, is a donative publicly supported organization. Individual A contributes $5,000 to M. M subsequently makes a $5,000 grant to X, an organization devoted to giving public performances of chamber music. The grant to X is fully includible in the numerator of X's support fraction for the year of receipt.[722]

---

[715] *Id.*; Reg. § 1.170A-9(f)(6)(v).

[716] The *stabilizing canons* offered by Antonin Scalia and Bryan A. Garner include the canon of imputed common-law meaning, which is that a "statute that uses a common-law term, without defining it, adopts its common-law meaning" (*Reading Law: The Interpretation of Legal Texts* 320 (Thomson/West, St. Paul, MN: 2012).

[717] Reg. § 1.170A-9(f)(6)(i).

[718] See Chapter 1, pp. 6-7.

[719] Reg. § 1.170A-9(f)(6)(v).

[720] *Id.*

[721] E.g., New Dynamics Foundation v. United States, 2006-1 U.S.T.C. ¶ 50,286 (U.S. Ct. Fed. Cl. 2006).

[722] Reg. § 1.509(a)-3(j)(3), Example (1).

Individual B gives M a donation of $10,000, requiring that M spend the money for the purpose of supporting organizations devoted to the advancement of contemporary American music. M has complete discretion as to the organizations of the type described to which it will make a grant. M makes a grant of $5,000 each to charity Y and Z. Y and Z may each include one of the $5,000 grants in the numerator of its support fraction. Although the donation to M was conditioned on use of the funds for a particular purpose, M was free to select the ultimate recipient.[723]

N is a national organization for the encouragement of art; it is a donative publicly supported charity. O, a charitable art workshop devoted to training young artists, persuades P, a private foundation, to make a $25,000 grant to N. P is a disqualified person with respect to O. P made the grant to N with the understanding that N would be bound to make a grant to O in the amount of $25,000, in addition to a matching grant of N's funds to O in the sum of $25,000. Only the $25,000 received directly from N is considered a grant from N (and public support in full).[724]

PROPOSAL

Back to the notice that Treasury published. Treasury officials writing the proposed regulations concluded—without publicly disclosing any data in support of it—that this ability to treat grants from donor-advised funds as public support is an abuse that has become too widespread to ignore. The Notice stated that the Treasury Department and the IRS are "aware" that "some" donors and distributee charities "seek to use DAF sponsoring organizations as intermediaries."[725] The Notice added: "Rather than making contributions, which would be subject to the 2 percent public support limitation, directly to charities, these donors make contributions to DAFs maintained by sponsoring organizations and then advise the sponsoring organizations to make distributions from the DAFs to the distributee charities."[726]

They see the practice as a form of "laundering" of grant funds in a nefarious attempt to artificially inflate organizations' amounts of public support. (A charitable

---

[723] Id., Example (2).

[724] Id., Example (3).

[725] The import of this "awareness" is not clear, inasmuch as sponsoring organizations are always intermediaries.

[726] This is a description of a typical gift to a donor-advised fund, followed by exercise of advisory privileges – a practice that may have nothing to do with avoidance of the public support limitations.

organization that cannot meet a public charity test is likely to lapse into private foundation status[727]—an outcome that is usually undesirable in relation to public charity status.) One of these officials was heard to say at a nonprofit law conference that donor-advised funds are being used to help charities "get around" the public support requirement.

Referencing this "potential for abuse," Treasury and the IRS stated in the Notice that they "are considering treating, solely for purposes of determining whether the distributee charity qualifies as publicly supported, a distribution from a DAF as an indirect contribution from the donor (or donors) that funded the DAF rather than as a contribution [grant] from the sponsoring organization." This approach would cause the grant to be subject to the two percent limitation, rather than be public support in its entirety. This treatment, Treasury and IRS wrote, "would better reflect the degree to which the distributee charity receives broad public support from a representative number of persons."[728]

The Notice then stated that it is anticipated that any proposed changes to the tax regulations would provide that a grantee organization, for purposes of determining the amount of public support, "must treat" (1) a sponsoring organization's distribution from a donor-advised fund as coming from the donor (or donors) that funded the advised fund rather than from the sponsoring organization; (2) all anonymous contributions received, including a donor-advised fund distribution for which the sponsoring organization fails to identify the donor that funded the advised fund, as being made by one person; and (3) distributions from a sponsoring organization as public support without limitation only if the sponsoring organization specifies that the distribution is not from a donor-advised fund or states that no donor or donor advisor advised the distribution.

The Treasury Department and the IRS stated that they recognize that a grantee organization may need to obtain additional information from the sponsoring organization in order to determine its amount of public support. It was noted that this additional information would only be needed if the grantee organization intended to treat as distribution from a sponsoring organization as public support.

---

[727] IRC § 508(b). See *Private Foundations* § 1.2.

[728] The very concept of an indirect contribution distorts the extent to which a charity receives broad public support. Apparently, this law change would leave existing law in place where the grantor is not a sponsoring organization, which does not seem fair or logical, and thus would not completely solve the perceived problem.

ISSUES

This dramatic proposed shift in approach by Treasury raises two issues. One, given the fact that the term *indirect contribution* is statutory, does Treasury have the authority to revise the definition of the term by regulation? As noted, the term is not defined in the existing statutory law, which came into being in 1964. It has been defined, however, in the tax regulations in the form summarized above since their origins in 1972. Congress has passed many tax laws, large and small, over the ensuing decades and has never even contemplated overriding today's interpretation of the term *indirect contribution* in the tax regulations. Thus, this definition may be presumed to have congressional imprimatur.[729]

The second issue is whether Treasury has the authority, based on the present-day record, to change the existing definition of the term *indirect contribution*, even by regulation. To be sure, government agencies may change an existing policy. To survive review under the Administrative Procedure Act, by not being arbitrary and capricious,[730] however, a government agency in this position must, as the Supreme Court directed, "provide a reasoned explanation for the change."[731] That is, the agency must at least "display awareness that it is changing position" and "show that there are good reasons for the new policy."[732] As a federal district court stated, "[u]nexplained inconsistencies in agency position are arbitrary and capricious and therefore unlawful."[733]

COMMENTARIES

As to the requirement for a "reasoned explanation" for a change in the public support rule, reference may be made to the observation by the Community Foundation Public Awareness Initiative to the IRS that "there is no showing of evidence that the perceived abuse is so common and widespread as to justify imposing a new rule

---

[729] E.g., Davis v. United States, 495 U.S. 472, 482 (1990).
[730] 5 U.S.C. § 706(2)(A).
[731] Encino Motorcars, LLC v. Navarro, 136 S. Ct. 2117, 2125 (2016).
[732] *Id.* at 2125–2126.
[733] Steele v. United States, 260 F. Supp. 3d 52, 61 (D.D.C. 2017).

creating significant administrative burdens on grantee organizations."[734] Likewise, the American Association of Certified Public Accountants stated to the IRS that use of a "DAF distribution to circumvent public support is likely rare" and that the proposal would "create significant complexity and administrative burden for publicly supported organizations receiving contributions from sponsoring organizations."[735] Similarly, the Tax Section of the American Bar Association wrote to the IRS, observing that "it is not clear to the Section that support from donor advised funds is, in fact, permitting charities that otherwise would be private foundations to be classified as public supported."[736] The Council on Foundations expressed its view that the proposals are "overbroad, administratively burdensome, and will serve to discourage financial support for many public charities."[737] Fidelity Charitable stated that it "do[es] not believe there has been any showing of abuse" and believes that the Department of the Treasury and the IRS are proposing a "baroque system of rules without sufficient cause or analysis."[738]

American Bar Association Tax Section

As to the concern at the Treasury Department and the IRS about use of a donor-advised fund to circumvent the two percent limitation and balloon public support ratios, the Tax Section of the American Bar Association, in its response to the Notice, pointed out the existence of the earmarking rule in the existing tax regulations.[739] The Tax Section stated: "To the extent that a donor makes a contribution to a donor advised fund with the express purpose of advising that such contribution be paid, as a grant, to a charity, the Service, under the existing Treasury Regulations, could deem such grant as having been earmarked by the donor for the charity."

The ABA Tax Section also noted that, "once a donor makes a contribution to a donor advised fund, that donor has relinquished control of the contributed funds, which become the legal property of the sponsoring organization of the donor advised fund." The Section continued: "While a Donor/Advisor may retain advisory privileges over such amounts, the sponsoring organization is under no obligation to heed the Donor/Advisor's advice with respect to a particular recommended

---

[734] CFPAI Notice Comments.
[735] AICPA Notice Comments.
[736] ABA Notice Comments.
[737] COF Notice Comments.
[738] Fidelity Charitable Notice Comments.
[739] ABA Notice Comments.

grantee."[740] Thus: "Should a sponsoring organization, in its diligence process with respect to a grant recommendation, determine that a Donor/Advisor is attempting to utilize his or her donor advised fund to circumvent the 2% Limitation, the sponsoring organization could decline the grant recommendation."

The Tax Section raised another point, rarely taken into account in analyses of donor-advised funds. This is that "[s]ponsoring organizations of donor advised funds include a broad array of entities—such as universities and religious organizations in addition to more traditional sponsoring organizations like community foundations and national donor advised funds." The Section stated that, "as a general matter, we do not see why, absent clear abuse, a donor advised fund's grant to an organization seeking to be classified as publicly supported would be treated differently from a grant from any other public charity." In the Section's view, "requiring public charities to differentiate between support received from many different public charities, including support from donor advised funds and other sources at the same public charity, would be complicated and unwieldy." The Section reiterated its argument: "We believe that compliance with proposed requirements that differentiate support received from sponsoring organizations from support received from different public charities will be extremely complex and burdensome for both donee charities and sponsoring organizations."

The Section further pointed to the fact that there is no evidence that the two percent limitation is being widely subverted. Its comment letter states that "it is not clear to the Section that support from donor advised funds is, in fact, permitting charities that otherwise would be private foundations to be classified as publicly supported" as donative publicly supported charities. It recommended that Treasury and the IRS "consider delaying implementation of any proposed regulations and instead study the issue."

The Section concluded its analysis with a statement of its "understanding" that "one of the underpinnings of Treasury and the Service's concerns with abuse of the 2% Limitation may be that Treasury and the Service perceive that donors to donor advised funds are entitled to a more favorable charitable contribution deduction under section 170 than donors to private foundations."[741] The Section wrote that, if this is the concern, the "regulations proposed in the Notice would not address

---

[740] In the Notice, the Department of the Treasury and the IRS conflated the statutory law's references to *donor, donor advisor,* and *related person* (see Chapter 4, p. 91) to *Donor/Advisor.* That formulation is sometimes followed in this chapter, although the words are not capitalized.

[741] This is odd phraseology; this is not a "perception," it is a fact.

that concern in any meaningful way." The Section noted that, "[e]ven if distributions from a donor advised fund are subject to the 2% Limitation, the donors to such donor advised fund still will be entitled to the more favorable charitable contribution deduction, as sponsoring organizations typically are classified as publicly supported" as a donative publicly supported charity. The Section's concluding thought: "If Treasury and the Service's concern does stem from section 170 charitable contributions deductions, then instead of implementing regulations to address potential abuse of the 2% Limitation, we recommend the development of procedures to ensure that sponsoring organizations exercise appropriate discretion and control over contributions made to donor advised funds."

National Philanthropic Trust

The National Philanthropic Trust agreed that "the use of DAFs to circumvent the public support rules is a potential area of abuse," then observed that the "proposed rules articulated in the Notice are overly broad and reach far beyond what would be necessary to prevent any such abuse."[742]

The Trust stated that it, "like most DAF sponsoring organizations, has procedures in place to prevent such an abusive scenario." In these circumstances, the Trust wrote that it looks to the donor's and donor advisor's relationship to the donee organization, the composition of the board of the donee organization, the list of donors to the donee organization, and whether the donee organization has made attempts to fundraise.

The Trust stated that any rule designed to prevent this type of abusive scenario should be "narrowly tailored," such as confined to situations where a single donor or family controls the board of the donee organization and is its principal supporter, and/or where the organization makes no attempts to fundraise.

Council on Foundations

The Council on Foundations expressed its view that these proposals are "overbroad, administratively burdensome, and will serve to discourage financial support for many public charities."[743] The Council urged Treasury and the IRS to "narrowly tailor any new regulations to be imposed on DAF distributions to address the very particular circumstances that could be viewed as abusive." It proposed a rule that a

---

[742] NPT Notice Comments.
[743] COF Notice Comments.

donor or donor advisor receives a more-than-incidental benefit in situations where the donor and donor advisor makes a contribution of appreciated property to a donor-advised fund and the sponsoring organization in turn (1) distributes the property to a public charity controlled by the donor or a related person and (2) the public charity could not have met the public support test had the contribution been made directly by the donor.

The Council wrote that a rule that would penalize all distributions from a donor-advised fund by imposing the two-percent limitation would "unfairly penalize the many grantee public charities—which would then incur additional administrative costs to collect information needed to properly calculate their public support." This "would be even more difficult if donor information were not available, precluding the public charity grantee from counting the distributions as public support and potentially endangering their public charity status." Similarly, "public charity grantees that have previously demonstrated a history of substantial public support should not be at risk for recharacterization as private foundations simply because of generous DAF distributions without any evidence that a Donor/Advisor is actually receiving any improper benefit if the donor is not related to the grantee." The Council concluded: "The Treasury proposal, which strongly discourages anonymous giving by placing more burden on organizations that receive such gifts, may have a disproportionate [adverse] impact on the charities supported by donors from certain religious backgrounds, which prize anonymous giving."

The Council concluded its comments on this aspect of the Notice by "call[ing] attention to the increased administrative burden such a rule would impose on sponsoring organizations with respect to the new reporting requirements and information to be provided to the grantee organization." Additional administrative expenses, the Council wrote, "for both sponsoring organizations and grantee public charities, result in less funding for charitable activities in communities across the country." The essence of the Council's submission is that "broad, burdensome regulations should not be imposed on all organizations, where a more narrow targeted approach is available."

Community Foundation Public Awareness Initiative

The Community Foundation Public Awareness Initiative submitted to the IRS that "there is no showing of evidence that the perceived abuse is so common and widespread as to justify imposing a new rule creating significant administrative burdens on grantee organizations, the clear majority of which would not be affected by this new requirement."[744]

This submission details the burdens on grantees from donor-advised funds in tracking and tracing the funds in relation to the two-percent cap. It also summarizes the administrative burdens that would be imposed on sponsoring organizations. The Initiative stated that the Treasury position "also belies a view that donor advised funds are improperly controlled by advisors and are not public charities themselves." That view, the Initiative wrote, "disregards the significant oversight and commitment made by DAF sponsors in reviewing and approving grant recommendations." The Initiative concluded: "Grants from DAFs are grants from public charities—and are public support to the grantee[s]—and this should not be changed or eroded by the adoption of the position contemplated by Treasury."

American Institute of Certified Public Accountants

The American Institute of Certified Public Accountants advised the IRS that the positions outlined in the Notice concerning this public support calculation issue would "create significant complexity and administrative burden for publicly supported organizations receiving contributions from sponsoring organizations."[745] The AICPA emphasized the "additional work" for recipient charities, as well as the sponsoring organizations that "will likely receive many requests and will be required to review and revise many procedures." The organization posited that "most" grantee organization would seek the information. It observed that this "look through" approach "seems to ignore that contributions to the sponsoring organization into the DAF are completed contributions and the sponsoring organization has exclusive legal control (and thus oversight) over the assets contributed."

The AICPA is of the view that "using a DAF distribution to circumvent public support is likely rare." Nonetheless, the organization acknowledged the "potential for abuse." It added: "A significant form of this abuse would possibly occur where a controlling donor prefers to structure an organization as a public charity rather than a private foundation, but the donor does not intend to seek broad public support." That observation led the AICPA to recommend that the IRS apply the existing guidance which addresses the abuse of a supporting organization by a donor who may control a supported organization.[746] If this approach were adopted, the AICPA wrote,

---

[744] CFPAI Notice Comments.
[745] AICPA Notice Comments.
[746] Reg. § 1.509(a)-4(f)(5).

if a public charity received a grant from a donor-advised fund that was created or substantially funded by disqualified or other related persons, the public charity would have to look through the grant and report it as being from the donor to the fund.

The AICPA concluded that if the public support tracking change proposed in the Notice was applied to all publicly supported charities that do not have public support issues and have a board of directors broadly representative of the public, the resulting burden would be "excessive." This change to the public support test "would require tracking by donor identification number to provide certainty [that] the recipient organization was aggregating and limiting contributions from the correct donors." By using this existing law, said the AICPA, the Treasury Department and the IRS "could curtail what are likely the most egregious cases of abuse while relieving compliant public charities of excessive administrative burden."

The AICPA also introduced data collection burden and privacy issues in this context, noting the "difficulty in obtaining reliable data on the underlying donor(s) to the DAF unless there is a taxpayer ID number available." Acknowledging that these numbers allow the Treasury and the IRS to trace the specific donors involved, the organization raised the point that "access to this information causes additional privacy and identity theft concerns."

AICPA's response to the Notice included the observation that the Treasury Department has previously removed proposals to obtain donor tax identification numbers.[747] Likewise, it was noted that Congress has removed the possibility of Treasury receiving a donor acknowledgment form.[748] "On numerous occasions," the AICPA wrote, "based upon privacy and identity theft concerns, Treasury has determined [that] the risk of obtaining the information outweighed the benefit (e.g., aggregation of direct and indirect gifts through a DAF, which is legislatively a completed gift)." Additionally, the AICPA stated, "there is difficulty in the ability to match the donors to determine who is an excess contributor."

New York State Bar Association

The New York State Bar Association expressed its view that these proposed "earmarking rules" represent "sound policy."[749] In the view of the Association, the proposal would prevent a "masking" of the amount of public support, "by preventing

---

[747] This is reference to Treasury's withdrawal, on Jan. 7, 2016, of proposed regulations to implement an alternative to existing donor acknowledgment rules (Prop. Reg. § 1.170A-13(f)(18)(i), issued on September 17, 2015, to implement IRC § 170(f)(8)(D))) because of widespread concerns about identity theft.

[748] This is reference to Congress's repeal of IRC § 170(f)(8)(D)) as part of enactment of the Tax Cuts and Jobs Act (Act § 13705).

[749] NYSBA Notice Comments.

an organization from treating as public support amounts received from another public charity that have been given to that charity for the purpose of making a further grant." The Association also observed: "Given the nature of public charities other than DAF sponsoring organizations, the earmarking rules [would] apply in a narrow range of cases."

Fidelity Investments Charitable Gift Fund

Fidelity Charitable wrote that "we do not believe there has been any showing of abuse" with respect to the existing law as to public support calculation and donor-advised fund grants.[750] The Treasury and IRS proposal was characterized by the Fund as "complicated," "unwieldy," "overly burdensome," and "baroque." Fidelity expressed its view that the "interests of the charitable sector would be better served by studying whether there is indeed a problem, the size and scope of any such problem, and other methods of addressing concerns."

Fidelity also made the point that, under existing statutory law, a sponsoring organization is a public charity. The Fund observed that the Notice "cites no authority by which a sponsoring organization's status as a public charity can be disregarded, cites no authority by which grants received by a public charity must be reattributed to donors to the sponsoring organization of donor-advised funds, and cites no authority by which a series of look-through rules and presumptions can instead be applied." Fidelity noted that "many sponsoring organizations, as charitable grant-makers, conduct their own review of potential grant recipients, including the breadth of support for those organizations," adding that that analysis "is best left to the individual sponsoring organization."

Author's Comments

Behold application of the doctrine of administrative convenience! Pursuant to contemplated forthcoming regulations, distributions from donor-advised funds would automatically not be considered forms of public support for distributee charities, irrespective of the degree of discretion and control the fund had over the funds involved. This approach would relieve Treasury and IRS of the obligation to make a determination, or propose rules concerning such a determination, as to whether a donor-advised fund is being operated as a mere conduit or in some other abusive fashion. But that is not the way the law should be.

---

[750] Fidelity Charitable Notice Comments.

The law should be the same as it is now, such as in the context of the deductibility of contributions to U.S. charities that operate to benefit foreign charities. In that setting, there is no deduction if the domestic entity is functioning merely as a conduit of the transferred funds. The IRS has, over the years, been quite adept at making these distinctions.[751]

The IRS should be required to do so in connection with distributions to and from donor-advised funds. The point is that not all distributions from donor-advised funds should be precluded as constituting public support in their entirety. Using the word in the best of senses, a donor-advised fund is always an *intermediary*.

If the Treasury Department cannot display the requisite awareness and showing of "good reasons," the existing law as to the definition of "indirect contribution" must remain in place. This law requires the IRS to examine the operations of donor-advised funds to determine whether they are functioning as a conduit. If they are, they are not operating as donor-advised funds to begin with but rather are donor-directed funds. Fair calculation of charitable organization's public support ratios dictates that the IRS should continue to make this distinction.

This type of analysis is a responsibility from which the IRS should not shirk, by hiding behind the doctrine of administrative convenience to blindly label all grants from donor-advised funds as made by their donors for purposes of the public support rules.

It may be noted that sponsoring organizations are making efforts to prevent abuses in this context. For example, Vanguard Charitable states that it "takes its due diligence process extremely seriously and reserves the right to take appropriate legal action if advisors are discovered to have made an improper grant recommendation or grantees have used grant funds improperly."[752] This sponsoring organization additionally states that "[g]rants from Vanguard Charitable should not be made for the purpose of enabling an organization that is controlled by a [d]isqualified [p]erson to avoid classification as a private non-operating foundation."[753]

The New York State Bar Association, pronouncing the proposed law change as "sound policy," does not explain why this matter of "masking" requires a new rule as to what *indirect contributions* mean, after decades of use of the existing definition. This is particularly the case where, according to the Association, the proposed earmarking rule would "apply in a narrow range of cases."

---

[751] See Chapter 1, pp. 17-21.
[752] Vanguard Charitable, *Policies and guidelines*, at 21.
[753] *Id.* at 22.

BRUCE R. HOPKINS

LEGAL ISSUE # 2: SHOULD CHARITABLE PLEDGES MADE BY DONORS AND DONOR ADVISORS BE ABLE TO BE SATISFIED BY GRANTS FROM DONOR-ADVISED FUNDS?

One of these five issues is whether a donor/advisor should be able to advise a distribution from a donor-advised fund in satisfaction of a donor/advisor's pledge to contribute to a charity.

Existing Law

The federal tax law backdrop as to this issue is that a private foundation's grant or other payment in fulfillment of the legal obligation of a disqualified person ordinarily constitutes an act of self-dealing.[754]

A payment by a third party to a charitable organization that explicitly is made to pay the legally enforceable pledge of a donor is to be treated as a gift from the third party to the donor and then a charitable contribution from the donor to the organization in satisfaction of the pledge.[755]

PROPOSAL

Treasury stated in the Notice that "[m]ost commentators favored allowing distributions from DAFs to fulfill a Donor/Advisor's charitable pledge." Some commentators expressed concern that requiring a sponsoring organization to determine whether such a pledge is "legally binding," under state law, may "unduly complicate charitable giving." These commentators "noted the difficulty inherent in determining whether a commitment identified as a 'pledge' is legally enforceable under state law or merely an indication of charitable intent."

Treasury and the IRS stated that they agree with these commentators. They declared their view that, in the donor-advised fund context, "the determination of whether an individual's charitable pledge is legally binding is best left to the distributee charity, which has knowledge of the facts surrounding the pledge." Accordingly, "to facilitate distributions from DAFs to charities," Treasury and the IRS stated

---

[754] Reg. § 53.4941(d)-2(f)(1).
[755] Rev. Rul. 81-110, 1981-1 C.B. 479.

they are "considering proposed regulations under § 4967 that would, if finalized, provide that distributions from a DAF to a charity will not be considered to result in a more than incidental benefit to a Donor/Advisor under § 4967 merely because the Donor/Advisor has made a charitable pledge to the same charity (regardless of whether the charity treats the distribution as satisfying the pledge), provided that the sponsoring organization makes no reference to the existence of any individual's pledge when making the DAF distribution."

Specifically, said Treasury and the IRS, "it is anticipated that under this approach a distribution from a DAF to a charity to which a Donor/Advisor has made a charitable pledge (whether or not enforceable under local law) will not be considered to result in a more than incidental benefit to the Donor/Advisor" where three requirements are satisfied: (1) the sponsoring organization makes no reference to the existence of a charitable pledge when making the distribution from a donor-advised fund; (2) no donor/advisor receives, directly or indirectly, any other benefit that is more than incidental on account of the distribution; and (3) a donor/advisor does not attempt to claim a federal income tax charitable contribution deduction with respect to the distribution, even if the distributee charity erroneously sends the Donor/Advisor a written acknowledgment[756] with respect to the distribution from the donor-advised fund.

Treasury and the IRS made it clear that this "special rule" regarding charitable pledges would only apply in the donor-advised fund context. The basis for this distinction is that the "relationship between a private foundation and its disqualified persons typically is much closer than the relationship between a DAF sponsoring organization and its Donor/Advisors."

COMMENTARIES

American Bar Association Tax Section

The ABA Tax Section stated that it "welcome[s]" the regulations proposed on this point in the Notice.[757] These regulations, wrote the Section, "will eliminate the need for Donor/Advisors and sponsoring organizations to answer the difficult legal question of whether a pledge is binding, will encourage grantmaking by sponsoring organizations and will decrease administrative costs."

---

[756] IRC § 170(f)(8). See *Charitable Giving* § 21.3.
[757] ABA Notice Comments.

The Section offered five refinements to this proposed rule. First, it recommended that the proposal that the sponsoring organization make no reference to the existence of a charitable pledge be abandoned, noting that this "formalistic requirement" does not appear to "address any substantive concern as to the character of the pledge." Second, it noted the need to amend the excess benefit transaction regulations to make it clear that fulfillment of a pledge will not be treated as an excess benefit transaction.[758] Third, the Section stated that, if this reference to a pledge is required, guidance is requested as to what will constitute a "reference" to a charitable pledge, with that guidance "preferably . . . limited to direct references." Fourth, the Section questioned the necessity of a reiteration of a prohibition on additional benefits, adding that if some form of acknowledgement is deemed necessary, it recommended requiring either (1) sponsoring organizations to obtain an acknowledgement from the donor/advisor or (2) donor-advised fund grantees to acknowledge this point in any appropriate material (including grant agreements, transmittal letters, or donor manuals) or on their websites. Fifth, it questioned the proposed rule about an inappropriate claiming of a charitable deduction, noting that that fact "should not affect [the] analysis of whether the fulfillment of a charitable pledge by a sponsoring organization is considered a more than incidental benefit," adding that if such a rule is considered necessary it should be added to the charitable contribution deduction regulations. As to this last point, the Tax Section also observed that "there is little that a sponsoring organization can do to police the actions of grantee organizations that may send acknowledgement letters to Donor/Advisors who have made charitable pledges, or Donor/Advisors who use such letters to claim charitable deductions."

National Philanthropic Trust

The National Philanthropic Trust agreed with the Treasury's and IRS's positions as to pledges, except for the proposed rule that, to avoid treatment as a more-than-incidental benefit, the sponsoring organization must not make any reference to the existence of any pledge when making the distribution from the donor-advised fund.[759] The Trust expressed its view that this proposed rule amounts to a "don't ask, don't tell" policy, "which would be difficult to administer and fraught with potential pitfalls." Under such a rule, the Trust noted, "it is unclear what would be the

[758] See *Tax-Exempt Organizations* § 21.4(a).
[759] NPT Notice Comments.

consequences of a DAF sponsor's actual knowledge of the existence of a pledge or even of the suspicion of the existence of a pledge." "It is also unclear," the Trust wrote, "what amounts to a 'reference'—would the inclusion of a Donor/Advisor's account number with the grantee charity constitute such a reference?"

The Trust concluded that "[d]istributions from a DAF in fulfillment of a Donor/Advisor's pledge should not be considered to result in a more than incidental benefit to a Donor/Advisor," adding that the "requirement that the DAF sponsor not reference the existence of any pledge is unnecessary to support this conclusion."

Council on Foundations

The Council on Foundations stated that it is "generally pleased with the recognition that it is often difficult for a sponsoring organization to differentiate between a charitable pledge and a mere expression of charitable intent and appreciates the approach that would leave this determination to the grantee charity rather than to the sponsoring organization."[760] In addition, the Council wrote that it "appreciate[s] the recognition of the significant difference between the relationship an independently-managed, sponsoring organization shares with its many DAF donors and the relationship between a private foundation and its substantial contributors, who are often managers of the private foundation as well."

Thus, the Council is supportive of proposed regulations "that would provide certainty to sponsoring organizations that DAF distributions will not result in a more than incidental benefit to the Donor/Advisor provided certain requirements are satisfied." Nonetheless, the organization requested that the forthcoming proposed regulations "confirm that the sponsoring organization does not have any affirmative obligation to determine whether the Donor/Advisor has received any other benefit as a result of the DAF distribution (requirement 2) or that the Donor/Advisor has not attempted to claim a second charitable contribution deduction as a result of the distribution (requirement 3)." In the alternative, the Council added, the proposed regulations "should provide specific guidance regarding statements or information the sponsoring organization must receive from the Donor/Advisor and/or the grantee organization in order to satisfy the three safe harbor requirements."

---

[760] COF Notice Comments.

Community Foundations Public Awareness Initiative

The Community Foundations Public Awareness Initiative "strongly support[ed] the thrust" of the proposed rule in the Notice concerning pledges—with "one suggested modification" (actually, two). It stated that "[d]etermining whether a pledge is legally binding rather than merely indicative of a donor advisor's charitable intent is a virtually impossible task for most" community foundations. This determination, it was said, "turns on facts and circumstances often unavailable to [community foundation] staff or even to the donor" and "requiring an analysis of legal enforceability requires knowledge of state law potentially beyond the capacity of [community foundation] staff, and the application of laws lacking bright lines tests." Moreover, the Initiative questioned the concept of "pushing" this determination "down" to the grantee organization, writing that that approach "perpetuates the conundrum." It also questioned the merits of the "don't-ask-don't-tell safe harbor," which "impedes transparency and works counter to the culture of accountability which benefits the [nonprofit] sector."

Thus, the Initiative's recommendation was a regulation "explicitly permitting the pledge of a donor advisor to be paid by distribution from a DAF without regard to the enforceability of the pledge or whether the sponsoring organization references or knows of the pledge." The Initiative added: "Regulatory clarity permitting distributions from DAFs to satisfy pledges will increase the already significant distributions from DAFs to charitable organizations throughout the United States."

American Institute of Certified Public Accountants

The AICPA stated: "Other than clarification on the application of the law between the use of the terms incidental and insubstantial," the organization "agrees with the conclusion of Treasury and the IRS in allowing the recipient charity to determine if a pledge is legally binding and whether the donation fulfills the pledge."[761]

The AICPA added that the "proposed guidance relieves the burden on the sponsoring organization for a legal determination of a contractual obligation while promoting the distribution of funds to public charities and ultimately the community at large."

New York State Bar Association

The New York State Bar Association believes that distributions from donor-advised funds to satisfy donor/advisors' legally enforceable pledges to make contributions

---

[761] AICPA Notice Comments.

174

to charity should be considered to confer a more-than-incidental benefit on the donor/advisors, largely because that is the rule in the private foundation context.[762] The organization did, however, propose a refinement, which is that if a donor/advisor represented to the sponsoring organization that the recommendation was not in satisfaction of a charitable pledge there would not be a penalty.

The Association wrote that the Treasury's position "appears" motivated by "practical concerns associated with the difficulty for sponsoring organizations to differentiate between a legally enforceable pledge by an individual to a third-party charity and a mere expression of charitable intent."[763] The organization expressed its "sympathy" with this dilemma but rejected the notion in favor of its proposed refinement.

Fidelity Investments Charitable Gift Fund

Fidelity Charitable "welcome[d] the outcome reached" as to this matter of pledges, "which has been an area of confusion and difficulty for donors, donor-advised funds, and recipient charities alike."[764] Having said that, the Fund noted that the second and third proposed requirements stated in the Notice "merely restate existing requirements in connection with any grant from a donor-advised fund" and "suggest[ed] that their iteration here confuses rather than clarifies the proper application of the rules." Moreover, wrote Fidelity Charitable, the first condition "only injects uncertainty and confusion." Thus, the Fund "suggest[ed] that [the] three stated conditions be stricken," so that the rule would simply be that the donor and distributee charity are responsible for determining whether a particular grant would constitute relief of an indebtedness of the donor.

As an alternative, Fidelity suggested that distributee charities provide sponsoring organizations with a certification, which could state that pledges received from the charity's donors are "never legally binding" or that the distributee charity will not accept a grant from the sponsoring organization that would satisfy a legally binding pledge.

Author's Comments

Contrast what is being proposed with the rule in the private foundation context that a grant made in fulfillment of the legal obligation of a disqualified person constitutes an act of self-dealing. With foundations, there is no expressed concern about "mere indications of charitable intent."

---

[762] NYSBA Notice Comments.
[763] This is not a matter of "appearances"; it is fact!
[764] Fidelity Charitable Notice Comments.

This distinction is justified on the rationale that the "relationship between a private foundation and its disqualified persons typically is much closer than the relationship between a DAF sponsoring organization and its Donor/Advisors." But not always. Originally, the IRS's biggest rap against donor-advised funds was that they are merely vehicles to use in circumventing the private foundation rules. Today, philanthropists of modest means utilize donor-advised funds in lieu of private foundations—and can be quite attached to them.

As to Fidelity Charitable's comments, it would be difficult (if not impossible) for a charity to "certify" to a third party that the pledges from its donors are "never" legally binding. Also, why would a public charity, knowing that a donor wanted to satisfy the donor's pledge by means of a donor-advised fund grant and knowing that such a grant would not trigger any federal tax law penalties, put itself in the position of not accepting the grant (and probably highly annoying the donor)? If the pledge was legally binding, the charity would still have to record it as such on its financial statements. Would the charity still be expected to try to enforce the pledge?

LEGAL ISSUE # 3: SHOULD DISTRIBUTIONS FROM DONOR-ADVISED FUNDS BE PART OF PAYMENTS ENABLING DONORS AND DONOR ADVISORS TO ATTEND OR PARTICIPATE IN CHARITY-SPONSORED EVENTS?

Treasury and the IRS stated, in the Notice, that guidance had been requested as to whether a distribution from a donor-advised fund to a charitable organization that enables a donor/advisor to attend or participate in an event results in the donor or other person receiving a more-than-incidental benefit.

EXISTING LAW

In the private foundation setting, self-dealing was found when a joint purchase of benefit tickets was made by a sharing of the ticket cost. The private foundation paid the deductible, or charitable contribution, portion of the ticket; the disqualified person paid that part of the ticket price allocable to the fair market value of the dinner, entertainment, and other benefits provided to contributors in connection with the fundraising event.

The IRS ruled that self-dealing occurred because the benefits were more than tenuous or incidental.[765] To be able to attend the benefit event, foundation representatives would have been required to individually pay the full amount of the ticket price. Thus, the IRS reasoned, they reaped direct economic benefit to the extent that the foundation paid a portion of the ticket price. (The nature of the charity-sponsored event is not discussed in the ruling. Some private foundations are of the view that it is appropriate for their managers to attend fundraising events as representatives of the foundation to evidence their support (with private benefit not occurring).)

A private foundation paid its trustee's church dues, thereby enabling the trustee to maintain his membership in and otherwise participate in the religious activities of the congregation. The dues payment was ruled to constitute self-dealing, with the IRS concluding that the foundation's payment of the dues "result[ed] in a direct economic benefit to the disqualified person because that person would have been expected to pay the membership dues has they not been paid by the foundation."[766]

PROPOSAL

Treasury and the IRS stated, in the Notice, that they currently agreed that the "relief of the Donor/Advisor's obligation to pay the full price of a ticket to a charity-sponsored event can be considered a direct benefit to the Donor/Advisor that is more than incidental." Therefore, the Notice stated that proposed regulations would, if finalized, provide that a distribution from a donor-advised fund pursuant to the advice of a Donor/Advisor that "subsidizes" the Donor/Advisor's attendance or participation in a charity-sponsored event confers on the Donor/Advisor a more-than-insubstantial benefit.

Treasury and the IRS added that they do not currently agree that a distribution made by a sponsoring organization from a donor-advised fund to a charity on the advice of a donor/advisor should be analyzed the same as a hypothetical, direct contribution by the Donor/Advisor to the charity. That is, a "Donor/Advisor who wishes to receive goods or services (such as tickets to an event) offered by a charity in exchange for a contribution of a specified amount can make the contributions directly, without the involvement of a DAF."

---

[765] Priv. Ltr. Rul. 9021066 (Mar. 1, 1990).
[766] Rev. Rul. 77-160, 1977-1 C.B. 351.

Treasury and the IRS, in the Notice, recognized that a similar issue arises if a sponsoring organization makes a distribution from a donor-advised fund to a charity to pay, on behalf of a donor/advisor, the deductible portion of a membership fee charged by the charity, and the donor/advisor separately pays the nondeductible portion of the fee. Thus, Treasury and the IRS expressed their anticipation that the same analysis would apply to a case where the donor/advisor receives these types of membership benefits, so that the sponsoring organization cannot pay the deductible portion of the membership fee without conferring more than an incidental benefit to the donor/advisor.

COMMENTARIES

American Bar Association Tax Section

As the American Bar Association Tax Section observed, the issue concerns a situation where an amount is distributed from a donor-advised fund to purchase tickets to a charity event, with the payment bifurcated, so that the amount from the donor-advised fund does not exceed the portion of the ticket cost that would be deductible as a charitable gift if paid by the donor/advisor directly and the donor/advisor separately pays the nondeductible portion.[767]

The Tax Section offered this example. A ticket to a charity-sponsored event costs $1,000. The fair market value of the ticket (the value of the goods and/or services to be provided) is $100. Some commentators argued that an arrangement where the donor/advisor pays the charity the $100 and the donor-advised fund involved, advised by the donor/advisor distributes $900 to the charity in respect of the remaining cost of the ticket does not violate the donor-advised fund rules because the tax law outcome would be the same as if the donor/advisor paid the $1,000 cost of the ticket and claimed a $900 charitable deduction. As noted, the Treasury and the IRS disagree with this interpretation of the law.

The ABA Tax Section took the position of these commentators, noting that, as reflected in the statute's legislative history, Congress intended that application of the more-than-incidental-benefit standard turns on whether a donor/advisor making a direct payment to a charity would have received a benefit reducing or eliminating a charitable contribution deduction to which the donor/advisor otherwise would

[767] ABA Notice Comments.

have been entitled. This legislative history, the Tax Section stated, supports bifurcation in this context "because the portion of a bifurcated distribution from a donor advised fund would be fully deductible if paid directly by a Donor/Advisor." The Section recommended that Treasury and the IRS rely on this legislative history and not adopt the position taken on this topic in the Notice.

National Philanthropic Trust

The National Philanthropic Trust disagreed with the Treasury and IRS position on bifurcated payments to events.[768] The Trust is of the view that the payment by a donor-advised fund of the tax-deductible portion of a ticket to a charity-sponsored event or a membership fee should not constitute a more-than-incidental benefit to a donor/advisor. It noted that if the donor/advisor paid for the ticket or fee, the person would be entitled to a charitable contribution deduction only for the deductible portion of the ticket. The donor/advisor, wrote the Trust, "would not receive any benefit in connection with the payment of the tax deductible portion of a ticket or membership fee from a DAF that would reduce or eliminate a charitable contribution deduction if received as part of the contribution to the sponsoring organization."

Council on Foundations

The Council on Foundations advised the IRS that, since passage of the Pension Protection Act, it has, taking a "conservative approach," advised its membership to not engage in these bifurcation practices.[769] Nonetheless, the Council recognized that these practices persist. The organization wrote that, "[s]ince the donor pays the full fair market value for any benefit received from the charity, it is difficult to imagine what additional benefit the donor receives from the DAF distribution." Therefore, the Council stated, "because maximizing attendance at fundraising events is critical for many grantee charities . . ., and because disallowing contributions from DAFs often reduces attendance, the Council believes that prohibiting all such distributions would be a mistake."

The Council wrote that if there are "particular situations in which donors are deriving inappropriate benefits, it would be extremely helpful to have from Treasury additional guidance, and examples of when a DAF distribution would be permitted

---

[768] NPT Notice Comments.
[769] COF Notice Comments.

versus when it would result in too much benefit to a donor." "Safe harbor" guidance regarding what is considered a more-than-incidental benefit with respect to donor-advised fund distributions has, the Council stated, "long been sought by the field, and the Council is hopeful that this opportunity will result in such guidance."

As a fallback position, the Council wrote that, "[i]f, after more than a decade of tacit agreement with a range of practices[,] the IRS now wants to adopt a conservative position in regulations," it should do so only prospectively.

Community Foundations Public Awareness Initiative

The Community Foundations Public Awareness Initiative requested that Treasury and the IRS reconsider their position on this bifurcation issue.[770] It asked that proposed regulations be issued "mirror[ing] the law already in place" that allows for the division of such payments. It suggested that legislative history of the donor-advised fund rules shows that bifurcation is to be allowed and noted that the statutory law does not prohibit bifurcated payments.

The Initiative also noted that the typical sponsoring organization knows the tax law and has professional staff that "serv[es] as a backstop against abuse," in contrast with individuals who are less likely to properly calculate the appropriate charitable deduction. Thus, it wrote, "the involvement of a DAF sponsoring organization can increase the likelihood of the proper bifurcation being made between charitable and noncharitable portions of a total payment for an event or membership," adding that this approach "will facilitate more money coming out of DAFs, which is consistent with public policy objectives."

Further, the Initiative stated that it is "unaware of any policy rationale for the notion that paying the charitable portion of an event from a DAF is inherently abusive, whereas it is not abusive when an individual taxpayer makes such a payment directly to a charity." This matter of using the charitable portion of the payment to get the donor "in the door" should, the Initiative asserted, be regarded as a "pure recognition benefit, which the IRS already has recognized as having no financial value."

American Institute of Certified Public Accountants

The AICPA is of the view that "[p]rohibiting bifurcation is inappropriate for several reasons."[771] One reason given for this position is the creation of "additional com-

---

[770] CFPAI Notice Comments.
[771] AICPA Notice Comments.

plexity for individuals and companies as they undertake charitable gift planning during a time when it is otherwise understood there is a goal of simplifying overall tax compliance/administration and encouraging continued support of the charitable community." Another is that there is the same tax law outcome with bifurcation and direct charitable giving.

The AICPA also noted that "[m]any charities' budgets depend significantly on events-based fundraising and their overall goals include both dollars raised and actual event attendance (often attendance at such a function is a significant part of donor engagement and relationship building)." The organization stated that, "[i]f potential donors cannot fund an otherwise charitable contribution (i.e., the amount in excess of any quid-pro quo determination) from funds they have already irrevocably donated to charity through a DAF, the added cost of supporting the event through a separate contribution pool provides another reason for them to deny support." The AICPA added: "Alternatively, they will reject the offer of tickets provided in order to comply with the tax law, causing a negative financial impact on the charity due to smaller event attendance." Overall, the AICPA concluded, "there are substantial benefits to organizations having donors attend various charity events," with these benefits "provid[ing] an incentive to allow the use of funds currently held in DAFs to be used for the charitable portion of these events if these funds are transferred out of the DAFs and into the charitable sector."

New York State Bar Association

The New York State Bar Association supports the Treasury and IRS position that the bifurcation arrangement in connection with charity-sponsored events causes donor/advisors to receive a more-than-incidental benefit.[772] The Association's view is that these grants from donor-advised funds "enable" the donor-advisor to receive the inappropriate benefit.

The Association first observed that, where the donor-advised fund funded the entire amount of the contribution, the benefit received by the donor-advisor is the monetary value of the benefit assigned by the recipient charity. That is true; that also is not the issue. The Association then stated that the "better answer" in the bifurcation context is the same because it follows the law in the private foundation self-dealing setting. The Association added, however, that a resulting benefit that has no monetary value should not be considered as giving rise to a more-than-incidental benefit (analogizing to gifts generating naming rights to a building).

---

[772] NYSBA Notice Comments.

Fidelity Charitable

Fidelity Charitable believes that the Treasury's and the IRS's position as to this matter of bifurcation is "wrong."[773] Fidelity essentially argued that the standard to be applied in this context is not that of the rigorous private foundation self-dealing rules but rather the statutory donor-advised fund rules and the excess benefit transactions rules, the former set of rules with the more-than-incidental benefit test. That is, assuming the two amounts in the bifurcation arrangement are properly calculated,[774] "there is no place for the invention of any additional" element of benefit to the donor.

The Fund also noted that "there is no showing, nor even a reasonable assertion in the Notice, that there are any abuses that would be presented by" a rule permitting a "split" or "bifurcated" grant from a donor-advised fund.

Author's Comments

The notice and the above commentaries completely miss one of the principal aspects of this topic. They treat all charity-sponsored events alike. This is not reflective of the real world.

The notice does not, and thus presumably the proposed regulations will not, differentiate between the flashy mega-galas, with fabulous entertainment, ample drink, and excellent food (where patrons really want to attend) and events with nothing more than the proverbial rubber chicken and boring speeches (where just about everyone would just as soon be elsewhere). A donor/advisor may accede to be in attendance at an event to support a charity and help provide dutiful applause as awards are being handed out, even though that individual really did not want to go. There is no private benefit being provided on these occasions. If, on the other hand, a donor/advisor truly wants to attend an event, such as because of the nature of the entertainment or the popularity of the speaker, attendance at the event in accordance with a bifurcated payment arrangement may provide a more-than-incidental benefit to the donor/advisor. But, apparently, Treasury and the IRS does not want to make these distinctions either.

---

[773] Fidelity Charitable Notice Comments.
[774] In the Treasury/IRS illustration, the $100 and $900 amounts.

LEGAL ISSUE # 4: SHOULD PRIVATE FOUNDATIONS BE ALLOWED TO UTILIZE DONOR-ADVISED FUNDS

IN CONDUCTING THEIR PROGRAMS AND MEETING THEIR MANDATORY PAYOUT REQUIREMENT?

The Treasury Department and the IRS, as part of the Notice, requested comments with respect to (1) how private foundations use donor-advised funds in support of their purposes and (2) whether, consistent with the private foundation mandatory payout rules, a transfer of funds by a private foundation to a donor-advised fund should be treated as a qualifying distribution only if the sponsoring organization agrees to distribute the funds for charitable purposes (or to transfer the funds to its general fund) within a certain timeframe.

Of particular concern in this regard is the ability of private foundations to, under current law, satisfy their payout requirement by making grants to donor-advised funds.[775] The private foundation community made its case for foundations' use of donor-advised funds in connection with their charitable undertakings.

COMMENTARIES

Philanthropy Roundtable
The Philanthropy Roundtable submitted comments in the form of examples that "demonstrate how important donor advised funds can be for private foundations in sustaining our nation's diverse, abundant and vibrant civil society."[776] Donor-advised funds are, wrote the Roundtable, a "valuable tool for private foundations, which use them for a wide variety of purposes consistent with their purposes and federal law."

Here are some of the illustrations:

SAFETY AND SECURITY

A private foundation makes grants to a donor-advised fund to support charities in foreign countries where the foundation has staff working in the country, accompa-

---

[775] See *Private Foundations*, Chapter 6.
[776] Letter from the Philanthropy Roundtable to the Department of the Treasury and the IRS commenting on Notice 2017-73 (Mar. 5, 2018).

nied by their families. Many of these countries are unstable and dangerous; the lives of the foundation's staff and family members would be in jeopardy if this foundation made the grants directly to the charities. This use of a donor-advised fund keeps the identity of the foundation private and protects the safety and well-being of those connected to it.

A foundation makes grants to a donor-advised fund to support organizations that oppose terrorism, some of which have fatwas against them. This grantmaking protects the foundation's trustees from the threat of violence.

COLLABORATION AMONG FOUNDATIONS

A foundation utilizes a donor-advised fund at a community foundation as part of a collaborative effort with several other foundations that also make grants to the fund to jointly fund local economic development projects. This donor-advised fund is a vehicle that can accept and manage grants from multiple sources without the need for establishing an additional management structure for the collaboration.

A foundation makes grants to donor-advised funds at community foundations in order to participate in multi-foundation collaborative funding efforts, which it finds more efficient than coordinating direct grants by the participating foundations. This approach also allows grantees to have a single entity to which to report.

SUPPORT OF LOCAL PROJECTS

A foundation makes grants to a donor-advised fund at a community foundation in a geographic region as to which the foundation lacks significant local knowledge. This grantmaking allows the foundation to access the local knowledge and experience of the community foundation's staff.

A foundation supports, in collaboration with other foundations, a project collecting data about city and county governments. All of these foundations fund this project at a community foundation.

FUNDING OUTSIDE NORMAL AREAS

A foundation uses a donor-advised fund when it supports organizations and projects outside of its typical areas of grantmaking.

A foundation normally does not provide support for fundraising events. The foundation decided to make a one-time exception, funding a major fundraising event for a charity. By granting to a donor-advised fund and recommending a grant to the charity, the foundation avoided sending a signal to other charities that might encourage them to seek a similar funding exception.

A foundation allows its board members to make discretionary grants. By keeping these gifts private by use of a donor-advised fund, unsolicited proposals from similar organizations, that might otherwise waste time and effort, are reduced.

A foundation allocates annual grants to a donor-advised fund for innovative programs that are outside the foundation's normal grantmaking procedures. The foundation established a donor-advised fund to be paid out over three years to help drive these programs.

ALIGN FUNDING WITH PROGRAM SCHEDULE

A foundation made a grant to a donor-advised fund to support a large capital campaign commitment to a university. The foundation wanted to fund the commitment in a year where its investments performed well, then distribute the funds over several years as elements of the project are completed and the grant contingencies are met.

A foundation makes grants to donor-advised funds at community foundations because this approach enables the foundation to make distribution decisions with respect to projects based on the projects' timeline and achievements rather than be constrained by the annual distribution requirement.

BRUCE R. HOPKINS

MAXIMIZE FUNDING AND EFFICIENCY

A foundation uses a donor-advised fund to make international grants to foreign charities. This is seen as a more efficient use of charitable funds inasmuch as the fees are nominal.

A foundation supports programming at a university's law school that provides training and professional development for federal judges. The organization providing the programming will apply for recognition of exempt status but has yet to do so. The foundation makes grants to a donor-advised fund for this funding, finding this approach more efficient and less costly than making expenditure responsibility grants.

A foundation used donor-advised fund to support a consumer education project sponsored by a tax-exempt business league. The foundation utilized this approach because a new organization that is administering this project has yet to receive its determination that it is a charitable organization. Again, this avenue of funding was used to avoid more costly and less efficient expenditure responsibility grants.

INSTILL FAMILY GIVING

A family with a private foundation uses a donor-advised fund to encourage the next generation to be more philanthropic. The family created the fund, with their children as advisors, to provide the children with a giving vehicle. Due to the children's busy lives, this donor-advised fund turned out to be an ideal charitable giving entity, enabling the children to learn about funding philanthropy and making an impact, in advance of involving them directly in the management of the foundation.

A foundation terminated and distributed its assets to a donor-advised fund to bring multiple generations of family members into the grantmaking process, and document and create the vision for the family's legacy in philanthropy in perpetuity, without the continuing administrative burden of the foundation. This donor-advised fund will become an endowed fund that distributes income each year to causes the family members champion.

A foundation uses a donor-advised fund during times of economic downturn to maintain granting levels.

186

A foundation created a donor-advised fund to create an endowment for an impact investment fund at a university's business school. This investment fund allows students to make investments and learn from the experience.

A foundation allows its board members to make discretionary grants to a donor-advised fund as to which the foundation is the advisor. By keeping these grants separate from the foundation's general accounts, use of this fund makes accounting easier because the discretionary grant ledger is managed by the sponsoring organization with respect to the fund.

A foundation allows board members to make discretionary grants, utilizing the due diligence screening capacity of a donor-advised fund sponsor to ensure that the grantees are qualified and have a mission that is aligned with that of the foundation.

American Bar Association Tax Section

The Tax Section of the ABA provided Treasury and the IRS with a summary of several ways in which private foundations may use donor-advised funds in furtherance of their purposes.[777] One of these ways is in connection with foundations' grant-making programs, where a sponsoring organization may be better positioned than individual private foundations to engage in appropriate due diligence with respect to potential grantees. A comparable use is in connection with grants to foreign organizations, where a large sponsoring organization is likely to have greater experience with the expenditure responsibility requirements than a small private foundation.

The Tax Section noted that sponsoring organization may have in place better infrastructure than smaller foundations, creating cost savings and efficiency in the grantmaking process. An example was provided of a small private foundation that may elect to make an annual grant to a donor-advised fund and thereafter advise as to distribution of the grant funds to multiple public charities. This practice was said to save the private foundation the "administrative burden of itself issuing multiple checks and grant award letters to such charities."

The Tax Section also observed that a private foundation may terminate into a donor-advised fund. That is, a private foundation that distributes all its net assets to a donor-advised fund at a sponsoring organization that has been in existence for a period of at least 60 calendar months may, after the distribution, terminate without incurring a termination tax.[778] Terminating a private foundation into a donor-ad-

---

[777] ABA Notice Comments.
[778] IRC § 507(b)(1)(A)). See *Private Foundations* § 13.3.

vised fund can result in lower administrative costs, because of absence of requirements to file an annual information return, adhere to recordkeeping requirements, and make state-level filings. In the family foundation context, where division of the foundation is necessitated, an alternative is establishment of two or more donor-advised funds at a sponsoring organization, with different family members named as donor advisors. Terminations of this nature, because of a decrease in administrative costs, is likely to result in more money used for charitable purposes.

In the Tax Section's view, proposals to impose a time limitation as to the subsequent distribution of foundation grants (qualifying distributions) to donor-advised funds are unnecessary. Imposition of limitations of this nature "risks harming what can be effective and useful collaborations between private foundations and donor advised funds."

Also, the Tax Section opposed the idea of excluding grants from private foundations to donor-advised funds from the definition of qualifying distributions, on the ground that law change would place "unneeded restrictions" on private foundations. This type of exclusion, the Section wrote, "could both increase administrative costs for private foundations and, potentially, decrease regulatory compliance by private foundations that otherwise rely on donor advised funds for [advancement of their charitable] purposes."

National Philanthropic Trust

The National Philanthropic Trust stated its view that "any rule regarding the treatment of private foundation transfers to DAFs should be tailored and should focus on the specific scenarios of concern."[779] The NPT observed that "[t]here are many legitimate uses of DAFs by private foundations, which should not require distribution of the funds transferred to DAFs within a specified period of time."

The NPT stated that private foundations use donor-advised funds in support of their purposes in a "number of effective and permissible ways." All illustrations, the Trust wrote that private foundations "have used DAFs and NPT to fund collaborative funding projects (i.e., projects funded by multiple foundations), to make anonymous grants in support of their charitable purposes, and to fund charitable projects that may be outside the clear scope of their missions." The NPT said that it also has had several private foundations "conclude that a DAF would be a more efficient vehicle for carrying out the foundation's mission"; in each of these instances,

---

[779] NPT Notice Comments.

the foundation board decided to terminate the foundation and distribute its assets to a donor-advised fund, which is to be used to carry out the foundation's mission.

Council on Foundations

"Recognizing the value of relationships between community foundations and private foundations," the Council on Foundations combined membership asked the Treasury Department and the IRS to consider the following examples of "successful collaboration" and "avoid any regulations that would discourage private foundations from utilizing the resources at community foundations."[780]

A private family foundation is developing a program designed to support community efforts and charitable causes in all "company communities," namely, towns where the family had owned businesses years ago. To efficiently facilitate this charitable program, the private foundation established two donor-advised funds at a community foundation, with each intended to focus its grantmaking activities in one of these communities.

As is common at many community foundations, one of the foundation's board members has other philanthropic interests, including an active private foundation. While the board member is not interested in terminating the private foundation into a donor-advised fund, he is interested in building the assets of, and providing support for, the operations and programs of the community foundation. The board member decides to establish a donor-advised fund with a grant from the private foundation to support the community foundation's grantmaking and administrative costs.

A private foundation with limited staff and research capabilities established a one-million dollar donor-advised fund at a community foundation. The private foundation looks to the community foundation to help it make "smarter grants" with greater impact. The private foundation partnered with the community foundation in the most recent community grants round, helping to make several grants possible in counties that previously did not receive the same level of funds.

As an incentive to serve on a private foundation's board, instead of paying compensation to its trustees, a private foundation may create a donor-advised fund for each trustee to advise, designating the trustee as the donor advisor. This approach ensures that these trustees will not receive impermissible benefits as a consequence of fund distributions because the community foundation must approve all grant rec-

---

[780] COF Notice Comments.

ommendations and conduct due diligence. Further, these funds are remaining in the charitable sector rather than being paid to private individuals.

The Council also reported that it occasionally sees private foundation-established donor-advised funds used to show appreciation for CEOs retiring from private foundations. While there is no private benefit or private inurement in any of these instances, the advisory privileges associated with a donor-advised fund may feel like a meaningful "gift" that allows the trustee or retiring executive to be active philanthropically.

Community Foundation Public Awareness Initiative

The Community Foundation Public Awareness Initiative observed that donor-advised funds "have become a vitally important philanthropic tool for [community foundations], their donors, and nonprofit organizations in our communities."[781] It "support[s] changes that will open up more opportunities for charitable giving" and it "oppose[s] any regulations that will discourage charitable giving by making the process more complex for donors, sponsoring organizations, and beneficiary charities to understand."

The Initiative "disagree[s] with the implication by some DAF critics that if a private foundation meets a portion of its payout requirement with a grant to a DAF, this is prima facie suspect or nefarious." It added that for a private foundation to make a grant to a donor-advised fund at a community foundation "is not uncommon" but "in the vast majority of cases, these grants fulfill a genuine charitable purpose and are not meant to skirt the five percent payout requirement." The group offered a list of the "myriad ways" a private foundation may use a donor-advised fund—a set of examples along the lines of those provided by the Philanthropy Roundtable.

The members of the Initiative are said to work with donors at all income levels, noting that many of the wealthiest donors maintain a private family foundation. The Initiative wrote that "[f]or a [private foundation] to make a grant to a DAF at a community foundation is not uncommon—but in the vast majority of cases, these grants fulfill a genuine charitable purpose and are not meant to skirt the five percent payout requirement." The organization "disagree[d] with the implication by some DAF critics that if a private foundation meets a portion of its payout requirement with a grant to a DAF, this is *prima facie* suspect or nefarious."

---

[781] CFPAI Notice Comments.

American Institute of Certified Public Accountants

The AICPA recommended that Treasury and the IRS proposed regulations that allow private foundations to utilize donor-advised funds in support of their purposes in a number of ways, including grantmaking to DAFs prior to liquidation, facilitating international grantmaking, leveraging joint grantmaking efforts, and unitizing donor-advised funds in grantmaking decisions.[782]

The AICPA observed that "[p]rivate foundations and DAFs have historically worked together to provide a greater benefit to the philanthropic community." For example, some sponsoring organizations work in specific communities and "[m]any private foundations utilize the resources of those community foundation sponsored DAFs to fund projects and build on the local knowledge of those foundations." Likewise, sponsoring organizations with international grantmaking knowledge enable private foundations to "make international grants more effectively without having to directly perform expenditure responsibility oversight reporting or make an equivalency determination." Private foundations utilize donor-advised funds to "make better grant making decisions based on the community data that the sponsoring organization typically gathers in suggesting [grantee] organizations or areas that would make the most impact in the community."

The AICPA recommended that Treasury and the IRS propose regulations that state that a transfer of funds by a private foundation to a donor-advised fund is treated as a qualifying distribution only in specific circumstances, such as a five-year mandatory distribution period and a counting of grants as qualifying distributions in the year of the grant where the foundation has more than 50 percent of the advisory privileges.

The AICPA concluded: "Grants distributed to DAFs from private foundations should enhance philanthropic efforts of private foundations and relieve administrative burdens, but not allow private foundations to thwart laws enacted to prevent abuses."

New York Bar Association Tax Section

The Tax Section of the Bar Association of New York recommended that a grant to a donor-advised fund by a private foundation not be considered a qualifying distribution unless the fund's sponsoring organization agrees to distribute the funds for

---

[782] AICPA Notice Comments.

charitable purposes within a certain timeframe.[783] This approach, the Section wrote, "will ensure that a DAF is not used merely as a parking place for funds by private foundation[s] in contravention to Congress' intent that private foundations distribute income currently as expressed in the required minimum distribution rules."

This group stated that, "[i]n the situation that the DAF is receiving the contribution [grant] from the private foundation, it is in substance acting as an intermediary between the private foundation and the ultimate recipient."[784] The statement observes that a donor-advised fund "is not directly using the funds for a charitable activity; rather it is using the funds only to make the grant to another organization."[785] Because of these circumstances, the statement continues, "there is no good policy reason to distinguish between the contribution to the DAF from the contribution to another private foundation," adding that "[r]equiring the contribution to be used for charitable purposes, and not be merely retained and reinvested [sic], is consistent with the underlying policy" of the private foundation mandatory payout rules. And: "In reaching this conclusion, we are relying upon the supervision of the sponsoring organization to insure that the distribution is actually made."

Fidelity Charitable

Fidelity Charitable Gift Fund opened its analysis of this topic by observing that "[t]here are many reasons individuals may choose different methods of giving—in addition to direct contributions to charities—to fulfill their charitable objectives."[786] Fidelity Charitable "believe[s] that donors should be free to adapt their giving patterns to fulfill their objectives in compliance with the law, and that the charitable sector as a whole is richer and best served by that flexibility and adaptability."

Fidelity Charitable observed that sometimes a private foundation decides to "collapse" (i.e., terminate) by transferring all its assets to a sponsoring organization, doing so on the basis of costs and efficiency. In other instances, a private foundation may make one or more transfers to sponsoring organizations, again perhaps for reasons of cost and efficiency, or does so to achieve a discrete objective, such as funding a particular program. In Fidelity Charitable's experience, "these decisions are based

---

[783] NYSBA Notice Comments.

[784] This is a true but odd observation. A donor-advised fund is *always* an intermediary between the donor or grantor and the ultimate charitable recipient, just as private foundations, supporting organizations, endowment and other funds (such as those for research or scholarships), and charitable remainder trusts.

[785] This is not a correct statement of the law. See Chapter 1, pp. 22-26.

[786] Fidelity Charitable Notice Comments.

on careful considerations of cost, efficiency and charitable purpose, and should in no way be a cause for concern."

As to the matter of a private foundation grant to a donor-advised fund being a qualifying distribution, Fidelity Charitable observed that the general definition of a qualifying distribution is an amount paid to accomplish one or more charitable purposes.[787] It noted that there is no requirement in that body of law that a qualifying distribution be spent on current programs nor is there any prohibition on a qualifying distribution being used as an endowment by a grantee. Again, Fidelity Charitable expressed its concern that sponsoring organizations will become subject to a "different set of rules without any showing of statutory authority, nor any showing of any abuse." Fidelity Charitable expressed its view that the definition of *qualifying distribution* should not be revised in this regard.

Author's Comments

Two aspects of this matter of the interrelationships of private foundations and donor-advised funds are clear. One of these aspects is that there is no evidence that private foundations are "gaming the system" by making grants to donor-advised funds as a means of avoiding their mandatory payout responsibilities at a level warranting a law change that would outlaw (or tax) these types of grants. This is another of these instances where critics seize on the fact that a practice *may* occur to try to generate interest in law revision on the (ostensible) ground that it *does* occur—and does so on a widespread basis.

The second of these aspects is that the private foundation, community foundation, and general public charity communities have assembled a splendid inventory of examples where private foundation grants to donor-advised funds superbly advance U.S. philanthropy. It would be a shame to wreck these abilities of foundations to effectively utilize donor-advised funds based on conjecture. These are valuable relationships and arrangements that enrich and expand the charitable sector—and should be appreciated and encouraged, not swept away.

These arrangements and relationships are impossible to value, yet they have great value. These aspects of the operations of donor-advised funds are thus often overlooked when assessing the use and importance of these funds. For example, one cost/benefit analysis of donor-advised funds, in concluding that the "predominance of the evidence . . . suggests" that these funds "are unlikely to stimulate more new

---

[787] See *Private Foundations* § 6.5.

giving than they cost in forgone tax revenues," admitted that the analysis did not take into account "benefits" that many DAF holders "feel," such as the "ease of online giving or the joy in bringing families together to decide on giving."[788]

LEGAL ISSUE # 5: SHOULD DONOR-ADVISED FUNDS BE SUBJECT TO A MANDATORY PAYOUT REQUIREMENT?

The grandest of the legal issues pertaining to sponsoring organizations and donor-advised funds is this matter of a mandatory payout of grants from these funds. Of course, existing law does not include a payout requirement in this context.

A mandatory payout requirement is, by definition, an artifice (a word with the same origins as *artificial*) in the sense that it is a contrivance or stratagem used to gain a desired outcome. (There can be a hint of trickery to the term.) It is an artifice because it forces persons subject to the requirement to do something they might not otherwise do or do not want to do, perhaps with good reason.

More specifically, a mandatory payout requirement is a law imposed on a pool of investment assets forcing a payment of income or deemed income, usually annually, from the asset base. Commonly, the amount of income generated by the investment assets would, in the absence of the mandate, be lower than the required amount. Such a mandatory payout forces one of two outcomes (or perhaps both): a dip into principal to make up the difference between the "normal" income flow and the mandated level of income to be distributed and/or a reconfiguring of the investment policy to ensure (or attempt to ensure) that the mandated income amount is the income amount that is in fact generated.

In this context of this analysis, the pool of investment assets is either in a tax-exempt charitable entity or is being otherwise held for charitable purposes. Thus, as illustrations, the investment assets may be held in a private foundation, an endowment fund, a charitable remainder trust, a supporting organization, or a donor-advised fund. A collection of assets held in an endowment fund for the benefit of a public charity may be invested primarily for asset appreciation and thus generate little income (e.g., 2 percent), while the same set of assets held in a private foundation would be invested differently, that is, to generate a higher income return (at least 5

---

[788] Andreoni, "The Benefits and Costs of Donor-Advised Funds," National Bureau of Economic Research 40, 32 (978-0-226-57752-4 (2018)).

percent (see below)), as would the assets held in a charitable remainder trust, to generate sufficient income to meet fund the required income interest (see below). (Under current law, these models are "legal.")

The point of the mandatory payout of this nature is, of course, to push out of the investment pool, for distribution elsewhere (usually for charitable purposes), a level of income that the policymakers deem sufficient under the circumstances to achieve the desired policy aims. In the private foundations context, for example, the purpose of the mandatory payout requirement is to ensure that a certain level of money is granted for charitable ends on an ongoing basis. Such a mandate is predicated on the assumption, obviously, that, absent the requirement, the payout would be less. This is the artificiality of the matter: law forcing individuals to do what they would not otherwise do (again, perhaps for quite sound reasons). It is an artifice designed to solve a perceived policy problem.

Those advocating more government regulation in an area love mandates. The members of the regulatory class are fond of dictating to others (or trying to) how to act and what to do. In most instances, the nature of the mandate is lawful, so that the issue is the policy aspect of the matter—the contours and content of the mandate. In a few instances, a government mandate may be illegal, as in unconstitutional. A mandatory payout in the donor-advised fund context would assuredly be lawful. Thus, the matter is solely one of policy, with the overriding issues being whether such a mandate is needed and, if so, what should it be.

CURRENT LAW

The federal tax law includes four instances of mandatory payouts involving tax-exempt charitable organizations or assets otherwise held for charitable purposes.

Private Foundations

Standard grantmaking private foundations are subject to a mandatory payout regime, which is enforced by a series of excise taxes.[789] A grantmaking foundation's mandatory distribution requirement principally is a function of the fair market value of

---

[789] IRC § 4942. Private operating foundations (IRC § 4942(j)(3) entities) have a different feature in this regard, in that they must make distributions directly for the active conduct charitable programs. See *Private Foundations* § 3.1.

BRUCE R. HOPKINS

its noncharitable-use assets. The amount that must be annually distributed is ascertained by computing the private foundation's *distributable amount*, which is equal to the sum of its minimum investment return, plus additional amounts, reduced by the sum of the foundation's unrelated business income taxes and the excise tax on investment income for the year. A foundation's *minimum investment return* basically is an amount equal to 5 percent of the value of its noncharitable assets, reduced by any outstanding debt. That amount must be distributed in the form of one or more *qualifying distributions*.[790]

This body of law was enacted in 1969. The rule that a private foundation must pay out at least a specified percentage of its average noncharitable assets was a product of a "current-benefits-to-charity purpose," that is, a correlation between the "substantial tax benefits" a donor to a foundation may enjoy "currently" and the timing of the receipt of grants by the ultimate charitable grantees. The reports of the House Committee on Ways and Means and the Senate Committee on Finance thus state that the committees concluded that "substantial improvement in the present situation can be achieved by providing sanctions if income is not distributed currently."[791]

The arguments for a private foundation mandatory payout are redolent of some of today's payout arguments in the donor-advised fund setting. A major factor underlying the foundation payout rule, however, which is not present in the donor-advised fund setting, was that it would remove the incentive to use a private foundation as a vehicle to control commercial businesses that do not provide much of an economic return.[792] Thus, two of the arguments for the foundation payout were that (1) it was needed "to insure that charity will begin promptly to receive benefits commensurate with the tax benefits available to donors and their foundations" and "[n]o private foundation should be permitted to use the tax laws to carve out a perpetual role in society without having to justify its continued existence to the contributing general public."[793] Analyses of this nature did not include any data

---

[790] In general, *Private Foundations*, Chapter 6.

[791] Committee on Ways and Means, U.S. House of Representatives, "Tax Reform Act of 1969" (H. Rep. No. 91-413 (Part 1) 25 (91st Cong., 1st Sess. (Aug. 2, 1969)); Committee on Finance, U.S. Senate, "Tax Reform Act of 1969" (S. Rep. No. 91-552, 91st Cong., 1st Sess. (Nov. 21, 1969)).

[792] E.g., Staffs of the Joint Committee on Internal Revenue Taxation and the Committee on Finance, "Summary of H.R. 13270, the Tax Reform Act of 1969 (as Passed by the House of Representatives)" 14 (91st Cong., 1st Sess. (Aug. 18, 1969)). Also, Staff of the Joint Committee on Internal Revenue Taxation, "General Explanation of the Tax Reform Act of 1969 (JCS-16-70 (Dec. 3, 1970)).

[793] *Id.* Arguments against a payout rule included the complaint that it would force private foundations to engage in investment practices that would not permit growth and that foundation managers should

196

as to payout amounts by foundations and, of course, there were no other payout rules by which to judge payout performance or outcomes (baselines).

Certain Type III Supporting Organizations

Of the four categories of supporting organizations,[794] only the Type III nonfunctionally integrated supporting organizations have a mandatory payout requirement. In general, this type of supporting organization must satisfy an integral part test, an attentiveness requirement, and a distribution requirement.

With respect to each tax year, a supporting organization must, to be in compliance with this latter rule, distribute to or for the use of one or more supported organizations an amount equaling or exceeding the supporting organization's distributable amount for the year. In this setting, the *distributable amount* is an amount equal to the greater of 85 percent of the supporting organization's adjusted net income for the immediately preceding year or its minimum asset amount for the preceding year. A supporting organization's *minimum asset amount* for its immediately preceding year is 3.5 percent of the excess of the fair market value of the organization's nonexempt-use assets in that year over the acquisition indebtedness with respect to the assets, increased by certain amounts.[795]

Charitable Remainder Trusts

A charitable remainder trust is an entity—a form of split-interest trust—by which money and/or other property is split into two types of interests: an income interest and a remainder interest. The remainder interest is the portion of the property that is destined for one or more charitable organizations, while the income interest is retained by and/or created for one or more noncharitable beneficiaries. The gift of the remainder interest gives rise to one or more federal tax charitable contribution deductions. Charitable remainder trusts are tax-exempt organizations.[796]

Charitable remainder trusts are basically of two types: the charitable remainder annuity trust and the charitable remainder unitrust. In the case of a CRAT, a sum certain (an annuity) is to be paid from the trust, at least annually, to one or more persons, at least one of which is not a charitable organization. This sum may not be less than 5 percent of the initial net fair market value of all property placed in

---

be the sole judges of the best timing for the charitable use of foundation income (*id.*).

[794] *Private Foundations* § 15.7(d)-(g).

[795] *Private Foundations* § 15.7, text accompanied by notes 331-343.

[796] IRC § 664. *Charitable Giving* § 12.8.

the trust and may not be greater than 50 percent of the initial fair market value of all property placed in the trust.[797] In the case of a CRUT, an amount equal to a fixed percentage of the net fair market value of the trust's assets, valued annually, is to be paid from the trust, not less often than annually, to one or more persons, at least one of which is not a charitable organization. The unitrust amount must not be less than 5 percent of the net fair market value of the trust's assets determined annually and may not be greater than 50 percent of the value of the trust's assets determined annually.[798]

This body of law was enacted in 1969.

Charitable Lead Trusts

A charitable lead trust is another form of split-interest trust by which money and/or other forms of property is apportioned into an income interest and a remainder interest. Pursuant to this type of trust, an income interest in property is contributed to a charitable organization, with the remainder interest in the property reserved to be distributed to one or more noncharitable beneficiaries. Like the charitable remainder trust, the income interest may be stated as a guaranteed annuity or an annual payment equal to a fixed percentage of the fair market value of the trust property, valued annually.[799]

This body of law was enacted in 1969.

Pooled Income Fund

A pooled income fund is a third form of split-interest trust; as the name indicates, this type of trust is a pool of many gifts. In this context, a remainder interest is contributed to charity and the income is paid to noncharitable beneficiaries. The income paid each year to the income interest beneficiaries is based on the rate of return earned by the fund for the year.[800]

This body of law was enacted in 1969.

Charitable Gift Annuities

Charitable gift annuities are based on agreements between the donors and the donees, where the donor agrees to make a gift and the donee agrees to provide the

---

[797] *Id.* § 12.1(a).
[798] *Id.*
[799] *Id.*, Chapter 16.
[800] *Id.*, Chapter 13.

donor and/or others with an annuity. Most charitable organizations that conduct gift annuity programs adhere to the suggested annuity rates established by the American Council on Gift Annuities.[801]

PROPOSALS

All major (and most other) critics of donor-advised funds are demanding enactment of a mandatory payout rule. It is a core mantra of the group. Thus, Dean Zerbe proclaims that "[p]ayout is the cornerstone of DAF reform."[802]

Mandatory payout proposals, with respect to donor-advised funds, generally come in two flavors: strong and stronger. The milder of the proposals is a mandatory payout on all funds held by a sponsoring organization; this would be a payout imposed on all fund amounts collectively. The other proposal is a mandatory payout on a fund-by-fund basis.

The matter of a mandatory payout came to the fore soon after enactment of the donor-advised fund statutory rules in 2006. That legislation included a congressionally mandated report from the Department of the Treasury that concluded, among other things, that it was "premature" to comment on the need for any donor-advised fund distribution requirement based on the data used in the report, which was for 2006.[803] It was noted, however, that the average payout rate across donor-advised funds in general, in 2006, was 9.3 percent and for the national supporting organizations was 14.2 percent.[804]

A subsequent report, from the Congressional Research Service, is based on data for 2008. This report, which is somewhat biased,[805] stated that the payout rate across all sponsoring organizations was 13.1 percent and for the national supporting organizations was 26.5 percent. The report advocated, not too subtly, consideration of a minimum payout rate for donor-advised funds. First, it rejected the notion that,

---

[801] *Id.*, Chapter 14.

[802] Zerbe, "DAF Reform – A Chance to Provide Real Benefit to Working Charities," 25 *Nonprofit Quar.* (Issue 2) 52, 53 (Summer 2018).

[803] See Chapter 3, pp. 73-75.

[804] *Id.*, p. 74.

[805] For example, the CRS report reflects the view that donors to sponsoring organizations actually retain control over the gift properties, which is not true (see Chapter 5, pp. 132-133), stating that "donors appear to have actual control of grant-making because sponsoring organizations typically follow their advice" (see Chapter 3, p. 78) Also, the CRS report bought into the notion that it is proper to refer to national sponsoring organization as "commercial" entities (see Chapter 2, pp. 45-46).

because donor-advised fund overall payout rates are higher than those for private foundations, there is no need for imposition of a minimum payout requirement for these funds—without saying why. Second, it stated that an overall payout rate on sponsoring organizations would be "relatively meaningless," apparently because it would "create an incentive" for donors who wish to avoid grantmaking to make their gifts to the larger sponsoring organizations, including the commercial ones.[806] The report concluded: "Requiring reporting on individual [fund] accounts is an option that could improve understanding of how [donor-advised funds] operate and provide better oversight."[807]

A more formal legislative proposal was advanced in 2014, as part of a tax reform legislative draft issued by the House Committee on Ways and Means, under the auspices of the Committee's then-chairman, Rep. David Camp (R-Mich.). One of the legislative "reforms" in that package was the idea that there should be a five-year payout requirement for all donor-advised funds, coupled with a 20 percent excise tax applicable to insufficient payout amounts.[808]

One of the more thoughtful analyses of this matter of payout requirements for donor-advised funds is found in an article by law professor Roger Colinvaux.[809] In this regard, he focused on the national sponsoring organizations. After making an argument that national sponsoring organizations have a "relatively weak case for exempt status" and that these organizations are to be differentiated from "active public charities,"[810] Professor Colinvaux advocated application of a version of the commensurate test,[811] pursuant to which national sponsoring organizations "should be required to ensure that each DAF under their control pays out contributions (measured annually) within a range of five to ten years."[812]

This is a striking proposal for two reasons. One, it posits that the federal tax law already imposes a mandatory payout requirement on sponsoring organizations or donor-advised funds themselves. Second, it offers a rationale that a mandatory payout requirement can be imposed on sponsoring organizations, national or otherwise, by tax regulation or revenue ruling.

---

[806] See Chapter 3, p. 78.
[807] Id. This report did not reference any of the reasons for not imposing a payout requirement on a fund-by-fund basis.
[808] See Chapter 2, pp. 51-52.
[809] Colinvaux, "Donor-Advised Funds: Charitable Spending Vehicles for 21st Century Philanthropy," 92 Wash. L. Rev. 39 (2017).
[810] Id. at 67. See Chapter 1, pp. 45-46.
[811] See Chapter 1, pp. 26-27.
[812] Colinvaux, supra note 809, at 67.

As Professor Colinvaux notes, one objection—actually, it is the principal objection—to a donor-advised fund payout regime is that it is unnecessary. That is, "many [national sponsoring organizations] claim to already pay out at high levels and so argue that a payout [rule] is redundant," citing data around 201-2106 showing payouts of 20 percent or more.[813] Roger, like so many donor-advised fund critics, denigrates this view, stating that these "robust" payout levels are "largely beside the point," in that the payout numbers are at the aggregate level, rather than the fund-by-fund level.[814] That is, "[h]igh payouts by some funds mean that many funds held by the same sponsoring organization pay well below the mean."[815]

Roger Colinvaux is also dismissive of concerns of donors in the face of the prospect of payout requirements—perhaps they will cease making these gifts. His answer—the one typical of academics—is that if a donor wants to establish a "perpetual institution," the private foundation is the "appropriate form."[816] If, he wrote, if a donor-advised fund is being used as an alternative to a private foundation, the donor-advised fund "represents a loophole,"[817] with a "high payout" having the virtue of closing the loophole,[818] as if that resolves the matter.

Another objection to a donor-advised fund payout regime is the administrative burdens and costs that would be imposed on sponsoring organizations. Professor Colinvaux concedes that sponsoring organizations "would have to calculate distribution requirements for each fund, inform donors of their obligations, and make distributions when donors fail to provide advice," with this acknowledged "burden" passed along to the donor account through higher administrative fees.[819] Ignoring the magnitude of the burden and the probable effect of curbing the use of donor-advised funds, Roger Colinvaux dismisses this burden argument with the proclamation that "[i]t should be within the competence of these sophisticated financial

---

[813] *Id.* at 68.

[814] *Id.*

[815] *Id.* While it is theoretically true that fund-by-fund reporting would yield more data and smoke out some funds that are not the source of grants, that does not render aggregate data "beside the point." Aggregate payouts of this magnitude – four and five times that of private foundations – are impressive and should be taken into account by policymakers in determining whether a fund-by-fund payout rule is worth the trouble.

[816] Colinvaux, *supra* note 809, at 69. This simplistic approach ignores the fact that many donors to donor-advised funds are contributing more than they may do otherwise but not at the level of giving that can absorb the expense of forming and operating a private foundation

[817] Here we go again! See Chapter 5, pp. 131-132.

[818] Colinvaux, *supra* note 117, at 69.

[819] *Id.*

intermediaries to track subaccount balances and payouts over time, without creating an undue burden,"[820] without citing any authority or justification for this purported "should."[821]

Roger Colinvaux's article has the virtue of setting the baseline for the other critics. Thus, Dean Zerbe writes that the "easy solution (also an anti-abuse measure) is to have a payout requirement for DAFs on an account-by-account basis."[822] He encouraged the proposition that a "greater proportion of the warehoused charity dollars" in donor-advised funds be transferred to "working charities."[823] Ray Madoff echoes that view, stating that statutory law could be enacted imposing a time period within which monies in donor-advised funds would have to be distributed for charitable ends.[824]

Not all commenters on the state of the donor-advised funds phenomenon are of this ilk, however. A striking comment came from Ruth McCambridge on the "one issue that is most talked about as in need of policy change," which is the issue of a donor-advised fund payout regime. Ruth notes that donor-advised fund payout rates have "compared very favorably to foundation payouts."[825] (This was as of mid-2018.) This statement is followed up by an odd one, which is that donor-advised funds payout rates do not "compare so favorably, of course, to direct giving, if you assume that the same amount would have been given elsewhere."[826] Those two comments do not make much sense, particularly when strung together. But, the two comments do serve as introductions to the remaining elements of the debate over mandatory payouts from donor-advised funds.

First, the donor-advised fund payout rate cannot compare with *any* aspect of direct giving because, with direct giving, there is no payout rate. That is true with any payout rate in the charitable sphere, whether imposed on private foundations, charitable remainder trusts, or charitable gift annuities. What Ruth McCambridge was alluding to, I believe, is the timing issue—the time gap between the date a

[820] *Id.*

[821] As discussed (see this chapter, p. 201), the most important argument against imposition of a donor-advised fund payout scheme of any sort is that the case has not been made that one is needed.

[822] Zerbe, "DAF Reform – A Chance to Provide Real Benefit to Working Charities," 25 *Nonprofit Quar.* (Issue 2) 52, 53 (Summer 2018).

[823] *Id.*, at 54.

[824] Madoff, "Three Simple Steps to Protect Charities and American Taxpayers from the Rise of Donor-Advised Funds," 25 *Nonprofit Quar.* (Issue 2) 46, 48 (Summer 2018).

[825] McCambridge, "Do Donor-Advised Funds Require Regulatory Attention?," 25 *Nonprofit Quar.* (Issue 2) 41, 44 (Summer 2018).

[826] *Id.*

contribution is made to a donor-advised fund and the date a grant is received by a charitable organization. Second, most discussions about the virtues of payout impositions on donor-advised funds "assume that the same amount would have been given elsewhere."[827] Little consideration has been given to how the universe of donor-advised funds and giving to them would change if a payout requirement were to be imposed.[828]

The "time gap" issue obviously is at the heart of the payout debate. If small sums of money were sitting around, not being paid out for charitable purposes right away, this debate would not be happening. Rather, there are stupendous sums being held in donor-advised funds these days, with the critics wanting all that money and property flowed out to charities today, with no care for what tomorrow may bring. Accumulations of charitable assets, while greatly suspect in the nation's early history of charity,[829] have become, in recent decades, acceptable forms of what Roger Colinvaux termed "perpetual institutions," such as private foundations, endowments, and charitable remainder trusts, with giving to them for accumulative purposes acceptable stratagems. Yet, the critics of donor-advised funds are trying to change the worldview here, eschewing words of nicety like accumulations and accretions, and turning instead to derogatory and inflammatory terms, such as warehousing, stockpiling, and hoarding. The advocacy strategy is that, to secure creation of a donor-advised fund payout rule, the case must be made that huge amounts of charitable dollars and other property are holed up somewhere,[830] stagnating, in the face of shrinking charitable giving, economic inequality, and human suffering.[831]

Just about the time I became confident that critics of donor-advised funds had exhausted their supply of derogatory terms—albeit concededly colorful ones—for sponsoring organizations and the funds they own, a fellow by the name of John Arnold proved me wrong. Writing that "tax-free hoarding" of charitable gifts in private foundations, donor-advised funds, and endowments "runs counter to the spirit of the rules concerning charitable deductions," he coined the phrase "zombie charity."[832] His premise is completely wrong, of course, as is evidenced by countless pages

---

[827] Id.

[828] The guess from here is that the growth of donor-advised funds would be stunted and giving to them would be slowed, at a time when the national level of charitable giving needs to be increasing, not slowing.

[829] See Chapter 2, pp. 34–36.

[830] Colorful language is also used in this context, to the same end; sponsoring organizations become "black-box charities," "black holes," and "donor-advised fund monsters."

[831] Thus, Paul Streckfus wrote that the "fact of the matter is that DAFs have pulled over $110 billion out of the charitable stream permanently" (*EO Tax Jour.* 2019-162 (Aug. 20, 2019)).

[832] Arnold, "Put a Stake in 'Zombie Charity.' Philanthropy Is for the Living," 31 *Chron. of Phil.* (Issue

of tax statutes, regulations, rulings, and court opinions concerning these institutions[833] but the premise nonetheless served as the springboard for his belief that a simple payout requirement of 7 percent should be applied to donor-advised funds, with the payout being the "stake" in the "zombie charity."[834]

I have concluded that (1) the proposals for a mandatory payout requirement on sponsoring organizations are not as "easy" and "simple" to implement as their proponents assert, (2) such a mandatory payout would have unintended and adverse consequences, (3) such a payout would pose enormous administrative headaches, and—this is the most important of the batch—(4) case has not been made that a donor-advised fund payout is needed.

I believe the Community Foundation Public Awareness Initiative has made the better case in this debate, showing why a mandatory payout in the donor-advised fund context is a bad idea. I think the trend toward the "institutionalizing" of charitable giving is a positive and healthy one, particularly in an era where overall charitable giving may be declining. This contemporary outlook on philanthropy, while difficult to quantify, appears to be making individuals and families more serious about charitable giving and causing them to give more.

The Initiative nicely summarized this matter of unintended consequences in a letter to the Senate Finance Committee in 2017.[835] Basically, the fear here is that, with imposition of a payout, contributions to donor-advised funds would decline.[836] A payout rule would prevent donors from making long-term commitments to their communities and grantees generally, precluding, for example, a build-up in pursuit of a larger grant or an endowment arrangement. Also, as the group observed, a forced distribution from donor-advised funds would "make[] it harder for the philanthropically inclined entrepreneur to make significant gifts at a point of liquidity (when the ability to give is high but the donor has not yet developed a philanthropic plan)."

---

11) 31 (Sep. 2019).

[833] Mr. Arnold also wrote that the "law requires that foundations spend at least 5 percent of their assets each year" (*id.*). First, no one can "spend' an "asset." Two, private foundations are not required to distribute chunks of their assets annually. Three, the general rule is that private foundations, to avoid excise taxation, are required to distribute an amount of money *equal to the value of* 5 percent of their noncharitable assets annually (IRC § 4942(d), (e)).

[834] No explanation is provided as to how this payout would apply in real life nor is there any rationale for the percentage; for DAF payout advocates these days all that is deemed necessary is the mere call for imposition of a payout regime.

[835] CFPAI letter to Senate Finance Committee leadership (Sep. 6, 2017).

[836] In addition to being an unintended and adverse consequence of a payout requirement, it would perversely also have the opposite effect from that that critics claim: it would reduce grants from these funds, not increase them.

Further, a payout rule would make donor-advised funds "so restrictive that it would virtually eliminate them as a tool for building family philanthropy" (involving children and grandchildren).[837] And, a payout rule would play havoc, legally and operationally, with endowed donor-advised fund arrangements.

As to the administrative "nightmare" for sponsoring organizations, the Initiative notes that many community foundations manage hundreds, if not thousands, of donor-advised funds and many of their donors are contributing to the funds on multiple occasions during a year. In the face of a mandatory payout, the Initiative asked, how are they supposed to manage that "unprecedented level of complexity"? For example, does a new payout requirement get triggered every time there is a contribution? Also, would a forced payout apply to investment earnings or just the contributed amounts? None of the payout proposals I have seen have even begun to consider, let alone answer, questions like these.[838]

I believe the biggest and best reason for not imposing a payout requirement with respect to donor-advised funds is that it is not necessary. As the Initiative wrote in 2017, payout proposals "impl[y] that inactivity of donor-advised funds is a pervasive problem that requires attention."[839] I think the Initiative's positive affirmation is true: "[T]he vast majority of DAFs are making grants regularly with deep engagement and input from the designated advisors." That is, "at community foundations, only a small percentage of DAF accounts would be considered 'inactive.'"

Moreover, as the Initiative pointed out, most community foundations have policies and or procedures in place to ensure that the donor-advised funds there remain active in accordance with established criteria. An accreditation program has been established by and for community foundations that requires compliance with best practices; pursuant to this program, donors must acknowledge and agree to adhere to a policy that outlines "fund activity."[840] If a fund becomes inactive, as defined by these criteria, the community foundation involved maintains a policy by which it will take steps to make grants from the fund.

---

[837] The Initiative's letter to the Senate Finance Committee observed that the "flexibility DAFs provide leads to greater charitable giving over time as donors become more engaged and see the results of their grantmaking."

[838] In its 2017 letter to the Senate Finance Committee, the Initiative wrote that these and similar questions "require serious thought from policymakers, and we don't believe the advocates for timed payouts on DAFs have adequately thought them through."

[839] In fact, *imply* is far too tame. Mandatory payout is the donor-advised fund critics' rallying cry. See, e.g., text accompanying *supra* note 802.

[840] This is the National Standards for U.S. Community Standards® program.

Critics of donor-advised funds base their position in this regard on the view that, inasmuch as, under the law, a donor *may* make a gift to a donor-advised fund and thereafter not recommend any grants, this is a widespread practice demanding legislative reform. I am unaware of any data evidencing lack of grantmaking from donor-advised funds, at community foundations or elsewhere, at a level even remotely approaching any need warranting legislative relief.

Therefore, I have concluded that the Initiative is correct in its position that, given that (1) relatively few donor-advised funds are truly inactive, (2) the average payout rate for donor-advised funds is significantly higher than the rate for private foundations, and (3) community foundation have a meaningful self-regulation program, there is no substantive merit in a statutory donor-advised fund mandatory payout requirement "given the risks and complexity it would entail."[841]

Having said that, I believe that the Treasury Department and the IRS have the authority to prescribe a form of mandatory payout on donor-advised funds by application of the law that has accreted in the form of the commensurate test. I'm not advocating that this be done; I'm merely observing that, as a matter of law, it could be done. For example, the rule of the test—that distributions must be made at a level that is commensurate with the fund's resources—could be articulated in a regulation, followed by illustrations of when the test is met and when it is not (taking into account elements such as the amount of the grant(s) in relation to the total of funds available and the timing of the grant(s) in relation to the date of the original gift). I suspect that is a controversy that the Treasury would sidestep.

LEGAL ISSUE # 6: SHOULD DONORS' CHARITABLE DEDUCTION FOR GIFTS TO DONOR-ADVISED FUNDS BE DEFERRED UNTIL CORRESPONDING GRANTS ARE MADE FROM THE FUNDS?

For years, critics of donor-advised funds have vociferously argued that DAF reforms are essential—and that the key reform device is a mandatory payout. This position is not based on anything resembling evidence but rather the speculation that, since a donor may conceivably contribute to a DAF and not advise as to a

---

[841] These positions of the CFPAI are also reflected in an earlier submission to Congress, in the form of a letter dated July 14, 2014, to the House Committee on Ways and Means, in response to the Camp Proposal (see this chapter, p. 200). In this letter, the Initiative expressed its members' concern that the proposal "seems to promote the perspective that DAFs *by their very nature* are somehow abusive."

distribution for a period of time, this is a widespread abusive practice requiring legislative reform.

The data I have seen show that DAF payouts are high, certainly higher than those of private foundations. Contributions to DAFs continue to grow, which I think is a good thing in an era where charitable giving overall seems on a decline. I continue to applaud the "institutionalization" of individuals' philanthropy, and recognize that DAFs are one of the chief vehicles for its accomplishment. I worry that a mandatory DAF payout scheme would introduce undue complexity and discourage giving to donor-advised funds. In short, donor-advised funds strike me as valuable and welcome charitable giving vehicles; statutory DAF payouts strike me as counterproductive and unnecessary.

The lack of necessity of a statutory payout regime in the donor-advised fund context is borne out by developments in the marketplace. One report notes that Fidelity Charitable requires at least one grant from a donor-advised fund within five years, Vanguard Charitable automatically transfers 5 percent of a fund's value to charity if there is no advised grantmaking over a five-year period, and Dartmouth has a 5 percent per fund annual payout requirement.[842]

Some of these critics are backtracking, conjuring up another type of donor-advised fund "reform": a delay of the contribution deduction until there is a comparable distribution from the fund. An example of such a proposal was published in late 2019.[843] The authors of this proposal concluded that "there is an even better approach [as compared to a forced payout] that could maximize contributions, help donors save on taxes, and avoid abuses that lose money for the Treasury." Pursuant to this notion, a donor "wouldn't get to take a charitable deduction just for giving to the fund" but would "get that deduction every time dollars are sent out of the fund," so that if the "property went up in value while sitting in the fund, the deduction would reflect that increase in value." These authors state that "[f]ixing the problem is simple," with the solution "based on the bedrock principle that no charitable deduction should be available until donors give up complete control of their gift."[844]

---

[842] Lorin, "Got $5 Million? Yale Will Invest It," *Bloomberg Businessweek* (issue 4596 (Dec. 17, 2018)).

[843] Colinvaux and Madoff, "A Donor-Advised Fund Proposal That Would Work for Everyone," *Chronicle of Philanthropy* (Sep. 23, 2019).

[844] This "fix" is not "simple" (see, e.g., the Internal Revenue Code sections referenced in *infra* notes 153, 154), there is no evidence of any "problem" warranting such a radical (and counterproductive) law change such as this proposal, and donors "give up complete control of their gift" (see Chapter 5, pp. 132-133) when they make their gifts to donor-advised funds and that is why the charitable de-

This is one of these reform proposals that may seem appealing from an academic standpoint but fail in the real world. This approach has been tried, for example, in connection with charitable contributions of vehicles[845] and partial interests in works of art,[846] the result being largely a drying up of those types of gifts. The administrative headaches and law complexities drag them down.[847]

If such a policy were adopted for DAFs, would it extend to comparable contexts? Consider these scenarios:

How about gifts to endowment funds? Perhaps a public charity is working to accumulate one. The institution does not pay out anything from income for over two years. No charitable deduction until the donors' third tax year?

Gifts to scholarship funds. Maybe the charity is building such a fund. Maybe suitable grantees are not available in a particular year. No charitable deduction until scholarships are granted?

A donor makes a gift to a supporting organization. No charitable deduction until the organization makes a grant to the supported organization or otherwise makes a charitable expenditure?

This deduction-delayed policy could be applied to all restricted and contingent gifts. Gaps between giving and granting are common in U.S. charity, as witnessed by gifts to private foundations, private foundation set-asides, and charitable remainder trusts. Lawyers, accountants, and writers of computer programs might benefit from these intricacies but the charitable sector would suffer.

The charitable sector would also suffer because of donor confusion and discouragement. In today's environment, donors are not likely to give, with the prospect of a deduction years later. Some will recall that planned giving was once termed *deferred giving*. That nomenclature was abandoned when donors stopped being donors because they feared it was their charitable deduction was deferred.

Just contemplating charities' administration of such a charitable giving deduction structure adds to its nightmarish aspect. The recordkeeping, tracing of dollars, sending of notices to donors every year (or perhaps more frequently). There are charities that still cannot cope with the gift substantiation rules, which have been

---

duction properly arises then (a "bedrock principle").

[845] IRC § 170(f)(12).

[846] IRC § 170(o). Also, IRC § 170(m), postponing portions of a donor's charitable deduction for a gift of intellectual property until there is an economic return to the donee charity.

[847] I contemplated writing a rebuttal to this article. My working title was "A Donor-Advised Fund Proposal That Would Be a Nightmare for Everyone." This paragraph and the next five paragraphs are from the draft of that rebuttal.

in the law for years. How will they engage in gift administration under a deduction deferral scheme?

Under some versions of a deduction delayed plan, donors would be able to take charitable deductions based on the appreciation of the value of the property in the funds, perhaps including earnings. That feature is not likely to go over well with tax law purists. Perspective needs to be kept in mind here; recall how "reforms" of supporting organizations have nearly wrecked what were once attractive and useful charitable vehicles. I think the best approach is to leave donor-advised funds and deductions for gifts to them alone from a regulatory standpoint—and welcome these funds as an enhancement of the sector.

A response to the Colinvaux-Madoff proposal was published shortly thereafter, with these authors observing (correctly, although it's an understatement) that the proposal "would have wide-ranging ramifications for DAFs and their donors."[848] The notion would "stymie taxpayers who seek to use DAFs to spread philanthropic activity across the life cycle," "dramatically reduce the tax benefits of DAFs for middle-income donors," and "raise the potential for unintended and unwanted consequences." Overall, these authors conclude that, although the "current regulatory regime for DAFs is certainly not perfect,"[849] the notion of "delaying deductions for DAF donors is no place to start." Not only would that approach "undermine the utility of DAFs to life-cycle givers and small-dollar donors but it also could cause high-bracket taxpayers to hold money in DAFs even longer." They conclude that, "[r]ather than the win-win that the authors describe, this is a DAF reform that should please no one."

---

[848] Harris and Hemel, "Don't Delay Deductions for Gifts to Donor-Advised Funds" *Chron. of Phil.* (Oct. 7, 2019).

[849] As examples of the imperfections of today's regulatory regime for donor-advised funds, these donors cite the ability of private foundations to use DAFs to satisfy mandatory payout requirements (even though there is no evidence of abuse in this area and there are many good reasons to allow foundations' use of DAFs (see this chapter, pp. 182-187). or to "skirt disclosure requirements" (no explanation for that one).

CHAPTER 7 CONCLUSIONS:
A Law Reality Check

As many articles, opinion pieces, and reports have reiterated over recent years, donor-advised funds are the nation's fastest-growing charitable giving vehicle. Today, these funds are also the most controversial of these techniques. There are many positive reasons for this growth but—such as is the tenor of our times—rapid expansion and popularity bring the inevitable raft of critics. One would think that, as charitable giving overall apparently is on the decline, any incentive to increase charitable contributions would be universally championed, but one would be wrong.

According to a recent report from the National Philanthropic Trust, U.S. donors gave $37.12 billion to donor-advised funds in 2018—or 12.7 percent of the total amount of money given by individuals to charities that year. In one of the many illustrations of the phenomenal growth of donor-advised funds in recent years, DAFs accounted for 4.4 percent of individual giving as recently as 2010.

As with any development that involves billions of dollars, scrutiny is warranted. Scrutiny, however, should be informed by facts—and the most vocal detractors routinely ignore crucial facts about how donor-advised funds actually work—and the law underlying them.

As a result, donor-advised funds are being labeled as "shams" and "tax shelters" that allow the wealthy to stash money for themselves at the expense of "starving" charities who are not seeing the benefit of this largesse—and never will. But these are allegations that are being spun and recycled in media coverage and in commentary—and they could lead to rules that would hurt charities and the people they help.

Here is a perspective that is informed by more than 50 years of working closely with charities and their donors. The simple truth is that donor-advised funds are helping to grow the pie for the charitable sector—not shrink it. They make it easy for donors to give and, without them, much less money would make its way to the homeless shelters, soup kitchens, and environmental charities that are being labeled as victims in many commentaries about donor-advised funds.

Donor-advised funds were created by community foundations nearly 100 years ago. Their rising popularity is a sign that more Americans are interested in being strategic with their philanthropy. DAF advisors want to help their communities, work with other donors to tackle persistent problems, and get their children involved in a lifetime of giving. Money contributed to donor-advised funds usually is granted out at a much faster rate than money that is invested in private foundations and other philanthropic vehicles. According to the National Philanthropic Trust, the average payout rate from DAFs was more than 20.9 percent—more than four times the required payout from private foundations.

NATURE OF CRITICISM

Over the decades, innovative charitable giving techniques and devices have emerged, followed by opposition and perhaps abuses. Planned giving techniques, such as charitable remainder trusts and charitable gift annuities, and private foundations went through these phases. Giving to and use of endowments is currently a subject of controversy. Today, center stage, when it comes to controversy, belongs to donor-advised funds.

This time around, however, the environment is different. Few topics presumably are beyond the reach of criticism. Yet arguments that are rational, not to mention civil and accurate, are normally the ones the carry the day. Not in the donor-advised fund setting; not today. Instead, we are witnessing an astonishing amount of vitriol, bombast, hyperbole, nonsense, and falsifications.

The intensity of this criticism started to peak around the time that the *Chronicle of Philanthropy*'s Philanthropy 400 began to include national DAF sponsoring organizations in the top ten. The critics went ballistic when one of these organizations, the Fidelity Charitable Gift Fund, became the nation's top fundraising charity (in 2015). (The *Chronicle* resolved this dilemma by creating a ranking called America's Favorite Charities, leaving the national sponsoring organizations out.)

The band of critics is quite small, yet they are having an impact far beyond their few number. Defenders of donor-advised funds have not (yet) achieved anywhere near a comparable impact. The defenders play nice, write gently. The critics fire away, terming donor-advised funds (in alphabetical order) black boxes, black holes, frauds, legal fictions, loopholes, monsters, shams, warehouses of wealth, and zombies, and pronounce them corrupt, immoral, and untrustworthy. The DAF critics are way ahead on point when it comes to hyperbole.

Three discrete sections of the Internal Revenue Code, of recent vintage, provide the statutory law basis for donor-advised funds. This body of law is supplemented by favorable court opinions, IRS rulings, and decades of history. Congress may enact laws that warrant criticism but the nation's legislature is not in the habit of creating shams, frauds, and the like. As a matter of law, then, these labels are unfair and inaccurate.

DONOR-ADVISED FUNDS ARE "ACTUAL" CHARITIES

Some critics of donor-advised funds contend that organizations sponsoring the funds are not really charities to begin with and thus, by extension, ought not be tax-exempt at all. These critics draw a distinction between "working" or "actual" charities and donor-advised funds. This distinction totally lacks merit from a law standpoint. The law is clear, and has been for nearly 100 years, that organizations that fundraise and make grants for charitable purposes are tax-exempt charities and are exempt on an equal basis along with charities that are exempt for other reasons. A well-known IRS ruling, issued in 1967, states explicitly that an organization that carries on no operations other than to receive contributions and investment income and to make distributions of income for charitable purposes at periodic intervals is an exempt charity. Likewise, a court observed that an organization need not engage in a "functional" charitable activity to be organized and operated for charitable purposes but that these purposes may be accomplished solely by providing grants to other charitable entities.

Indeed, the tax regulations expanding on the meaning of charitable, educational, and like purposes openly recognize and encourage this point. For example, schools are tax-exempt because they are educational institutions and various types of research facilities are exempt because they are scientific institutions. Yet, many types of nonprofit organizations are exempt as charitable organizations because they engage in activities that collaterally support and benefit these and similar institutions. These entities are termed the *advancement* organizations. Thus, an entity can be an exempt charity because it advances education, advances science, or ad-

213

vances religion. True, some of these advancement organizations have "functional" programming but others have "intermediary" functions, such as fundraising and holding of endowments.

Consequently, there is no basis in the law for bifurcating the charitable sector on the basis of these distinctions—the members of this sector have equal status when it comes to tax exemption. Efforts to downgrade and denigrate charities that focus only on fundraising and grantmaking are not supported by the law.

DONORS "CONTROL" OF DAFs

Despite crystal-clear law to the contrary, critics of donor-advised funds persist in arguing that transfers of money and other property to these funds are not "really" contributions because of the advisory privileges accorded donors. The ability to advise is equated with the ability to control. This viewpoint ignores, among other things, the distinction between donor-advised funds and donor-directed funds. To be clear, once money or other property is given to a DAF, it, as a matter of law, no longer belongs to the donor—and can only be given to a qualified charity.

Moreover, a provision in the Internal Revenue Code requires that donors to donor-advised funds be provided by the sponsoring organization a notice that the organization has "exclusive legal control" over the funds or assets contributed. There is no opacity in that characterization; the requirement is clear. That fact is also often stated in sponsoring organizations' policies.

Yet, the DAF critics soldier on, apparently of the view that mere repetition of a statement makes the statement true. Thus, one critic wrote that, while donors "part ways" with their money, "they don't give up control." One does not simultaneously part ways with and continue to control something. A favorite of the critics is that the donor-donee arrangement here is rested on a "wink and a nod." Some critics resort to terms such as *functional* control and *implicit* control.

As a matter of law, as noted, donors to donor-advised funds relinquish control—period. For example, the Tax Section of the American Bar Association observed that, once a donor makes a contribution to a donor-advised fund, that donor has relinquished control of the contributed funds, which become the legal property of the sponsoring organization of the donor-advised fund. The Tax Section also noted that, while a donor or donor advisor may retain advisory privileges over such amounts, the sponsoring organization is under no obligation to heed the donor's or donor advisor's advice with respect to a particular recommended grantee. The nation's tax lawyers have spoken—correctly.

DAFs as Alternatives to Foundations

Critics charge that donor-advised funds are being used as an alternative to private foundations. When the matter is stated that way (it usually is not put that way), the observation is quite correct. Recall the federal tax law definition of a private foundation—it is a tax-exempt charitable entity that cannot qualify as a public charity. Therefore, any type of public charity is an "alternative" to a private foundation. Schools, churches, hospitals, publicly supported charities. supporting organizations, and more are alternatives to private foundations. It is all rather logical—and legal. There may be as many as 80,000 private foundations; the close to 1.5 million public charities are hardly engaging in nefarious tax law avoidance.

Individuals involved as donors may wish to avoid the responsibilities imposed by law, including annual reporting to the IRS and other foundation regulatory requirements, of operating a private foundation. Use of a private foundation entails procurement of recognition of tax exemption and obtaining state and local tax exemptions. With the donor-advised fund, as opposed to a private foundation, there is no need to form an organization (no governing instruments or policies) or worry about personal liability.

Those who are very wealthy can establish private foundations. This initially is a time-consuming and costly undertaking. Costs and time commitments continue once the foundation is launched, as governing boards must be created and sustained, staff selected, a grantmaking program launched, and all the other necessities of starting and managing a nonprofit organization must be attended to, including the selection and paying of lawyers and accountants. Those who are well below the high-income wealth levels can now achieve the same ends using donor-advised funds. They too can now institutionalize their charitable giving pursuits and integrate them with their financial and estate plans.

Donor-advised fund critics do not use genteel terms, such as *alternative*. Rather, these critics say that donor-advised funds are a means to "get around" or "evade" the private foundation rules. These charges are not true. Sponsoring organizations are public charities and most of the private foundation regulatory rules simply do not apply.

DAFs AS INTERMEDIARIES

Another charge the critics muster against donor-advised funds is that they are "intermediaries." This is indisputably true. Until recently, however, intermediary was not a bad word. Now it is being used as if something immoral or evil is taking place.

The fact is that many categories of charities are intermediaries: they include private foundations, endowment funds, supporting organizations, and charitable remainder trusts. The definition of exempt charity is, of course, found in section 501(c)(3) of the Internal Revenue Code. This definition does not differentiate between working and non-working charities or engage in scare tactics by divining "monster" or "zombie" charities. This definition instead is sweeping, reflecting the fact that there are many pathways to achievement of charitable objectives. Donor-advised funds take merely one of these diverse paths.

This distinction has been baked into the tax law since the beginning of the tax regulations in the early 1970s. For example, as noted, some organizations are educational, scientific, or religious in nature, while others are charitable because they advance education, science, or religion. A case in point are charities that function to engage in fundraising efforts and grantmaking. These entities can be tax-exempt charities even though they do not have "programs" in some sense of that word.

PRIVATE FOUNDATIONS' USE OF DAFs

Then there is the matter of private foundations' grantmaking to donor-advised funds. The critics' thinking here is that because private foundations might use these funds in an effort to "get around" the foundation payout rule, this is an area of immense abuse. There is no data or other evidence to support this basis for a ban on foundations' grantmaking to donor-advised funds. The private foundation community has done a great job of demonstrating the many positive ways foundations utilize donor-advised funds. Even in a case of abuse, existing law is available to cure the matter. There is no need of "reform" in this area.

MANDATORY PAYOUT

Donor-advised fund critics insist the time lag between the gift to a DAF and the final grant to the charity is a problem. Why? Similar—if not longer—timelines exist for private foundations, supporting organizations, endowments, and charitable remainder trusts. Moreover, if a person chooses to make a large gift directly to a charity, the charity might also add that gift to its endowment and not "spend" the funds that year.

To solve this perceived problem, many critics are recommending imposition of a payout rate on donor-advised funds. But with mandatory payouts—such as the 5 percent payout rule for private foundations—floors becoming ceilings. Many private foundations tightly manage their expenditures to ensure that they pay out exactly 5 percent of their assets every year. This is not a criticism, it is just a fact. Take a donor-advised fund sponsor with an average payout of 20 percent, apply a 5 percent payout, and many DAF advisors will start granting 5 percent instead of 20. It seems foolish to drive total grantmaking down just to ensure each individual fund is making grants regularly. Many sponsoring organizations have rigorous inactive funds policies to ensure grants are being made from these funds.

Another favorite reform pushed by donor-advised fund critics is the timed payout, which would require all DAF contributions to be distributed over a certain number of years. But no other charitable giving vehicles are burdened with such a convoluted restriction. How could the nation's community foundations build an endowment for the future if all donor-advised fund contributions had to be paid out over 5 or 7 years? What about a family that wants to get its children involved in philanthropy, but lacks the resources to start a private foundation? Why should that type of generosity be limited to the very wealthy?

As to the issue of a statutory mandatory payout imposed on donor-advised funds, there is no need for that "reform" either, at least not at this time. The data does not support such a requirement. The critics' best argument is that the current state of the law allows the creation of donor-advised funds and thereafter a hoarding (or stockpiling or warehousing) of the gifted money or other property, and that thus there is a potential for abuse that warrants prophylactic reform. This does not appear to be a sufficient basis to support a legislative change. There may be a few outlier situations but these can be dealt with without statutory law revision. Worrisome is the prospect of unintended consequences of such a law change. With charitable giving declining, now is not the time to curtail use of the most popular of the charitable giving vehicles. Sponsoring organizations in general appear sensitive to this issue and are imposing policies to encourage payouts from the funds they maintain. The commensurate test remains in reserve should specific enforcement action prove necessary.

It is time to abandon the histrionics and get realistic. Money and property flowing into donor-advised funds is a good thing. It is just not sensible to think that the same amount of giving would be forthcoming in the absence of donor-advised funds. This is the case with private foundations, endowments, and the like, as well. Payout theoreticals (or theatrics) or not, all this value is being trapped for charitable ends. So, let the Fairbairns and their peers donate hundreds of millions of dollars, even if they are doing it purely for the tax savings. Overall, society benefits. The admonition of Oscar Wilde should be recalled in this context: "Nothing succeeds like excess."

DEDUCTION DEFERRAL

For years, critics of donor-advised funds have vociferously argued that DAF reforms are essential—and that the key reform device is a mandatory payout. This position is not based on anything resembling evidence but rather the speculation that, since a donor may conceivably contribute to a donor-advised fund and not advise as to a distribution for a period of time, this is a widespread abusive practice requiring legislative reform.

The data show that donor-advised fund payouts are high, certainly higher than those of private foundations. Contributions to DAFs continue to grow, which is a good development in an era where charitable giving overall seems on a decline. The "institutionalization" of individuals' philanthropy should be applauded, and it should be recognized that donor-advised funds are one of the chief vehicles for its accomplishment. Many fear that a mandatory DAF payout scheme would introduce undue complexity and discourage giving to donor-advised funds. In short, donor-advised funds are valuable and welcome charitable giving vehicles; donor-advised fund payouts seem counterproductive and unnecessary.

Indeed, some critics of donor-advised funds seem to be backing off the push for a mandatory donor-advised fund payout and are switching to an alternative "reform": deferring donors' charitable deductions until distributions are made from the funds to the ultimate charitable beneficiaries. This is an idea that is worse than the payout one, because of the immense complexity that would be introduced and the drop in giving to donor-advised funds that would surely ensue. This notion has been tried before, for example, in connection with charitable contributions of vehicles and partial interests in art, with the same predictable result: a plummet in the amount of charitable giving. Such a law change would probably wreck the donor-advised fund system as well. Again, this approach is not taken or advocated in connection with gifts to private foundations, endowments, and charitable trusts—all of which are granting money at a much slower rate.

This deduction-delayed policy could be applied to all restricted and contingent gifts. Gaps between giving and granting are common in U.S. charity, as witnessed by gifts to private foundations, private foundation set-asides, and charitable remainder trusts. Lawyers, accountants, and writers of computer programs might benefit from these intricacies but the charitable sector would suffer.

The charitable sector would also suffer because of donor confusion and discouragement. In today's environment, donors are not likely to give, with the prospect of a deduction years later. Some will recall that planned giving was once termed *deferred giving*. That nomenclature was abandoned when donors stopped being donors because they feared it was their charitable deduction was deferred.

Just contemplating charities' administration of such a charitable giving deduction structure adds to its nightmarish aspect. The recordkeeping, tracing of dollars, sending of notices to donors every year (or perhaps more frequently). There are charities that still cannot cope with the gift substantiation rules, which have been in the law for years. How will they engage in gift administration under a deduction deferral scheme?

Under some versions of a deduction delayed plan, donors would be able to take charitable deductions based on the appreciation of the value of the property in the funds, perhaps including earnings. That feature is not likely to go over well with tax law purists. Perspective needs to be kept in mind here; recall how "reforms" of supporting organizations have nearly wrecked what were once attractive and useful charitable vehicles. The best approach is to leave donor-advised funds and deductions for gifts to them alone from a regulatory standpoint—and welcome these funds as an enhancement of the sector.

ANONYMOUS DAF GIFTS

Still another unwarranted criticism of donor-advised funds is the fact that some donors choose to make their gifts anonymously. Anonymous gifts to charity have existed for decades. Overall, donors' rights to privacy are no different in the donor-advised fund context than in other realms of charitable giving.

DAF GRANTS AND FUNDRAISING EVENTS

Under consideration by the federal government is whether distributions from donor-advised funds to charities as part of fundraising events should be allowed where the donor and/or a donor-advisor attends the event. More technically, the issue is whether the donor or advisor in these circumstances is receiving an impermissible private benefit. The inclination of the Treasury Department and the IRS is that donor/advisor participation in the event confers a "subsidy" that amounts to a more-than-insubstantial benefit.

    The fundamental difficulty with most analyses of this issue is that they do not differentiate between the flashy mega-galas, with fabulous entertainment, ample drink, and excellent food (where patrons really want to attend) and events with nothing more than the proverbial rubber chicken and boring speeches (where just about everyone would just as soon be elsewhere). A donor/advisor may accede to be in attendance at an event to support a charity and help provide dutiful applause as awards are being handed out, even though that individual really did not want to go. There is no private benefit being provided on these latter occasions. If, on the other hand, a donor/advisor truly wants to attend an event, such as because of the nature of the entertainment or the popularity of the speaker, attendance at the event in accordance with a bifurcated payment arrangement may provide a more-than-incidental benefit to the donor/advisor.

DAF GRANTS AND CHARITABLE PLEDGES

Also under consideration by the federal government is whether a donor or donor advisor should be able to advise a distribution from a donor-advised fund to a charity in satisfaction of the donor/advisor's pledge to that charity. The government's inclination is to permit these distributions, even though in the private foundation context distributions of this nature are generally acts of self-dealing. Most of the analyses of this matter focus on whether the ostensible pledge is really one, that is, an enforceable one, and the difficulty in making this determination. The best answer seems to be to allow the distributions.

DAF SUPPORT AS PUBLIC SUPPORT

Critics of donor-advised funds muster their best argument for a DAF "reform" when the focus is on the existing law that a grant from a donor-advised fund can constitute, in its entirety, public support for the benefit of the recipient charity. This is particularly the case where the grantor DAF and the grantee are both the "donative" type of publicly supported charity. The "reform" proposal would treat a distribution from a donor-advised fund as an indirect contribution from the donor (or donors) that funded the advised fund, and thus make it subject to the two percent limitation, rather than a grant from the fund that is entirely public support.

The problem with this reform, if accomplished only by revision of the tax regulations, is that the change may violate principles of law. Although the term *indirect contribution* is not defined in the existing statutory law, which was enacted in 1964, the term has been defined in the regulations since their implementation in 1972. Congress has passed many tax law since then without contemplating law revision in this area; thus, the existing tax regulations' sole definition of *indirect contribution* may be presumed to have congressional imprimatur.

Another principle of law is that, while government agencies can change their policies, to survive review as to whether the policy change is arbitrary and capricious, the government agency must provide a reasoned explanation for the change. Most of the commentaries on the notice issued by Treasury and the IRS, as a precursor to proposed regulations, took the positions that the proposed rule would create significant administrative burdens on grantee organizations and that there is no showing of evidence that the perceived abuse is so widespread as to justify a rule change.

SUMMARY

Overall, the thoughts about donor-advised funds from here are twofold: we do not live in a perfect world and thus the operations of donor-advised funds are not ideal but many of the proposed reforms would likely cause more harm than good. Until and unless critics of donor-advised funds can base their calls for law change on meaningful evidence and not merely speculation, the law as to donor-advised funds should be left alone.

The United States is facing an era of a potential decline in charitable giving, due to recent tax law changes such as doubling of the standard deduction and modifications of the estate tax law. Vehicles like donor-advised funds are needed now more than ever. They presently account for about 13 percent of individual giving; that percentage continues to increase. They grant nearly as much as private foundations, yet the latter are nine times larger in asset size. Donor-advised funds should be protected and celebrated, not pummeled and criticized.

BIBLIOGRAPHY

American Bar Association, Section of Real Property, Trust and Estate Law, letter to Internal Revenue Service (Mar. 5, 2018)

American Bar Association, Section of Taxation, letter to Internal Revenue Service (April 19, 2018), commenting on Notice 2017-73

American Endowment Foundation, "What is a Donor-Advised Fund?"

Andreoni, "The Benefits and Costs of Donor-Advised Funds," National Bureau of Economic Research (978-0-226-57752-4 (2018))

Arnold, "Put a Stake in "Zombie Charity." Philanthropy Is for the Living," 31 *Chron. of Phil.* (Issue 11) 31 September 2019)

Beckwith and Woolf, "Donor-Advised Funds: Separating Myth from Fact," reproduced in *EO Tax Jour.* 2018-206 (Oct. 19, 2018)

Berman, "Donor Advised Funds in Historical Perspective," *The Boston College Law School Forum on Philanthropy and the Public Good* (2015)

Bloomberg BNA, *Daily Tax Report*, "Billionaires Funding a Goldman Philanthropy Charity Unmasked by IRS Snafu" (Mar. 14, 2018)

Blum, "In-House Donor-Advised Funds," 30 *Chron. of Phil.* (Issue 8) 28 (June 2018)

Borzykowski, "The Rapid Rise of Donor-Advised Funds," 201 *Forbes* (Issue 8 (Oct. 31, 2018))

Cantor, "A Gain to Commercial Funds Is a Loss to Charities," XXVII *Chron. of Phil.* (No. 2) 29 (Nov. 6, 2014)

Chronicle of Philanthropy, "California Bill Would Require Greater Disclosure of Donor-Advised Fund Activity" (Jan. 14, 2020)

Colinvaux, "Donor Advised Funds: Charitable Spending Vehicles for 21st Century Philanthropy," 92 *Wash. L. Rev.* 39 (2017)

Colinvaux and Madoff, "A Donor-Advised Fund Proposal That Would Work for Everyone," *Chron. of Phil.* (Sep. 23, 2019)

Committee on Finance, U.S. Senate, "Tax Reform Act of 1969" (S. Rep. No. 91-552, 91st Cong., 1st Sess. (Nov. 21, 1969)).

Committee on Ways and Means, U.S. House of Representatives, "Tax Reform Act of 1969" (H. Rep. No. 91-418 (Part 1), 91st Cong., st Sess. (Aug. 2, 1969))

Community Foundation Public Awareness Initiative, letter to IRS dated (Mar. 5, 2018), commenting on Notice 2017-73

Community Foundation Public Awareness Initiative, letter to Senate Committee on Finance (Sep. 6, 2017), commenting on proposed DAF law changes

Community Foundation Public Awareness Initiative, letter to House Committee on Ways and Means (July 14, 2014), commenting on DAF payout proposal

Congressional Research Service, "An Analysis of Charitable Giving and Donor Advised Funds" (R4259 (July 11, 2012))

Congressional Research Service, "Tax Issues Relating to Charitable Contributions and Organizations" (R45922 (Sep. 19, 2019)).

Council on Foundations, "Donor Advised Fund Timeline" (undated)

Council on Foundations, letter to Internal Revenue Service (Mar. 5, 2018), commenting on Notice 2017-73

Department of the Treasury, "General Explanation of the Administration's Fiscal Year 2001 Revenue Proposals" (February 2000)

Department of the Treasury, "Report to Congress on Supporting Organizations and Donor Advised Funds" (December 2011)

Ebeling, "The $80 Billion Charity Stash: Donor-Advised Funds Reach Record Highs" (Forbes.com (Nov. 15, 2016).

Fidelity Charitable Gift Fund, *2017 Giving Report*

Foord, "Philanthropy 101: Donor-Advised Funds," *Jour. of Financial Planning* (Nov. 2003)

Friedman, *A History of American Law, Third Edition* (Simon & Schuster, New York: 2005).

Gelles, "How Tech Billionaires Hack Their Taxes With a Philanthropic Loophole," *New York Times* (Aug. 3, 2018).

Giving USA, *The Annual Report on Charitable Giving* (2017)

Giving USA, *The Data on Donor-Advised Funds: New Insights You Need to Know* (Jan. 2018)

Government Accountability Office, "Tax-Law Enforcement: IRS Could Better Leverage Existing Data to Identify Abusive Schemes Involving Tax-Exempt Entities" (GAO-19-491 (Sep. 2019)).

Gunderson, "Current Trends in Philanthropy," 84 *Jour. of Jewish Communal Service* (No. 1/2) 91, 92 (Winter/Spring 2009)

Hammack and Anheier, *A Versatile American Institution: The Changing Ideals and Realities of Philanthropic Foundations* (Brookings Institution Press, Wash., D.C.: 2013)

Harris and Hemel, "Don't Delay Deductions for Gifts to Donor-Advised Funds," *Chron. of Phil.* (Oct. 7, 2019)

Haynes and Theis, "A Tough Year for Giving," 31 *Chron. of Phil.* (Issue 9) 22 (July 2019)

Hopkins, *The Tax Law of Private Foundations, Fifth Edition* (John Wiley & Sons, Inc., Hoboken, NJ: 2018); 2019 supplement

Hopkins, "Stunning Portrait of Donor-Advised Funds Issued," 37 *Nonprofit Counsel* (No. 1) 1 (Jan. 2020)

Hussey, "Avoiding Misuse of Donor-Advised Funds," 58 *Clev. L. Rev.* 59 (2010)

Hurtubise, "The Problem with Donor-Advised Finds – and a Solution," *Stanford Social Innovation Rev.* (Dec. 20, 2017)

Husock, "Growing Giving: American Philanthropy and the Potential of Donor-Advised Funds," Manhattan Institute Civic Report No. 97 (April 2015)

Institute for Policy Studies, "Warehousing Wealth: Donor-Advised Charity Funds Sequestering Billions in the Face of Growing Inequality" (July 25, 2018)

Internal Revenue Service, 1996 Exempt Organizations Continuing Professional Education Text, Topic M, "Shoemaker and Henchey, "Donor Directed Funds"

Internal Revenue Service, 2000 Exempt Organizations Continuing Professional Education Text

Internal Revenue Service, 2001 Exempt Organizations Continuing Professional Education Text, Topic G, Shoemaker and Brockner, "Control and Power: Issues Involving Supporting Organizations, Donor Advised Funds, and Disqualified Person Financial Institutions"

Internal Revenue Service, Notice 2017-73, 2017-51 I.R.B. 562

James, III, "Describing complex charitable giving instruments: Experimental tests of technical finance terms and tax benefits," 28 *Nonprofit Management and Leadership* (Issue 4) (Summer 2018).

Johnson, Sheka, and Weeden, "Give to Get: Magnifying the Impact of Executive Compensation through Charitable Giving," 69 *Jour. of Financial Serv. Professionals* (No. 1) 63 (Jan. 2015)

Joint Committee on Taxation (Staff), *Technical Explanation of H.R. 4, the "Pension Protection Act of 2006* (JCX-38-06 (Aug. 3, 2006))

Jones, "Regulating Donor Advised Funds," 75 *Florida Bar Jour.* (Issue 5 (May 2001))

Kalwinski, Stamm, and Briceno, "Can You Define a Community Foundation?," 29 *Tax'n of Exempts* (No. 3) 36 (Nov./Dec. 2017)

Knoepfle, "The Pension Protection Act of 2006: A Misguided Attack on Donor-Advised Funds and Supporting Organizations," 9 *Fla. Tax Rev.* 221 (2009)

Kridler, Phillipp, Slutsky, Seleznow, and Williams, "Donor-Advised Funds: How to Make Sure They Strengthen Our Communities," *Nonprofit Quarterly* (Aug. 20, 2018)

Lee, "Regulating Donor-Advised Funds: Not Everyone's a Fan of IRS Plans," Bloomberg BNA, *Daily Tax Report* (No. 63) G-7 (April 2, 2018)

Levine, "The Political Quicksand of DAFs and Supporting Foundations," *Nonprofit Quar.* (Oct. 16, 2018)

Lindsay, "Raising Money From Donor-Advised Funds: It's There for the Asking; You Just Have to Ask," 31 *Chron. of Phil.* (Issue 7) 47 (May 2019)

Lorin, "Got $5 Million? Yale Will Invest It," *Bloomberg Businessweek* (issue 4596 (Dec. 17, 2018))

Ludwig, "Donor Advised 'Dark Money'?," *Philanthropy Daily* (Aug. 12, 2019)

Ludwig and Hartmann, "How Much Regulation of Donor-Advised Funds Is Enough?," *Philanthropy Daily* (Sep. 23, 2019)

Madoff, "5 Myths About Payout Rules for Donor-Advised Funds," *Chron. of Phil.* (Jan. 13, 2014))

Madoff, "Charities and Taxpayers Deserve More From Donor-Advised Funds," 29 *Chron. of Phil.* (Issue 1 (Nov. 2016))

Madoff, "Three Simple Steps to Protect Charities and American Taxpayers from the Rise of Donor-Advised Funds," 25 *Nonprofit Quar.* (no. 2) 46 (Summer 2018)

Mankiw, "DAFs Should Be Applauded," blog posted Aug. 5, 2018, reproduced in *EO Tax Jour.* 2018-157 (Aug. 10, 2018)

McCambridge, "Do Donor-Advised Funds Require Regulatory Attention?", 25 *Nonprofit Quar.* (no. 2) 41 (Summer 2018)

Metcalf, "Billionaires Funding a Goldman Charity Unmasked by IRS Snafu," Bloomberg BNA, *Daily Tax Report* (No. 51) G-8 (Mar. 15, 2018)

Mittendorf, "Fairbairn vs. Fidelity: The Lawsuit That Reflects Rising Concerns About the DAF Boom," reprinted in *EO Tax Jour.* 2019-114 (June 12, 2019)

Mullich, "Donor-Advised Funds: The Fastest-Growing Vehicle for Charitable Giving," 200 *Forbes* (Issue 5 (Nov. 14, 2017))

National Philanthropic Trust, *The 2019 DAF Report* (made public on November 12, 2019)

National Philanthropic Trust, letter to Department of the Treasury and Internal Revenue Service (Mar. 5, 2018), commenting on Notice 2017-73

New York State Bar Association, Tax Section, letter to Department of the Treasury and Internal Revenue Service (Feb. 28, 2018), commenting on Notice 2017-73

New York Times, "Lawsuit Could Cool a Fast-Growing Way of Giving to Charities" (May 31, 2019)

Nopar, "Savvy Nonprofits Can Reap Big Benefits," XXVII *Chron. of Phil.* (No. 2) 29 (Nov. 6, 2014)

Osborne, Jr., "Voices from the Field: Fidelity's 2019 DAF Grants Spike – How Donor-Advised Funds Changed Giving for the Better," *Nonprofit Quar.* (July 29, 2019) (online).

Philanthropy Roundtable, letter to Department of the Treasury (Mar. 5, 2018), commenting on Notice 2017-73

Pike, "How I Helped Create the Donor-Advised Fund Monster – Inadvertently," *Chron. of Phil.* (Aug. 22, 2018)

Ries, "First Look at the Tax Cuts and Jobs Act: The Impact on Donor Advised Funds," 88 *CPA Jour.* (Issue 4 (April 2018))

Roady and Madrigal, "Integrated Philanthropy Using Private Foundations, Private Operating Foundations, Public Charities and Non-Charitable Organizations," presentation at 10th Annual Rocky Mountain Tax Seminar for Private Foundations (Sep. 19, 2019)

Rothey, "A Surprising Benefit of the New Tax Law," 65 Bloomberg BNA, *Daily Tax Report* (No. 65) G-11 (April 4, 2018)

Schlesinger and Goodman, "Advance Peek at Proposed Regs. for Donor-Advised Funds," 45 *Estate Planning* (No. 8) 45 (Aug. 18, 2019)

Sheppard, "Disciplining Donor-Advised Funds," *Tax Notes* 795 (Aug. 5, 2019)

Shoemaker and Brockner, "Control and Power: Issues Involving Supporting Organizations, Donor Advised Funds, and Disqualified Person Financial Institutions," Topic G, IRS 2001 Exempt Organization Continuing Professional Education Text

Shoemaker and Henchey, "Donor Directed Funds," Topic M, IRS 1996 Exempt Organizations Continuing Professional Education Text

Smith and Morris, "Donor-Advised Funds: A Well-Kept Secret," 71 *CPA Jour.* (Issue 9 (Sep. 2001))

Staffs of the Joint Committee on Internal Revenue Taxation and the Committee on Finance, "Summary of H.R. 13270, the Tax Reform Act of 1969 (as Passed by the House of Representatives)" 14 (91st Cong., 1st Sess. (Aug. 18, 1969))

Stiffman and Haynes, "Can the Boom Times Last?," 32 *Chron. of Phil.* (Issue 1) 8 (Nov. 2019)

Streckfus, *EO Tax Jour.* 2018-50 (Mar. 12, 2018), 2018-158 (Aug. 13, 2018), 2018-163 (Aug. 20, 2018), 2018-176 (Sep. 7, 2018), 2019-156 (Aug. 12, 2019), 2019-159 (Aug. 15, 2019), 2019-162 (Aug. 20, 2019), 2019-187 (Sep. 25, 2019), 2019-217 (Nov. 6, 2019), 2019-223 (Nov. 14, 2019), 2019-245 (Dec. 18, 2019), 2019-247 (Dec. 20, 2019), 2019-252 (Dec. 31, 2019)

Theis, "Fidelity and Schwab Ban Gifts from Donor-advised Funds to NRA-Affiliated Charities," *Chron. of Phil.* (Dec. 4, 2019)

Vanguard Charitable Endowment Program, *Policies and guidelines*

Woolf, Senior Tax Policy Counsel, The Jewish Federations of North America, email message published in EO Tax Jour. 2019-159 (Aug. 15, 2019)

Woolley, "The Super-Rich Are Stockpiling Wealth in Black-Box Charities," Bloomberg BNA (Oct. 5, 2018)

Zerbe, "DAF Reform – A Chance to Provide a Real Benefit to Working Charities," 25 *Nonprofit Quarterly* (no. 2) 52 (Summer 2018)

TABLE OF CASES

TABLE OF IRS REVENUE RULINGS

Table of IRS Revenue Procedures

TABLE OF IRS PRIVATE LETTER RULINGS, TECHNICAL ADVICE MEMORANDA, AND CHIEF COUNSEL ADVICE MEMORANDA

INDEX